STRATEGIC MANAGEMENT

STRATEGIC MANAGEMENT: INDIAN EXPERIENCE

Editor:
DILIP ROY
Foreword by:
SUJIT K. BASU

GYAN PUBLISHING HOUSE
NEW DELHI-110002

The responsibility for the facts stated, and the views, if any expressed or conclusions drawn in any article of this book is entirely that of the author(s). The editor is in no way responsible for the same.

Strategic Management:
Indian Experience
(Management)
ISBN : 81-212-0546-8

Published in 1997 in India by
Gyan Publishing House
5, Ansari Road,
New Delhi-110 002

Laser Typesetting at Manas Typesetter,
New Delhi
and Printed at Mehra Offset Press,
New Delhi.

Contents

Foreword

This volume is a collection of articles presented at the National Seminar on Strategic Management organized by the Department of Business Administration, Burdwan University on February 3-4, 1996.

The importance of strategy in the context of management of organization cannot be over-emphasized. In today's competitive and complex scenario in any sphere of human activity, strategy is more than a mere buzz word, drawing up of plans and programmes and implementing these to the desired effect calls for an effective strategy or a set of interacting strategies. The appropriate strategic approach to issues depends not only on their nature but also on their time and the relevant environment-sociological, political, economic and a variety of other relevant factors and thus strategic handling of issues ought to be usually a very complex game.

I am very pleased to note that the Department of Business Administration of the Burdwan University has taken the initiative to emphasize and understand the role of strategic management by organizing the seminar which was attended by not only academicians but also some leading practising managers. As articles included in this volume would testify, the Department's basic strategy of offering a common platform to all those academicians and practising managers to effectively interact and share views on strategic management has largely been successful. As one would normally expect most of the articles in the volume are theoretical in nature and a few are survey based; there are some case studies with complete analysis. Interestingly, they all come under the perview of current scenario. The works are of immense help in the field of management of knowledge and information under the area of strategic planning.

I appreciate the editor Professor Dilip Roy for his efficient managing of the editorial work.

I expect that the volume will attract the attention of a large number of readers of varied backgrounds.

Sujit K. Basu, Ph.D.
Professor of Operation Management,
Former Chairman, PG Programme, IIMC

Preface

The complexion of the global business environment has changed beyond recognition in the last decade. Many countries have opened up their doors for transnational companies and entered into others' territories for locating new markets and opportunities. As a consequence of these global ventures the business world is passing through a state of high volatility, turbulency and complexity.

In India, sensing the global mood the government has eschewed its original posture and has embarked on a new economic policy unleashing wide reforms in many dimensions. Caught in the grip of competition, management functions have undergone sea-change. The age old system of single-state-planning has found its place in the shelf of old records and now the vital force has been the strategic one.

Since external unpredictability has its effect on internal stability there is a growing need to understand and apply the concept of strategic management for long run survival. Unfortunately, environmental changes have induced a lot of conceptual changes in strategic planning and the subject has been passing through continuous reforms over the last few decades.

In the late 40's we noticed a predominant war-fare approach in the subject. Terms like 'attacking, defending, defeating' were of frequent use. Infact the term strategy itself was borrowed from defence wordbook. Later in 50's it was realized that unlike a dead enemy a defeated competitor could come back from the brink of divestment for competing with more vitality. As a result during 60's we noted a movement towards meticulously drawn planning for diversification of business activities in multiple directions with emphasis given on structural implementation. Thus, the emergence of a system approach with an orientation towards tools and techniques was the marked outcome of those years. During 70's we observed the negative impact of overzealous diversifications raising doubts about the workability of many of the sophisticated tools developed for strategic planning. Success of Japanese firms that used to pay very little attention on exhaustive planning even quaked the base rock of the subject. Attempts to rebuild the subject came out with the concept of directed trial and error method for strategy formulation highlighting on continuous and intellectual aspects of the process. And this happened during 80's. The subject has taken a new turn in the present decade when it has been pointed out that many marginal players have outplayed their giant rivals with gritty determination only and have achieved their skyhigh ambitions.

That no concept is error-free and no concept is outrightly crashable can be seen from the repeated reemergence of those earlier concepts. We still look for ideas from warfare; sometimes we depend on detailed forecasting; we mostly go by directed trial and error method; and we also appreciate muddling through. Probably, we looked at this vast subject with a tunnel vision in the past. Our present desire is, therefore, to see the complete image of it by putting together all the 2D pictures snapped from different angles at different points of time.

To move one step forward towards that objective the Department of Business Administration of the University of Burdwan organised a National Seminar on Strategic Management on 3rd and 4th of February, 1996. We are extremely happy to be able to bring out this edited volume which is a selective collection of referred papers embracing different areas of strategic planning. It covers invited curtain raising talks and survey results, papers presented during the seminar days and cases developed in the workshop sessions.

Our thanks are due to the contributors who took lot of

interest in meeting our deadlines which were often not reasonable. We would like to put on record our appreciation for the help we received from the following members of the publication cell: Pradip Mallick, Tanmoy Dasgupta, Uddipto Roy and Isita Lahiri.

Last but not the least we are also grateful to Gyan Publishing House for kind patronage in publishing this esteemed volume for the benefit of management practitioners, researchers, teachers and students.

We offer a blanket apology for any lapse on our part.

16.4.97 **Dilip Roy**
Burdwan

Introduction

If we critically examine the life cycle of any enterprise, in the infancy stage we are likely to find the organizations usually striving for survival in the relevant product field and market. However, no sooner it attains a viable position, the organization driven by its expansion needs is forced to go beyond making only operational decisions. And going beyond operational management system means at first developing structural decision-making system and then transforming distinctive competence into competitive advantage. The later philosophy of managing business firms has no doubt evolved out of the concept of long range planning but this evolution is so prominent and distinct that it has been well recognized as the key to success in the today's dynamic corporate world. This comprehensive management approach is now known in the literature as the strategic management approach.

A strategy is a commitment to undertake one set of actions rather than another and this commitment necessarily describes a relationship between a firm and its environment. Organizational strategy, when left to itself, begins with the desire to out perform the competitors in the market. As a result such an organization follows an expansion strategy in a traditional fashion by extending its activities in the same or similar product field. And a time comes when a crisis of concept creeps in. It is, therefore, absolutely necessary to continuously search for a new concept, which may even include an attempt to redefine the existing business time and again. In this sense, a strategy is centered around a few fundamental issues such as: What is our business?

What should it be ? Should we stay or get out of this business? Should we slow down or accelerate our activities? What should be our business in future?

It is clear from the above mentioned issues that strategic planning is not a simple long-term planning though it is futuristic in its approach and tries to anticipate the forthcoming changes in the environment. Under strategic planning contingency schemes are drawn for each of the likely future states of the environment and are aimed at creating favourable changes in the market along with providing ways to manage environmental changes. The basic inputs to this second generation planning process are the enterprise strategists, the enterprise objectives and the managerial awareness of the past strategies. The strategic management process combines these elements and goes for analysis and diagnosis of the external and internal environments for determining the present potential opportunities and threats and the organizational strengths and weaknesses. Depending on the significance of external changes in the economy, technology and market and in the roles of competitors, suppliers and the regulatory bodies and examining the size and distribution of firm's resources, corporate planners make the final choice of the strategy. The underlying analysis we have referred to is also known as SWOT analysis where 'S' stands for strengths, 'W' stands for weaknesses, 'O' stands for opportunities and 'T' stands for threats.

It is needless to mention that a strategic planning becomes meaningful only when it is followed up with utmost sincerity and zeal. Implementational success for a corporate strategy largely depends on the strategy—strategist matching. It is also necessary to ensure that the organizational structure remains unidirectional with corporate and divisional strategies. Factoring of strategy at every lower level must flow in a cascade fashion and implementational difficulties, if any, must trickle up without unwanted delay to retain the unified, comprehensive and integrated nature of the corporate strategy.

In India the study and practice of strategic management have gained momentum from the turbulent state of the business environment induced by the new economic policy of the government. Earlier, the business environment was nearly predictable with limited competitors and minimum variations. As a result strategic planning was more of a long-term planning and less of an environmental matching. But now there is a need to switch over to continuous monitoring and planning and following the theoretical base developed in the literature on this subject. However, one major hindrance in coopting the existing theories lies in their limited applicability in the Indian context. While business ethics, corporate climate and core proficiencies are different in nature planners are virtually copying the Western style of management without recognizing the need to evolve a new style of functioning based on our internal experiences and values. It is also important to note that at the time of developing a corporate strategy every manager must be a corporate visionary rather than a corporate gambler.

The present work is born out of this gap and describes Indian experiences in respect of various stages of strategic planning. We have presented the view of a successful strategist who has re-expressed faith in the doctrine of Karma, covered the effects of global treatise on Indian economy, indicated the importance of different internal and external factors for SWOT analysis in the Indian context, highlighted the strengths and probable strategies of regional business organizations, described different functional strategies which can be successful in the Indian condition, emphasized on the integration of human resource planning with strategic planning, stressed on strategic management of small scale industries and presented a few cases with complete analysis.

environment induced by the new economic policy of the government. Today, the business environment [illegible] with limited resources and minimum [illegible] analysis [illegible] of environmental [illegible] managers and planners [illegible] the [illegible] major [illegible] corporate [illegible] management [illegible] the need to [illegible] a corporate [illegible] and [illegible] the [illegible] corporate [illegible] every manager [illegible] a corporate [illegible]

[illegible] of this [illegible] and [illegible] various stages of [illegible] a view of [illegible] successful [illegible] the [illegible] of [illegible] and [illegible] business organisations [illegible] can be [illegible] the integration of human resources [illegible] strategic [illegible] and [illegible]

1

Strategic Management and my Days in Peerless

P.C. Sen

Any discussion on strategic management just starts off with the words—attack, defend and so on. Although experts claim that these words belong to the 50s and are outdated. I do not accept this thinking that these words are not relevant today. I believe these words are still very strong.

Strategy—in General Sense

Now, the word "Strategy" has descended from its Greek origin *'Strategia'*—the office of the General. The 'General' necessarily means the General in charge of the soldiers. And what comes out of the office is strategy, what does come out really is the method of conducting a war. It is also applicable to skilful planning in business to attain a business objective or it can be used even during an interaction with your wife. You always have to use strategy, even when you want something from your wife or vice versa. You just cannot say 'I want this'. So strategy is important in every sphere of life.

Types of Strategy

According to my long industrial experience there are mainly two types of strategies. One is the General Strategy and known as a long-term strategy and the another is short-term strategy.

A company is known by the type of people who work there because a company is run by people not by machines. Often a recruitment policy says 'pick up the best'. Now what is meant by 'the best'. If there is an IIM graduate and another is a University MBA, I would prefer the University MBA. Why? Presumably he is not the best because he is not supposed to be as good as an IIM graduate. But unfortunately or fortunately he is. He is cheaper, less flamboyant, he won't go telling everybody how to do their work from the very first day, he will last longer, and most importantly, he will, rock the boat less. An MBA from IIM rocks the boat so much that all the large industries are also very scared. So this is a general type of strategy—what type of personnel you require.

Here is another example, how should the company move—a dare devil strategy, an opportunistic strategy i.e. when there is an opportunity jump in your way. The glorious example of this is industrialist Mr. Dhirubhai Ambani. Yes, I know, because of this, he spends sleepless nights, he has had innumerable heartaches and physically he is really rundown. But that is what has built the Ambani and Reliance Empires. In a small way I have imitated him. Retain his sentence as it is. Only repeet and by. But there is a difference between the working styles of manager and the managing director of only organization. I will come to it at the end. So this is General Purpose Strategy.

Strategy and Tactics

Then coming to strategy, we have a planning called tactics. It is widely used in army. Both strategy and tactics could emanate from a General's office. When the tactics go down to the Divisional Commander, then these become a strategy. We can say it is the science of achieving objectives set by strategy. That means you have a broad strategy and it is broken up into small and small tactics. Now, you have ten Divisional Commanders, you give them ten different tactics and by each one of them achieving their tactics, the strategy or the objectives are obtained. It could be "look here you lose the battle, but ultimately you win the war". But why should you want to lose the battle? Most of you are familiar, I mean in the 50's when I did management, Hannibal was a great Commander. You have what is called a pincer of attack. It is still used today. What happens is that when you are face to face with enemy you are told to start falling back so they come attacking you. And then you start attacking them in a pincer-like fashion. They again go down and attack you from the back. Then you start attacking from the front. This is called pincer attack. It started a thousand years ago and is still used today. At that time what would happen—the Commander facing the enemy not appropriate were told to retreat. And that's tactics—to do what? The strategy—to win the war you have a pincer attack, for example, in the Second World War the British lost Singapore in 24 hours—they also lost Burma, and ran away from Burma without putting up much of a resistance. This was tactics. You retreat—what was the strategy? It was to get the U.S.A. to join the war. Now, Churchill convinced Roosevelt that the U.S.A. must join the war. But Roosevelt was scared that he neither convince the Senate nor the people of America why U.S.A. should join the war. So both leaders decided a strategy that they would show that Japan had attacked the U.S.A. So lot of dirty things were done in the war and Japan attacked Pearl Harbour—they were egged on. U.S.A. public went into furore and as earlier said "You must declare war." So, what was the strategy, to get U.S.A. to join the war. What was the tactics? Retreat from the scene, from the far east—let U.S.A. take over. So both the tactics and the strategy paid off because ultimately U.S.A. won the war in the far east.

Now coming closer to home, let us see what I did in Peerless. When I joined Peerless in 1986, I was C&MD in Burn Standard. I am a mechanical engineer from the Railways and I was trained in England. Peerless was a company which was then known as chit fund company. And the personnel of the company was that type of people whom I never had dealt with. The owner of the company told me that I must bring my own team. So I got some people from Railways and Burn Standard who filled the top slots. What we found that the only strength of the company was Rs. 600 crores and a broken down agent's force. SWOT analysis is a very important thing. That is what we did then and found that money was the only strength of the company.

Tactics Adopted in Peerless

What do we do now? Bring more money. Now move to tactics. First motivate and bring up the field sales force that is the agents. Increase them and bring in more money. What did we find? That the branches were very sparce, very few. So the agent has to collect money, travel 500-600 kms.—deposit in the branch, stay there overnight and come back. So what should be done? Bring the branches closer, so that they can deposit money and get back home. He spends less and he comes back frequently, because if he tends to keep the public money he may spend it.

So from our 50 odd branches we branched upto 155. I am proud to say that till the day I left the branch in Srinagar, it is still operating and collecting money. It is the only private sector company that is still working in Srinagar. And every month we send someone to visit that office to boost the morale of the people who are working there. So one has to proliferate the branches.

The Art of Making Peerless a Household Name

Now, the agents do not get salary, but they always used to feel jealous of the people working in the office—the clerks, the cashiers etc. At the end of the month they get salary regularly, but for them, there is no such provision. So we made it a point, that these agents should get their, commission on a fixed day of the month. So to him, slowly it started looking like a salary. When he came on the 28th day of the month, he got a packet waiting for him in the branch. In this way his family was relaxed. They knew that on a particular day they could definitely get their commission. When the agents go to get a new depositor, he would say—"Peerless? Oh! I heard it was like a Sanchayita, a cheat fund." So what we had to do was make Peerless a respectable household name. How to do it? The first thing that I did and for which I faced tremendous opposition in my company was to lend money to state Governments. The moment we lent money to state Governments, we became respectable. And what happened is, when one goes to places like Assam and Andhra Pradesh people generally say. "Look, you collect money from here and take it to West Bengal". The agents can say—"Now we take money and give it to the Government." So immediately the collection outside West Bengal shot up. The day I left Peerless, there were 13 state Governments whom we had lent money. This helped the agents enhance the business quicker. He did not have to say "Peerless, Peerless, Peerless" many times. Because the moment he pronounced "Peerless", people recognised it.

Then came the turn of sponsorships of popular games. As faras West Bengal is concerned, football is a popular game. Unfortunately it is the only state whch is a one cty state—everything is based on Calcutta. What we tried to do was to sponsor the events in districts because our collection is in the districts. People in Calcutta will no like to go in for Peerless.

Then we did a very peculiar thing. We published very cheap editions of questions and answers for secondary and Higher Secondary examinations. And I saw to it that it was timely distributed. And what happened was that, boys of 16 to 18 years old said, "Oh! this is Peerless." So from 16 we started brainwashing of boys into Peerless. When they grow up and somebody goes to them for deposit they would say that it is a good thing. It was very mild brainwashing. Again we were committed to the community. We had many clinics where for Rs. 2 one can consult with a good doctor. So in a village or in a slum if there was a problem they would say "Oh! Let us go to the closest Peerless Clinic." We not only gave a free check up but even the medicine were also free. And this strategy helped us to make Peerless a household name.

Drawing up of Strategy

How does one draw up strategy? I will be slightly theoretical here and then proceed with lists of examples from industry. Normally there are 3 types of approaches—a very planned and methodical approach, whereby this planning is done, SWOT analysis is made and strategy is chalked out. You have a planning group, they are all the time getting feedback. Sometimes they are advising you to go off the path because Government has changed rules, you cannot go this way to achieve the goal. You have to go another way by changing your strategy. This is the theoretical way. This practice is practised mainly in large

Public Sector Units. I have been the General Manager of 4 to 5 Public Sector Units. There we had to tell the minister that yes, we have a strategic planning department and after every 3 to 4 months, we had to tell the minister, yes, this is how I am planning, this is what is to be done. So at least for show purpose, these P.S.Us. have to have a strategic planning department where strategy is formulated. How much is followed I will not tell you but it is certainly there.

The other type is intuitive. This is more in my life. Let us take the case of a chief executive of a company. It can be only one man—the chief executive. He has got to just dream of the company, think of the company, when he is going to bed he has to think of the company, he has to get up thinking of his company, in the bathroom too he has to think of his company, if he ever goes to a club, which he should not, he has to think of the company. He should devote all the 24 hours to his company. Then this feeling creeps into his blood. He knows what his people are feeling. He knows what the people dealt with are feeling and he knows what his customers are feeling.

This man says "You are gonna do this." This looks very ad hoc, very autocratic, but this is the real private sector growth companies—this is what they follow. A big executive—again I go back to Dhirubhai Ambani—because it is a one-man show and now his two sons are there.

But this oneman concept is very dangerous—if Hitler brought Germany up, see from where he brought Germany up. Most of us probably do not know what he did. I do, because I have read his works, I have read what he did through and through. What he did for Germany in 1930s is something worth looking at. So it has to be one man—but he must be totally dedicated, devoted and he must know what he is doing, doing not for himself, not to put money in his pocket but to make the company grow. So only the Chief Executive will say—O.K. this is it—go and do it. This is intuitive entrepreneur, whatever you may call it. Quinn advocated—trial and error. A little bit of trial and error is needed because one man certainly can make a few mistakes. So trial and error. He is very right—because chief executive, concerned, I must admit, does not want to do this. Well I think we made mistakes. So trial and error is a very important thing for strategy. The director of planning must accept the errors and they must change directors where it is called for. A few academicians speak what the 50's, 60's, 70's and 80's said, what the 90 is saying—but no method has been proved foolproof. Otherwise that method would have continued right down the ages. Every decade, every 5 years you find a new fad, there is nothing foolproof.

Then there is the adaptive approach. It is something like Government's planning and I call it muddle throw approach. This is also a very efficient way of doing things. Because if you have the steady footing you can muddle through a lot of different things. For example, the Government have their plans, but there are so many things that go wrong midway. They just like to go and say, "O.K. Hang on ! Let us see what happens. Let things serve themselves out." This is a very good way of doing things and in this method you may have long term plans, and objectives (goals). But you have to continually change your objective based on how the environment is reacting. So these, by and large, are the methods. But actually no company, worth its name, will follow one method. So it is a mixed approach. When you are drawing up a strategy, you have to have a mixed approach. You have to consult with people and have planning—which is a mixed one. So the best thing is a mixed approach and to decide when to decide which approach is best for a particular time. This is what I feel strategy is all about and what should be done.

Setting up of Goals

Now, drawing up the goal is very important. When you make a strategy, what should be the strategy and how to reach there—everything depends on what is your goal. When you have a goal you have to reach there by any means—either you may follow main line or you may follow chord line. So which strategy you take depends on what is your goal.

Now, I narrated what we did in Peerless, while drawing up the goal. The goal was to make Peerless a big respected financial company. So how did we achieve that? What was our next goal? There were too many eggs in one basket. And I told the people in Peerless about that 6 years ago and I get literally beaten up for that. I advised them, "Look, you will not be able to run this company in future because slowly other players will come in. And one day the Government of India will not let you carry on this type of business. "But I was called out, because of this fact, hammered and I went to hospital. And those days are going to come true in the next 2 years. Practically all the financial companies have been hot. ITC Classic is in very serious trouble. It should be noted that, one and half years ago everyday, at least one or two financial companies were coming up and were paying atrocious salaries—ranging from Rs. 40,000 to Rs. 80,000 per month. All the companies are now falling by the wayside and their people are looking for jobs at half of their previous salaries.

I could see this was going to happen, but unfortunately nobody believed me. So what was my idea? Let us diversify in two fields. So 5 years ago we thought of hotel business which is going to prosper for the next 50 years because tourism and commercial travel are increasing like wild fire. So the hotel group has paid-off. And what else for the future? I thought the future of a company would be best in oil business and I still dream of the day when the Bay of Bengal will be giving oil to this nation. I practically lost my job in my last company—Burn Standard as I spent Rs. 30 crore at Haldia to build offshore platforms with American collaboration without taking Government of India's permission. And that Rs. 30 crore is still there in Haldia for the whole world to see as they are still making offshore platforms at Bombay High. But I still dream of the day when those platforms will be useful for Bay of Bengal. Now oil, working toward what we called Peerless Drive, actually Drive was the name of the original company, Peerless makes a profit of Rs. 6-7 crore a year. This year Peerless Shipping and Oilfield has made a profit of Rs. 30 crores. It is in the core sector of the business which sooner or later will become a big name in India. So we have to diversify the company in order to save the company and those agents-and so we went into what is called Peerless Developers. What is the idea of Peerless Developers—to carry on the name of Peerless in the household. Those of you who have been to England must have heard of the chain stores—which have become legend in the countries of both U.S.A. and U.K. So I thought we should also have something like that. So if someone wants to buy a shirt he will say—let us buy a Peerless shirt because it has the best value for money and the agents would easily sell. Let us buy Peerless tea, because that has the best value for money and the agents would sell it and would have their income augmented by doing this business. Peerless Developers would also work as developers and build flats for MIGs and LIGs and as a result the agents could get the flats booked and make their commission. We had another project in collaboration with a U.K. company dealing in 4-wheel and 5-seater electric auto-rickshaw. It is meant for the small towns in India and is pollution free, noise free and trouble free. Only thing needed is a charged battery.

Then I had the Peerless infotech computer project. This project was catchy but it did not pick up in India because computers were too expensive. Now if in a middle class family, a boy, student of class X, wants to have a computer in his house, the father will not agree with the boy and say, "I do not have enough to eat and you want to have a computer." So I have been trying to manufacture computers of Rs. 10,000 or even less than that.

The Strategist

The chief executive must try to have the qualifications of a Sanyasi (saint). He has to tend to be a sanyasi. And when he comes closer to sanyasiship, his performance and the decisions taken by him will be more correct. The more closer he quite comes to sanyasiship his behaviour will be more impartial and he will be more temptationless. In today's world these are quite different for a chief executive, because all the temptations are lined up before him. So for him becoming a sanyasi, is very important. It is through rigorous self-discipline, daily practice of both physical and mental renunciation and sacrifice that you can tend to become a sanyasi. This is all I had to say about strategy and strategist and would like to tell you that forming a strategy is not just laying down the policy and forget it.

Interaction During Presentation

Q. In your paper you have said that Peerless wanted to provide computers at an affordable price. Was it because the company wanted to come out of a niche at the lower end of the market or was it because Peerless wanted to serve the society, pushing its business interests to the back ?

P.C. Sen : No, I will tell you what had happend, I tried to slightly serve our own ends because the society that we look after is not the one that would buy computers for personal use as they cannot afford to spend Rs. 10,000 for computers. This was far slightly selfish purpose. We had very big computer installations where out of 155 branch offices 100 have computer installations. I was also going to network it through satellite in the next 6 months. And we have very big computer installations in the 4 metros. So we have a host of hardware and software engineers who are getting a little fed up of doing the same work, time and again. What I was going to do would serve many purposes. If I could bring this computer of Rs. 10,000 in the market which young and bright boys would like to use. Then you have a wide area in which computers are being sold, they have a wider area to go and repair the computers, teach people and also run classes for teaching computers.

So, automatically these boys and girls would come to us for learning computers all over India. If would spread the network of Peerless Infotech into this large area which is not being attached by large players like WIPRO, DCL etc.

Q. It is mentioned in your paper that you prefer one man one direction and at the same time mentioned the importance of flat strategy. What is your opinion, which strategy would be helpful in India ?

P.C. Sen : It is a very very good question. Ours is a society, where although the joint family is broken up but the remnants are still there. Ours is a society where there is one father figure—Grandfather, Eldest uncle, or whatever. And we are used to it with one person dictating terms. We are used to one man-one boss. This matrix has failed because this one man-one boss is not there in the matrix and in oneman two-boss system, there is more fighting than the work done. So with Indian society you still have to follow the hierarchical system because it is still in our blood. This may not remain correct after 15-20 years, when we come to a nuclear family, then this tradition of 'listen to the top man' would have gone or may not. I do not know. But still today people, as I said so the hierarchical system is in our blood. But we try to wash it off quickly, it is like trying to remove a scab from a wound which is not healed properly. So the scab will fall off in its own time. May be in a hierarchical system in the next 15-20 years we fall-off. But do not try to change it because we are not ready for it. That is what matters.

No. 2 is, you have referred to one-man organization, which has to be given very-quick directions.

It cannot have a committee management. It is usually a dangerous trend to have a one man show because the organization collapses after that one man leaves. I am sorry to say that, it is exactly what had happened with me in a number of organizations like Sacksbee and Burn Standard. I was the C&MD of Burn Standard which made a profit even one year after I left, but thereafter it is in shambles. I do not know what will happen of Peerless. But all I can say is that if I had done a committee management in Sacksbee and in Burn Standard and in Peerless, one would have been just dribbling around without achieving the goals.

Q. Is it the money or facility that should be given to the managers? What should be the strategy?

P.C. Sen : Meet the individual inside or, outside the office and find out what makes him, I am using a very colloquial English expressions, what makes him tick. Now X may be a person. I know if I give him a nice new car and some extra money, he will move ahead. I may have to face the problem, wants his son to go to a good college or he wants to put him into a medical college. If I can put his son into a medical college, he will be totally devoted to the organization. Similarly Z may have a dream to visit Europe with family, you send Z to Europe. Look there is no single answer to that particular question because every man has something which makes him tick.

Q. Sir, is over-diversification detrimental to a company's future growth? And if not so, according to the Peerless Group, what have you adopted in Peerless? At which state should a company follow diversification?

P.C. Sen : Decade of the '70 is acquisitions and mergers, that is, I am talking of western world while 80's was the decade of diversification.

Today you will learn the term core competency. You stay in the area of core competencies and shed the companies which are not in the areas of core competencies. What I have done today has been in the best interest of the company at heart. I should not say that one should over diversify. It is very dangerous. But what was in the heart really?. The heart was our beloved state—West Bengal. It was West Bengal where the process of progress was stopped. We had to revive it. There is a fly ash brick manufacturing company near Bandel.

The Government of West Bengal was the owner of the company and it did not run for a day. It is with us now. We are 49% shareholder. But we should not have taken this, it is nothing to do with us. But government of West Bengal has started something and you cannot let it fail. You have to look at the circumstances in which we try to do certain things. Which posterity cannot understand. Only 5 years hence West Bengal will be back to its own glory. People will not know that in the 1980's what was the situation. I tried to push it up. Lot of my actions were dependent on the environment which need not necessarily have been correct management practice. But that it is not for a man who wants to do something for his country, for the men, for his company.

Q. Is it not more of flaunting rather than get the thing for the company's sake?

P.C. Sen : I expressed sometime back that I wanted Peerless to be a household word. You just cannot do one thing and become household word. You have to do many things. It is quite possible that 50% of them are wrong but it become a household name. Rs. 600 crores became Rs. 4500 crores in a matter of 6 years. Unless it was a household name, that Rs. 600 crores would not have become Rs. 4500 crores. The question may be what was my goal. My goal was to make this company a money-spinner which could even lend to the government if needed and to earn the respect of people. I had to do a lot of things to achieve that goal.

Q. You pointed out that if necessary company should adopt different strategies in different situations. Don't you think that such strategy could be rewarding in the short run, but it could be suicidal in the long run?

P.C. Sen : No, you are making a mistake between strategy and goal. You have got a strategy, you could change your strategy, but not your goal. If you cannot attack Mount Everest from the Indian side, your strategy has to change.

Q: According to you a campany cannot become a household name by sticking to only one area of operation—then what could be the secrets behind the success of companies like Coca-Cola.

P.C. Sen : See there is a bit of difference. If you are distributing a product having product excellence, customer satisfaction, penetration in the market and if it is a customer wanted consumer product, it automatically goes into every house. If you have an excellent product, with good after sales service and, if your complaint cell is very active to rectify things, it becomes a household name because the product is meant for the house. Here in case of Peerless, I knew the resistance that the agents were facing it was equated with Sanchayita when I joined. To make a household name then with that particular product was impossible, because it was branded as a bad product. So I had to go to make the company big and famous by a new route.

Addendum

Now, after the resignation of Mr. P.C. Sen, Ex C & MD, a number of 'professionals' are to be inducted to the board of Peerless General Finance and Investment Company Ltd., According to a spokesman of the company, Peerless has decided to concentrate only in the parent company with subsidiaries to fend for themselves.

The company's field force have been agitating over commission rate which has virtually stopped new deposit collection for nearly nine months. But, the Peerless management has already prepared a revised table of commission and has waived interest charges for the certificate holders owing to a favourable RBI directive stipulating a one time service charge of Rs. 80 for a deposit of Rs. 500.

The company is also considering a thorough restructuring of the boards of the subsidiaries. In fact, the process has already started with a couple of renowned doctors being inducted into the board of Peerless Hospital and B.K. Roy Research Centre Limited.

The company has diversified into many other areas with new subsidiaries such as Peerless Technologies Limited, Continental Commercial Company, Pulver Ash Projects Limited, Peerless Infotech, CAD CAM Consultants Pvt. Ltd. and Conforms Pvt. Ltd.

2

Liberalized Corporate India : A Strategic Perspective

Shyamal Sen

Theoretical Perspective

Strategic management is the formulation and implementation of plans and the carrying out of activities relating to matters which are of vital, pervasive or continuing importance to the total organization.

Corporate level strategic management is the management of activities which define the overall character and mission of the organization, the product/service segment will enter and leave the allocation of resources and management of synergies among its business units.

Procedure

Embarking on the process of strategy formulation setting of organizational objectives is the first major step. Before establishing objectives a thorough environmental and resource analysis will have to be undertaken, strategic options will have to be generated and the strategy which provides the optimum results will be selected.

Critical Considerations

Internal Considerations : Strategy activation seeks to

determine whether structure follows strategy, whether centralization or decentralization of authority is the best strategy, the degree of departmentalization that is the most beneficial for the organization etc.

External Considerations

At this stage organizational strategists must be concerned with relationships involving other organizations of similar kinds such as competitors and vastly differing organizations.

Due consideration will also have to be given the organization's obligations to the government and society. Laws have become numerous and propensity of citizens to litigate has increased. Business organizations find themselves in a sea of political forces. Political facet of environment is concerned with the organizations relationships with government officials, individuals and groups holding power.

Evaluation of Strategic Efficiency

Once activities are initiated in accordance with strategic plans, strategic evaluation should be undertaken by comparing actuals with standards and depending on the result of such evaluation, strategic control should be affected either by changing the strategic plans in the light of the changed conditions or additional knowledge and/or taking corrective action.

Indian Economy: A Derivative Discourse

Time has gone when companies struggled in a restrictive business environment. With thrust on economic liberalization and integration with the global markets, the business scenario is fast changing. The successful penetration of Indian markets by multinational companies effect of deregulation of industry and trade, rising trend of financial restructuring have created business environment in which only the fittest will survive.

India's efforts to accelerate industrialization and improve international competitiveness received a boost with the announcement of new Industrial Policy in July 1991. Launched in conjunction with liberalized trade policy and vigorous reform of monetary and fiscal sectors, the Industrial Policy is a part of the comprehensive programme of economic reform that ends at better macro-economic management and full realization of the country's economic potential. The new Industrial Policy is attracting significant capital flows on a sustained basis. Majority of foreign equity even up to 100% is encouraged under the new policy. Today India has more than 20 million investors, the second largest in the world. Efforts must be made to increase this number. Foreign investment upto 51% in a number of industries is eligible for direct approval.

Single market-determined exchange rate for the rupee has evolved with foreign exchange freely available for payment of royalties, lumpsum fees, dividends etc.

Rapid integration with the global economy has opened the Indian capital markets to overseas investors. These include entry of Foreign Institutional Investors (FIIs) into the capital market, foreign investment in off-shore funds promoted by Indian Financial Institutions and allowing Indian companies to float Global Depository Receipts which are traded in major international stock exchanges. The promulgation of the Depositories Ordinance in 1995 is a positive step towards integrating the Indian securities market with the global market and attracting foreign investment.

Strategic Restructuring

In this age of transition and transformation all major companies are engaged in undertaking major corporate restructuring exercise. Companies are discovering new opportunities and encountering issues that require quick decision making. Companies are beginning to form strategic alliances to become market driven and pursue competitive as well as co-operative strategies. Companies are focussing on consolidation of their business through corporate and financial restructuring which include mergers, amalgamations, acquisitions and concentrating only on those sectors where discernible or distinctive competitive advantage exists or can be created and leveraged.

In this changing economic scenario as companies grow from domestic firms into multinational corporations globally oriented executives shift their primary focus from domestic planning to management of world opportunities, markets and world resources. Strategic managers must continuously consider and assess both the international and national environments in which their activities can be carried out as they work within the culture and structure of the firm. Some of the basic areas from which planning has to be formulated are:

(i) assessment of external environment

(ii) degree of risk both on macro and micro level based on analysis of host country's economy.

(iii) behaviour of domestic and foreign currencies in world money market and opportunities for international financial investment

(iv) strength weakness analysis of the company—the state of its resources, cash flow, long and short term availability of capital, profits and human resources.

(v) formulation and implementation of strategy with competition in mind.

(vi) economic forecast.

Companies engaged in international business face special challenges in evaluating and controlling those businesses. Establishing standards of performance for foreign subsidiaries is difficult. Useful approach would be to use multiple performance criteria keeping in mind the necessity of developing criteria which are truly comparable.

Strategy Alternatives

Marketing Mix : Adoption of the marketing concept in strategic management suggests complete focus on the customer through 5 'P's of Marketing.

The first 'P' or Product refers to the total bundle of goods and services which should be produced efficiently but with attention to the purchaser in terms of both quantity and quality. Quality can be improved through statistical quality control efforts, quality circles and suggestion system among other methods.

The second 'P' or Price is an important strategic weapon which has a clearly predictable direction or impact. The price-quality trade-off determines whether the customer will buy better quality goods at higher prices and vice versa.

The third 'P' or Promotion strategy is the plan for informing and convincing the customer through advertisement, personal selling etc. about the superiority of an organization's products in comparison to that of others.

Place the fourth 'P' often called physical distribution relates to how the product or service is delivered to the end user.

Packaging the fifth 'P' refers to the get up, the final form in which the product will be available to the customer.

Growth : But at What Cost

Strategic management guides the executives in taking growth, stabilization or retrenchment decisions. Larger company size usually carries with it prestige and power and huge over-head expenditure. Growth becomes an objective, profitability—a constraint. If the objective is to maximise return for shareholders this concentration upon growth may not be entirely appropriate. If growth is achieved at the expense of future profitability it may be to the detriment of all concerned. A company may choose to cut product costs by sacrificing quality and then compete on the market place on the basis of price. This may increase sales and profit until the change in product quality becomes apparent to customers. In the long run sales may decline and the company's reputation for quality would be permanently hurt. Like decisions about other objectives like those relating to whether and to what extent to seek growth should be based on sound business reasoning and not on an emotional aversion to retrenchment.

The most important strategies for growth relate to growth through cost reduction, promotion, product development, integration, purchase of technology, technological innovation, market area expansion; market area intensification etc. Retrenchment though not a popular decision there have been cases where companies have followed the most extreme retrenchment policy, liquidation with distribution of proceeds to shareholders with excellent results. If a company's liquidation value is above the market value of its securities, liquidation may be a reasonable alternative.

While considering stabilization a well administered company will recognize the trade-off between growth and profitability. Gaining a market share at the expense of current profitability may be justified by the prospect of future profitability the added market share brings. But if a company believes it will be unable to capitalise on added market share, it might be better to stabilize sales and increase profits today. Efficiency improvement, risk management are some of the strategies for stabilization. The most important criterion for growth, stabilization or retrenchment decision is the company's degree of distinctive competence in the product or service area. Undoubtedly, The decision should be based on these two factors :

(i) company's strength and weakness compared to those of its competitors in the particular product or service field.

(ii) the permanence or otherwise of those strengths and weaknesses.

The Leap Forward

As we march towards the 21st century, business organizations must realize that to carve a niche for themselves, it would be necessary to extensively use strategic management techniques to make a thorough in-depth analysis of their strengths, weaknesses, opportunities and threats; to take corrective, remedial and preventive action to ensure that the organisations can survive and prosper in today's competitive business scenario. Special vision and foresight are required to visualise and appreciate not only the economic and technological forces operating in the country and the world at large but also the social and political environment which influences the business activities of the company. Strategic management if properly practised will help today's business executives to successfully meet the evergrowing business challenges and seize emerging opportunities.

3

Corporate Strategy in the U.S.A., Japan and India : A Comparative Analysis

Rakhal Datta

Corporate organizations and management differ from country to country. So do corporate goals and strategies. The present study is aimed at analysing the corporate goals and strategies generally observed in two leading industrial countries of the world: the United States of America and Japan. It should be pointed out at the very outset that the treatment of the subject in this study is somewhat general and simplified. For, not every corporate unit in any country might have the same goals and strategies. However, to believe that there may be exceptions here and there, but by and large different patterns are clearly discernible in different countries insofar as corporate goals and strategies are concerned. The primary concern of this work is to highlight these patterns in the two countries taken up for study and draw lessons for Indian management from them.

A corporate entity is an organization and thus implies that its activities are coordinated with a purpose. What, then, is the purpose or objective of a corporation? How are the goals of a corporation related to its strategy? Who or what groups of people establish and develop strategy? These questions are crucial to our understanding of the behaviour of corporations in different countries.

The Role of Ideology

In this connection, we have to recognize the role of ideology. An ideology is a complex combination of ideas, beliefs and attitudes and guides choice and action. A corporation, being a social organization, is guided in its choice and action by its own ideology. Sometimes corporate ideology is referred to as corporate philosophy, corporate values and corporate belief systems. These terms are generally used interchangeably.

Again, ideologies do not exist in isolation as abstract principles. Rather, they are embodied in, and reflected by, the thought processes, choices, and actions of the various constituent groups within the organization. There may exist numerous ideological configurations inside a corporate organization, but the dominant ideology of a given corporation, by definition is that of the controlling power group.

A strategy is a grand design for implementing an organization's objectives. It outlines a unified direction and often implies a competitive posture towards rival organizations. A strategy consists of a group of policies aimed at propelling the organization in a given direction that is in accordance with its objectives. For example, an automobile manufacturing firm's strategy for achieving the objective of profitable growth may include such policies as producing only smaller cars for the domestic market while importing larger cars from overseas, subsidiaries etc.

Strategy, goal and ideology are closely interwoven. Different goals call for different strategies. Goals are determined by ideologies, and choices of strategies is constrained by the ideological orientation of the organization. Even the question of who sets the goals and chooses strategy and how the goals and strategies are determined are the functions of ideology.

It is commonly accepted that the primary goal of a capitalist enterprise is to make money. Neo-classical economics is based on the assumption that the ultimate goal of a private enterprise is to maximise profits. However, the development of the theory of the autonomous management group that is divorced from ownership interests has produced a series of new hypotheses of management goals and motivations. Now a days, objectives such as growth in sales volume or corporate size, maximisation of executives' perquisites and achieving a 'satisfying' level of profits are emphasized. J.K. Galbraith in his popular book. *The New Industrial State* argued that the techno-structureregards growth in sales revenues as the primary goal of its organization. According to him, the members of the techno-structure are more interested in improving their own chances of promotion and salary increases through the growth of the company than in maximising profits for remote and faceless shareholders. However, the techno-structure may be more interested in growth than in profit but the effective power of strategic control in large U.S. corporations resides with top management, not with the professional and technical staff. And the primary objective of top management is more closely tied to the ownership interest in growth of earnings than to the organizational interests in growth *per se*.

Profitable Growth

Growth and profits are complementary goals. Growth means greater economies of scale and competitive strength, which lead to greater earnings, which in turn enable the firm to grow further. Maximum profits in reality means maximum growth of earnings over times, and the earnings are not likely to grow much unless the company's scale of operations also grows. The most commonly used measure of corporate performance in the U.S.A. today is improvement in earnings per share. Edward Herman sums up this widely held view by stating that "profitable growth is a reasonable summary of the primary objective of the large managerial corporation today" (Corporate Control, p. 86). Profitable growth is a more flexible concept than profit maximisation. In Herman's words, "it does not assume that the quest for profits is always of constant, unremittingly high intensity but may vary from maximising to satisfying or worse, depending on challenges, pressures and individual or organizational special

* John Kenneth Galbraith coined the term 'techno-structure' in his book *The New Industrial State* (1967) to refer to professionals and specialists in large bureaucratic organizations.

circumstances; and it stresses the expansive and non-static nature of the profit quest".

Top management's interest in profits is heightened by the widespread practice of time managerial compensations to earnings performance. Again, stock (share) options permit managers to purchase their own company's shares from the company at a predetermined price. Thus, rising stock prices bring handsome capital gains to successful managers.

Stock prices play an extremely important role in managerial motivation and behaviour. Not only they are important in affecting the size of managerial incomes through bonuses and stock option plans, but also influence the financial health of the company and thus ultimately affect the job security and mobility of the executives. Low and declining stock prices adversely affect the company's stock prices, which in turn make external financing difficult and expensive. Healthy share prices are not only regarded as a sign of the capital market's approval of the ways in which the company is managed but also keep shareholders happy and are the best protection against takeover bids. When the share price is depressed below its asset value, an outside interest may be tempted to make a merger bid or a takeover bid in order to acquire the assets at a cost below their market value.

Herman mentions yet another reason that tends to identify managers with ownership interests. In relative terms, the holdings of officers of the voting stock of their companies are rather small. In qualitative terms, however, their holdings have been very significant to their owners. "Small percentages of ownership in very large companies can amount to large absolute values and possibly large fractions of the personal wealth of the officers" (Herma, *Corporate Control*, pp. : 92-93). They would naturally like to see the value of their stock appreciate and the quickest and surest way of making that happen is to improve the earnings of the corporations they control.

Profitable growth is also pursued by managers for the sake of enhancing their reputation among professional colleagues in the business community at large. Improved reputation also means improved marketability of their talent and enlarged future earnings potential. Finally, many top-level executives in American corporations view their jobs primarily as games. Profits in the context of corporate game-playing become important for two reasons. First, they are the best measure of success of winning. Second, they provide the game players with large resources to play with.

The prevailing strategy of the great majority of large American corporations can be described by such terms as bottom line operations, emphasis on the return on investment, management by the numbers and obsession with short-term earnings. The essential nature of this strategy is to regard a corporation not as a community of people but as a money-making machine or a portfolio of assets from which as much profit as possible is extracted.

The preoccupation with short-term result has deep roots in American socio-cultural values. Corporations are not thought of by their managers and workers as communities of people who work towards common goals and share common interests over a long period of time. With some exceptions, corporate managers of many of the U.S.A.'s large companies want to receive quick and handsome return for their performance and then move on to greener pastures.

Familistic Groupism

The ideology of the Japanese corporation is rooted in Japan's familistic groupism. A corporation is, first of all, a family-like community, which is organically integrated into the larger family-like community of the national economy. Individuals are integrated into the societal whole through memberships in successively larger groups organized into a hierarchy, and the individuals and groups in the hierarchy are related to each other in a complex network of interdependency and reciprocity.

A Japanese corporation is a social group as well as economic unit. As such, the quality of interpersonal relations is very important. Harmonious and emotionally satisfying human relationships must prevail if the community can function effectively as such. The basic unit of work in a Japanese corporation is not an individual position, but a team work. For the team members, peer evaluation and pressures and the primary motivation for hard work and achievement. Individuals work out so much for their self-realization as for the sense of satisfaction of being able to contribute to their group's welfare, being fully aware that what is good for the group is good for its members in long run.

This brief discussion of the Japanese corporate ideology has been made to facilitate our understanding of the difference of basic corporate goals of Japanese and American firms. In short, Japanese firms' value growth more highly than profits and are less concerned with short-term financial performance than their American counterparts.

The separation of ownership of control in a typical large Japanese corporation is even more advanced than that in an American counterpart. The top managers of large japanese companies tend to view their companies as communities and all the regular employees as members of the corporate family without a clear status distinction between managers and employees. Again these business corporations, as members of the national family, are held responsible for contributing to the welfare of society by producing useful products. These ideological convictions tend to generate a preference for growth in production and an increase in market shares as the primary goal of the corporate organization.

It is of course recognized that no corporation can survive long without making a reasonable amount of profit. But beyond a certain minimum or reasonable amount of profits, pursuing profits solely for profit's sake is selfish or even unethical.

In an interview survey of 64 presidents of large Japanese electric equipment manufacturing firms conducted in 1970, the presidents were asked to chose from seven business goals, the three they considered the most important. As each president chose three items, there were 192 items chosen in all. The four most frequently chosen were growth (50), profits (49), market shares (30) and the ratio of new product sales to total sales volume (30). These results show that :

(1) Both growth and profits are important business goals for a great majority of Japanese firms,

(2) But, when the other two growth-related objectives (market shares and new product ratio) are considered, growth as a corporate goal appears more highly valued than profits.

In this connection, it must be remembered and pointed out that most Japanese corporations depend largely on borrowings from banks rather than the equity markets as sources of their investable funds. The banks and related firms—the large shareholders of companies—holds shares in these companies for the purpose of maintaining good business relations with the company, not as a source of investment income. Since the small investors tend to benefit from high profitability are relatively less important to the management, and since the large investors are not much concerned about the dividend rate, the management has little reason to be preoccupied with high profitability. The total absence of fear of corporate takeovers that could be triggered by falling stock price contributes to the lower degree of importance of Japanese corporate managers attach to high profitability.

By contrast, the growth of sales volume and market share are considered very important by every Japanese management. Japanese corporations as well as individuals and other groups are extremely rank conscious. The reputation of a firm enjoys in a given industry depends almost exclusively on the firm's share in the market. As the Japanese companies tend to specialize in one industry, the market share becomes doubly important; a firm cannot compensate for the decline in the market share in one industry by the increase in another. Then, the market share becomes one of the most important indicators of success of a Japanese firm.

Growth in sales and expanded market shares are important also for reasons of better employee morale.

To achieve the goals of growth and expanded market share three major practices characterize the typical Japanese strategy :

(1) Long-term outlook

(2) Emphasis on manufacturing excellence and product quality and

(3) Productivity through people.

The long-term outlook of Japanese corporations is a concomitant of the long-term employment of Japanese managers. Since, almost all managers are expected to stay in the same company and promoted as a group, there is no need to evaluate and reward their performance in the short run.

The Qualities of Japanese Management

Japanese managers tend to stress on better product quality as a primary means of increasing their company's market share. This is in striking contrast to the American practice in which managers use cost cutting as the primary weapon for improving their company's financial performance. Thus quality consciousness has a root in the traditional Japanese respect for craftsmanship and perfection.

Perhaps the most important single quality of the Japanese management system is its unfaltering belief in the importance of the human factor in the production process. That people—not machines, techniques or theories— make products and that good products can be made only by people pulling in the same direction is deeply ingrained in the Japanese management psyche. Again, this is in striking contrast to the view of American management that workers are merely suppliers of labour that the buyer may choose to buy by the hour, week or year.

The two models of corporate goals and strategy discussed above need more detailed analysis for finding out their relevance to Indian conditions. But certain preliminary statements can be made. To start with, let us stress the point that by and large the western model of business organization has been accepted in this country. Management education in this country has been completely patterned after the courses in American Business Schools. The financial institutions developed in this country, particularly in recent years, are also of western type. So, certain steps have already been taken towards the western corporate management system. At the same time, it is also true that this system does neither consider Indian condition nor adapted to it. It is almost bodily lifted to an alien soil.

Keeping this in mind, it becomes a moot question whether at least some features of the Japanese corporate strategy could be introduced in India. The answer is in the affirmative. In particular, Indian manufacturing companies, working for decades under sheltered markets, have not yet been able to develop brand names that are internationally accepted. Most of the products are shoddy by international standard. It is clear that we can learn considerably from the Japanese. Their "total quality movement" based on firm-based quality circles have worked miracles in improving quality of our products.

Secondly we can also emulate the Japanese labour relation practices. Since conditions in India and Japan are not exactly similar, some modifications again would be necessary here. But the essential point is that we should not blindly follow the western pattern of labour relations.

Last but not the least, growth should receive greater interest as a corporate goal in the Indian context as most Indian manufacturing companies are very small by international standard.

4

GATT, Liberalization and Globalization: A Strategic Readings of Trips

Sarmila Banerjee

Since 1990 India has adopted a series of economic reforms branded as New Economic Policy (NEP). These policies indicate a clear drifting away from the philosophy of planning and the attitude to concede more and more to the market (price) mechanism as an instrument to guarantee allocative efficiency (*Economic Survey*, GOI, 1991-92). Another distinguishing feature of this policy prescription was the perception of Indian economy, as an integrated part of the world economy, and, therefore, the influence of International Monetary Fund (IMF) and World Bank was deeply suspected to be the motivational force behind this policy formulation.

At present the global economic order is getting highly dominated by the IMF-World Bank nexus and this has become quite explicit in the latest round of General Agreement on Tariffs and Trade (GATT). The Uruguay Round is the most comprehensive set of multilateral negotiations undertaken so far under the auspices of the GATT.

The global assurance in technology today by a handful of countries is a determinant in structuring global relations both economically and politically. The opening of third world economics under Fund-Bank aegis is providing the multinational corporations (MNCs) entry into larger and larger areas of global economy, with technology playing a vital role in this process (Purkayastha, 1994).

Among the new areas those have been included in the Uruguay Round is the trade-related aspects of intellectual property rights (TRIPS). The Spectacular technological advances in the field of genetics and bio-technology, computer software and satellite communications have opened up new areas of Intellectual Property Rights (IPR). At the same time, this technological progress has made the implementation of IPR more difficult because piracy has become more feasible than ever before. This situation has created a need for fresh thinking on this issue. We are going to elaborate this point shortly.

Aurther Dunkel, former Director General of GATT, has formulated a package of proposals known as Dunkel's Draft. Final Agreement which involves the extension of IPR to many new areas and provides for across the board punitive measures in cases where the implementation of IPR is found to be lax. The industrially advanced countries differ amongst themselves on several other issues that are being negotiated in the Uruguay Round, but they seem to be unanimous in insisting that the Dunkel Draft inso far as it relates to IPR, be accepted as it is in order to establish a uniform, broad-based and effective world regime (Dhar, 1994).

To be a party to this broad-based world regime, India has also chosen the path of liberalization and globalisation. The purpose of this study is to show that why the developed bloc did not have any other option but to force World Bank-IMF to give the call of an integrated world economy along with the rigorous enforcement of IPR and why the contemplated utopia of economically more prosperous and equitable future on the part of any developing country (of course, including India) by participating in this integrated world, is a more wishful thinking.

The Dunkel Draft is recommending a rigorous enforcement of Patent Act which has some far reaching implications for the welfare analysis of the trade sector. We are choosing only the debate related to IPR because there the apparent argument of 'level playing field' can be established to be an incredible excuse in the face of standard results suggested by economic theory.

R & D and Patent Protection

Let us first talk about the fairly well-known argument of why to give patent protection to encourage research and development (R & D) activities. According to Stigler (1968), the production of knowledge differs from the production of other common investment goods in three respects:

(i) The economic outcome of research expenditure is much more uncertain compared to that of any other investment;

(ii) The knowledge, once produced, is usually cheaply appropriated by any other enterprise which wishes to use it, in the absence of legal barriers to appropriation; and

(iii) When the legal protection is granted, a monopoly position is conferred.

So, patent protection confers exclusive right to the inventor to earn rent from that knowledge over a certain period of time. Thus, there is not much conflict between the path of allocative efficiency through competitive market and the assurance of temporary legal monopoly power to encourage research expenditure.

Here it is important to reiterate the phrase that the monopoly power is temporary and sometimes given the nature of the knowledge it may be highly costly to enforce the Patent Act. Sometimes the product carries the knowledge to every buyer or the process may be used in a clandestine manner—so free riding is likely. Thus, knowledge carries elements of public good.

Role of Technology in International Trade

In the theoretical literature strong arguments have been advanced to justify the fact that why the developed countries have to take lead in the production of knowledge (technology). Vernon (1966) in his product cycle hypothesis has shown that to retain its leadership in the international trade the developed country has to keep on innovating new products. Because when a new product is innovated in the developed country, it gets standardized in the home market and then gets exported to the developing country. After a while, through reverse engineering the developing country would acquire information regarding the technology of that product and she would also produce the same for her internal (local) market. Now her import demand for the product would keep on diminishing and will gradually approach to zero. To maintain the lead, by this time the developed country has to innovate new products. One cycle completes, but when one product cycle is in its peak the next one has to start to maintain continuity of dominance. It may not be out of place here to recall the Schumpeterian theory of innovation for the retention of market power. Vernon's hypothesis was later extended by Krugman (1979), Dollar (1986), and others. For a brief discussion of the issue confer Kabiraj (1994).

Reverse Engineering, Technology Transfer and R & D

Now the developed country has to keep on innovating, but the benefit from innovation depends on the length of the product cycle and this length in its turn depends on the speed of reverse engineering this day we observe quite a few newly industrialized countries (NICs), like South Korea, Hong Kong, Taiwan etc., which are growing fast and making their progress mostly on the basis of technology imitation and not product innovation. Since the expenditure on R & D is quite risky, being backward in nature, initially these countries did not have the risk-bearing ability to undertake R & D. What they did was mainly process innovation. Either they directly copied the products or innovated cheaper processes, or both. Whatever be the case, the principal innovator could not appropriate the total benefit of producing the knowledge—the rent dissipated and some of these less developed economics became developing and finally newly industrialized by adopting free-ridding strategy. Their collective efficiency has significantly accelerated the speed of reverse engineering. Moreover, compared to immediate post world war period, the technological focus has shifted from metal-based engineering to chemical-based engineering, where for the latter, because of the inherent nature of the product, it is easier to be copied. It has been observed by Purakayastha (1994) in the Indian context that the post world war scenario had a number of new factors which were to change the nature of technological relations between nations. The newly independent nations had come on the global scene with little industrial base and a clear desire to industrialize. The emergence of a powerful socialist bloc did provide the possibility of retaining relatively more initiative with the developing countries than their technological development might have otherwise allowed.

But technologies of the 50's and 60's were relatively different compared to today's technologies. They were relatively mature, i.e., had been developed sometime back and were not subject to rapid changes. Thus a scheme of indigenisation of such technologies is different from a technological scenario where continuous change is the order of the day. Principles of steel-making, development of turbines, etc. changed for slower than the current technologies which are being driven by the micro-electronic revolution. The development of micro-electronics and cheap computing power was to introduce a new dynamism in almost all production technologies and the capital goods sector.

During 70's and 80's the information sector grew real fast in the advanced countries. Globally, the development of information technologies led to the increasing importance of knowledge intensive industries. Hitherto R & D intensive industries were largely chemicals, pharmaceuticals, aerospace and materials. With micro-electronics and information technologies, a much larger domain of R & D-intensive or knowledge-intensive industries have been established. Now, if the producer of the knowledge cannot be properly protected against the possibility of free-ridding, then it would be almost impossible for the developed countries to carry on the R & D programmes profitably.

Dunkel Draft and Trade Related Intellectual Property Rights

The Provisions of Trade Related Intellectual Property Rights (TRIPS) discussed in the Dunkel text are chiefly geared towards protecting the interest of the developed country. Before going into the details of that a few observations may be extended here to show exactly how the developed bloc tries to use the LDC's market as a convenient dumping ground. Hazardous industries are moving to third world and India after they are banned in the advanced countries. Cases may be referred from the asbestos production, infamous for asbestosis and lung cancer, or the production of benzidine dyes known to cause bladder cancer. In both the cases the plant-location has been shifted to India, Egypt, Mexico, etc.

Moreover, technology itself has become a strategic weapon in the hand of the advanced countries by using which they are contemplating on twisting the hands of the developing bloc. As a result the initiative for enlarging the negotiating mandate of the GATT by including IPRs has come entirely from the developed industrialized countries (Dhar & Rao, 1994). These countries have argued that inadequate and ineffective protection provided to intellectual property in several countries has given rise to production and trade in counterfeit goods, as a result of which conduct of fair trade has been affected. They expressed the desire of competing on the 'level playing field' so that no one can take any undue advantage from the rival country. Consequently GATT has recommended uniform patent provisions for all the member countries and the provisions can be summarised as follows:

(i) Provisions Regarding Patentable Subject Matter

There are two contentious issues here, raised by the Dunkel Draft. The first concerns the field of activity that the patent system encompasses. The second concerns the future status of a process patent regime that many countries like India have adopted.

An extension of the field of activities to cover selected forms of life (which were hitherto not considered patentable by most countries) has been proposed in the Draft. This includes patenting of micro-organisms and plant-variety protection. The adverse implication of these provisions on the agricultural sector would be analysed shortly.

Again, instead of process patenting the Draft recommended product patenting. Product innovation implies creation of new goods and services, and process innovation reduces the cost of producing existing products. So, product protection implies protection of the new active compound or the good itself, irrespective of the method by which they are produced or the form or manner in which they are used or sold. But process protection implies that only chemical methods by which an active substance is produced can be protected (Landien, 1986).

This shifting to product patent from process patenting is expected to check the speed of imitation and technology diffusion—the developed countries do not want to ease their access over this rent-earning asset, viz. technological know-how. Moreover, the risk of imitation has further been raised through the reversal of burden of proof. According to Dunkel text, if a patented product is made by a process other than that covered by the patent, it is incumbent on the usurer of the process to prove that the process does not infringe the rights of the patentee. This is the reverse of the existing procedure which stipulates that the patentee is responsible for gathering the documents required to prove the allegation. Instead of plaintiff proving the defendant to be 'guilty', now it has become the responsibility of the defendant to prove himself 'not-guilty'. Moreover, the patent protections are extended over identical products (or, sui generies). Identical products are not same products. Therefore, this provision seems to extend the rights of the process patentee to rub out the possibility of developing any substitute products and getting their processes patented.

(ii) Duration of a Patent-grant

Previously, the duration of patent varies across countries, but now with the contention of integrated world economy, a uniform patent duration of twenty years has been recommended for all the member countries of GATT.

(iii) Conditions Governing Working of the Patent

Patents assure technology transfer only if the patent is worked in the patent granting country (Rao, 1989). The developing countries have a particular stake in this and most of them have provisions to ensure working of the patent. One of the ways of ensuring that the patent is worked in the country of grant is the system of compulsory licensing. Compulsory licensing is given by the state when the patentee does not work the patent himself and refuses to give a voluntary licence.

Now in the Trade Related Intellectual Property Rights (TRIPS) negotiations, controversy over the balance of rights and obligations between property holders (patentee) and government, to be incorporated by the developing countries in their national legislation, is the most crucial area of conflict. The manner in which this is resolved is important for the developing countries because the degree of monopoly will be ultimately determined by the actual balance that the licensing provisions will establish (Abrol, 1994).

The Dunkel proposals have produced a one-sided agreement which gives absolute rights to, and abolishes the obligations of property holders. Article 28.1(a) includes importation as one of the exclusive rights of the patent holder. The implication is that without an authorization from the patent holder, it will not be possible any more for the government to permit a third party to import the product from a country where the invention is in the public domain.

Thus, Dunkel proposals attempt to curb the power of the national government in every possible way, so that they cannot create any barrier in the uncontrolled exercise of monopoly power of the owner of technological knowledge in the integrated world economy. All the national boundaries are to be removed and the market power of the multinational monopolists of the developed bloc is to be raised.

Indian Economy and the Dunkel Proposals

Living aside civil aviation as a special case, the Dunkel Draft (Art. 8.2 (a), Section I) limits subsides on R & D to 50% for 'basic industrial research' or 25% for 'applied research' (Creation of new products, processes and services). These restrictions do not apply to a developing country until its per capita income reaches $ 1,00,00 per annum; once the threshold is attained, there will be a further grace period of eight years (Art. 27.2, Section I). Chandra (1993) argued that this relaxation may be more ephemeral than what it appears at the first sight.

To see the real threat of being subjected to these clauses let us look at India's Gross Domestic Product (GDP) statistics. Over per capita GDP in 1990 was $ 316 and going by the growth trend over the previous 40 years (1.8 p.a.) we are likely to cross the threshold of $ 1,000 in not less than 60 years; and that too, if there is no further real devaluation of rupee.

However, the IMF has already declared that the GDP measures in national currencies converted into dollars at the nominal exchange rates are misleading as against those in 'international' dollars, i.e. at the Purchasing Power Parity (PPP) of each country vis-a-vis the US dollar. There is a strong possibility that the IMF, World Bank and the post-Dunkel GATT will move over to the new system in the not-too-distant future. In that case from the World Development Report (1982 and 1992) it can be seen that India has already crossed that $ 1,000 barrier.

Even if India remains below the threshold for the next few decades, she will still be adversely affected. For many large R & D projects, India might require partners on a more or less equal footing, whether in co-financing, or in ensuring a larger market for the new products. The partners can hardly come from the TNC-dominated countries from the north; one would have to look for them elsewhere in the third world, far or near, and in the erstwhile socialist countries of Europe.

Chandra (1993) has cited quite a number of instances where the relatively developed countries with per capita income greater than $ 1,000 per annum have expressed interest in entering into R & D collaborations with India—but these efforts will all be barred by the subsidy provisions of Dunkel Draft.

When countries are allowed process innovation and patenting thereof, then the general environment of R & D would be created and that may lead to some genuine product innovation. But in the absence of R & D activities in South, if the South-South trade expands, then owing to its extended monopoly rights all the benefit will be appropriated by the trans-national corporations located in the South. Because, they would be the only parties having access to technological information.

Regarding subsidy provisions of Dunkel text and those of

Indian Constitution, Kumar (1993) has pointed out the major areas of conflict. In Dunkel Draft while both in the case of manufactures and agricultural products subsidies for disadvantaged regions are allowed, they have to be given to all enterprises located there. No exemption is allowed for assistance given to a section of the people. Whereas in Indian Constitution we have the provisions for launching target-group oriented special assistance programmes (Art. 46). We know that in certain industries mostly persons belonging to the backward classes participate. It will be possible for another country to argue that goods exported by such industries (handlooms, carpets, etc.) or from such enterprises (National Textile Corporation, etc.) carry more than 5% subsidy, causing 'serious prejudice' to its interests and are actionables.

The second area of focusing attention is Art. 48 of the Constitution where the state has given exclusive right to decide actions to be taken to organize agriculture and animal husbandry on modern and scientific lines and, in particular, to take steps for preserving and improving the breeds of cows and calves and other cattle. There may be hindrance in achievement of this objective by state due to proposed provisions regarding patents (Art. 27 of Annex III of Final Act on IPRS). Since no exception is being made for pesticides and agricultural inputs and even for plant varieties and animals, a regime of patents or sui generies system is to be established, there can be problems in making available the genetic materials and propagation of improved breeds for general distribution to farmers.

Prices of agricultural inputs are very likely to rise due to the introduction of product plants in these areas (the argument is only about the extent) and their use or consumption which is strongly correlated to prices, will be adversely affected and in turn this will affect agricultural production. Difficulty may also arise in multiplying and supplying new breeds of plants and animals (Thomas et. al, 1994) which would negate Art. 48.

The New Economic Policy and TRIPS

From the foregoing analysis it is clear that the Dunkel Draft is aiming at removing all the trade barriers in a global economy and at the same time it is trying to protect market power to encourage R & D activities. Now, India is a developing country and she is aiming at rapid industrialization (and quick prosperity thereof) by initiating a series of economic reforms including liberalization and globalization on the one hand and being a signatory to the GATT proposal on the other. The contention of this sub-section is to show that under this "integrated world economy framework there would be the international economic unification, but that new international world would have her own disparities. Previously, some of the less developed countries like, South Korea, Taiwan, Hong Kong, could have taken off as newly industrialised nations through imitation of technology and process standardisations, but now under TRIPS—protection the developing countries would permanently enjoy this status of backward region (South) and North would be the dominant leader for ever.

When free-trade stand had been advocated as the first-best welfare maximising device, then all the markets are assumed to be perfect (absence of market power), all information are assumed to be 'common knowledge' and resource allocation through price mechanism is considered to be efficient.

Now, India is going for free-trade by lifting up barriers and signing the GATT proposal, but now the markets are not perfectly competitive—strategic R & D for rent shifting reveals the presence of market power at both the domestic and the international markets. Moreover, information is no longer common knowledge. In fact, TRIPS, among others, aimed at making information a private knowledge as far as practicable. It has rightly been pointed out by Chandra & Shukla (1994) that the macro-economic policy reforms are opening the flood-gates of global competitive forces for the Indian economy, a strategy merely based on exports to combat the might of multinationals can prove to be dangerous, causing erosion in the strength of Indian companies in the home market.

Macro-policy reforms encourage competition, but the ability to compete depends on the dynamism of industrial firms to develop competitive management practices. Besides, the competitive ability of national industries also depend on the endowment factors like infrastructure, human resources, and scientific and technological research and development, and the existence of related industries, especially the capital goods industries. These factors are also, traditionally, inadequate in all developing nations, including India.

To make the product competitive in the global market India has to produce quality, but most of the indigenous Indian products (manufacturers) are not capable enough to produce quality efficiently. The domestic market would be flooded by the MNCs and the export market may remain beyond reach. Besides any short-term gain, no permanent solution to India's problem seems possible from this newly emerging global structure.

It has been noted by Patel (1989) that the developed countries have placed themselves in an embarrassing position. They want to move in the mutually conflicting directions. On the one hand they want the liberalization of trade in goods, even in services, thereby removing all tariff and several non-tariff barriers so that free competition among nation states could extend the benefits of comparative advantage to all. At the same time, they want to impose and enforce their mirror-image of an intellectual property system, which constraints and binds the world production and trading system to a further consolidation of the already highly privileged monopolistic interests of their enterprises. Thus, on the same platform, they plead for freedom for their traders and protection for their manufacturers. They cannot really free Prometheus by binding him further and more tightly.

The North is fighting vigorously to open up other economies while closing theirs. The prospect of the emerging global economy, from the standpoint of the developing countries like India, seems rather bleak—particularly when advanced countries are seeking much greater protection of their 'right' to monopoly over knowledge through new patent/IPRs. Of course, this scenario has been made bleaker by the collapse of the Soviet Union and the absence of any countervailing global force vis-a-vis the North. And even if there are mutual contradictions among advanced countries/groups such as the USA, Japan, EEC, etc., these may be of little help to the third world. When it comes to transfer of technologies in "strategic" industries, they all act essentially in concert.

**This paper draws heavily from the M. Phil level dissertation of Mr. Banhi Baran Ghosh prepared under my supervision.—S.B.

References

Alagh, Y.K. (1994), : The Dunkel Proposals and India's Strategic Interests', in Nair and Kumar (ed.), *Intellectual Property Rights*, Allied Publishers Ltd.

Abrol, D. (1994) : Intellectual Property Rights in the Uruguay Round : A Review of the Indian Debate', in Nair and Kumar (ed.) *op. cit.*

Chandra, N.K. (1993) : 'Industrial R & D in Developing Countries and Dunkel Draft", Economic and Political *Weekly*, Nov. 27.

Chandra, P and Shukla, P.R. (1994) : 'Manufacturing Excellence and Global Competitiveness—Challenges and Opportunities for Indian Industries', *Economic and Political Weekly*, February, 26.

Dhar, P.N. (1994) : Foreword', in, Nair and Kumar (*ed.*) *op. cit.*

Dhar, B and Rao, N. 1994 : 'The Dunkel Draft on TRIPS : An Assessment' in Nair and Kumar (ed.) : *op. cit.*

Dollar, D. (1986) : 'Technological Innovation, Capital Mobility and the Product Cycle in North-South Trade' : *American Economic Review.*

Kumar, P. (1993) : 'Dunkel Text and the Constitution—Areas of Conflict', *Economic and Political Weekly.*

Kabiraj, T. (1994) : 'Intellectual Property Rights and Technology Transfer', *Economic and Political Weekly*, Nov. 19.

Krugman, P.R. (1979) : 'A Model of Innovation, Technology Transfer, and the World Distribution of Income', *Journal of Political Economy.*

Laudien, D. (1986) : 'Benefits of a Patent System—Product Versus Patent Protection". — Pharma Patent Seminar, Jakarta, Indonesia, Oct. 30.

Nair, K.R.G. and Kumar, A. (ed.) (1994). : *Intellectual Property Rights'*, Allied Publishers Ltd.

Nambiar, R.G. (1977) : 'Import Substitution, Domestic Resources Cost and Key Sectors in the Indian Economy", *EPW*, June 11.

Patel, S.J. (1989) : 'IPRs in the Uruguay Round', *Economic and Political Weekly*, May 6.

Purkayastha, P. (1994) : 'New Technologies and Emerging Structure of Global Dominance', *Economic and Political Weekly*, Aug. 27.

Rao, N. (1989) : 'Trade Related Aspects of IPRs', *Economic and Political Weekly*, May 13.

Stigler, J. (1968) : *The Organisation of Industry*.

Thomas, P, et. al. (1994) : 'Dunkel Text : Implication for Rural Sector', *EPW*, March 26.

Vernon, R. (1966) : International Investment and International Trade in Product Cycle', *QJE*.

5

Strategic Issues in Factoring Business : An Analysis of Business Environment

T. Mallikarjunappa

Theoretical Backdrop

Working capital finance has been occupying considerable importance in the wake of growing industrialization in India. The Reserve Bank of India has been framing guidelines for working capital finance from time to time. Various Committees appointed by the RBI observed that cash credit system of lending has been the most prevalent and bill finance has only been a negligible portion of bank credit. To encourage the bill culture, the RBI took various measures from 1952. In spite of all these measures bill finance formed only about 5% of bank credit in 1991. In order to help companies in meeting their working capital needs, the RBI appointed a committee headed by Kalyana Sundaram in 1988 to examine the introduction of Factoring Services.

The Present Status

Acting on the recommendations of Kalyana Sundaram Committee, the RBI introduced factoring services in India. The RBI allowed four major commercial banks namely Canara Bank,

State Bank of India, Punjab National Bank, and Allahabad Bank to offer factoring services in southern, western, northern, and eastern regions respectively. While Canara Bank and State Bank of India have opened their factoring subsidiaries and operated for nearly three years, very little is known about the initiatives taken by Allahabad Bank and Punjab National Bank. Although factoring organizations were initially allowed to operate in their respective regions, this restriction has been removed following complaints about operational difficulties. Initially these factoring organisations had projected huge businesses but, the first full year of operation showed that their projections went awry. For example, *Canbank* factors had projected a total business of Rs. 2000 crore for the first year of operation but the actuals turned out to be about Rs. 149 crore.

At the international level the RBI has permitted Exim Bank of India to offer forfiting (international factoring is called forfeiting) services in 1992. Exim Bank has been offering forfiting services to exporters as an intermediary for the last two years. The bank has reported a total volume of about $ 40 million for the two financial years while the potential of this market is estimated to be about $150 millions at India's current market share of 0.6 % of the international trade (Bhattacharya, (1988)). Bhattacharya also reports that at the international level forfiting is being used as a trump card to enter and capture the virgin markets of Asia, Africa and Latin America. Given the fact that the MNCs will have to spend lot of time, money and efforts and to understand the markets in an alien country, forfeiting agencies could use this as the strategic opportunity. The announcement of short-term export strategy by the commerce ministry based on a matrix containing 15 countries and 15 products, the export of which will be pushed aggressively by about 200 export facilitators, is likely to open new opportunities for forfeiting services.

The present volume of business recorded by both domestic factoring organisations and forfeiting agency indicates that factoring/forfeiting as a trade finance is yet to become popular and there is a vast potential to popularise this service. This paper discusses some of the strategic management issues that are to be considered by factoring/forfeiting organizations while formulating their business strategy. Specifically, this study highlights the environmental analysis in strategy formulation.

Issues in Strategy Formulation for Factoring Business

Every organization should commence its strategic planning process with a set of objectives (incorporating financial or accounting targets which it wants to achieve) and a broad and long term view of the product-market areas in which the firm wants to operate. In this context, Howe (1986) argues that statement of financial objectives in comparison with the existing performance of the organization indicates the extent of strategic decision-making process necessary. The analysis of variance between objectives and the current level of performance lead to an understanding of the reasons for shortfall in the performance. Periodic variance analysis reports could also focus on the extent of strategic decision-making that is necessary and indicate the broad strategies that might be adopted. Business firms which have a minimum variance need to undertake less strategic analysis, whereas the existence of a large variance indicates the need for a fundamental reappraisal of a firm's strategy. Since there has been a large gap between the projected performance and the actual performance in the case of factoring organizations in India, there is a need for fundamental reappraisal of their business strategy. Factoring organizations seem to have based their projections on methodology used by the RBI committee. But it is important to understand that the RBI committee had estimated the potential volume of factoring business based on likely credit sales (obtained by opinion surveys). Since factoring organizations were operating in specific areas they should have first understood whether or not they have the potential to exploit the whole of the market in the light of their resource positions and the fact that they are entering the service industry which is yet to become popular in the trade circles. It is also relevant to note that the RBI committee had ignored the introduction of short term money market instruments like commercial papers which are used by highly rated companies to finance working capital for a short period. The fact that only 'with recourse factoring' service is being offered by factoring subsidiaries is a negative factor for attracting the potential customers. These factors were not reckoned by the RBI committee while estimating the potential volume of business. So factoring organizations were caught unawares when they found that they did not come anywhere near their projected business. This indicates that factoring organizations have not undertaken environmental analysis to identify who their customers are, and what business strategies are required to convert the potential customers into actual customers. Further, they seem to be lacking in analysis of the relevant product-market environment and the assessment of the appropriateness of business resources. This indicates that it is futile on the part of factoring organisations to focus attention on a market merely because there exists a transaction of continuous credit sales. Unless factoring organizations are able to tap this market by offering their services at most competitive rates, these markets are unlikely to contribute to the financial targets of factoring organizations. Therefore, factoring organizations should strengthen their resources on those market segments which are likely to be their strongholds. This brings us to the question of focusing strategy to identify potential markets in which the goals of factoring organizations may be achieved. Environmental analysis relative to its current and potential resources is an extremely important exercise to identify the potential markets and to formulate business strategy. This type of exercise may result in modifications in firms' objectives and financial projections. Thus all factoring organizations have to modify their original aspirations, which were based on the methodology of the RBI committee, in the light of their own capabilities to create niche market for their services and the alternative avenues (by way of new financial instruments like debt securitizations) for financing trade debts. The discussion to follow focuses on the environmental analysis for factoring organizations which is a crucial issue in formulating business strategy.

Environmental Analysis for Factoring Business

Strategy formulation for factoring organizations would require an assessment of the external environment in which they operate and internal assessment of an audit of their own resources. This process will result in SWOT analysis. While the assessment of external environment would lead to identification of opportunities and threats, the assessment of internal environment would lead to the assessment of strengths and weaknesses. Depending upon the impact the environmental factors can have on a firm, Paine and Anderson (1983) have classified these factors into general and task environment. This classification assumes special significance for factoring organizations. Therefore, a detailed analysis of the factors to be considered by FOs in the environmental analysis is presented below.

General Environment: This comprises of those conditions which have a broad and less direct impact upon the business. Normally, even if there are quite significant changes in these conditions, the impact of such changes is likely to be felt only after some time gap. Such factors include the changes in the GDP of a country, government policy to privatise/nationalise the industries, labour policies (like exit policy, retrenchment, lay off etc.) of a government, changes in legal enactments (like MRTP Act, FERA, Companies Act, Contract Act, Negotiable Instruments Act, Law of Agency, direct and indirect tax policies), government policies on mergers, acquisitions, and joint ventures, the philosophy of a ruling party towards industrialization. All these factors influence the potential growth of various industries which in turn constitute the potential market for factoring organizations. The scanning of general environment will indicate the emerging market conditions for factoring/forfaiting services.

Task Environment: Changes in task environment will have direct impact on a firm's strategic decision-making. Therefore, an understanding of the impact of task environment can highlight the potential opportunities and threats to FO/FAs. Factoring organizations will have to consider two dimensions of task environment. One is the task environment of various industry groups which constitute the market for factoring business and the other is the environment in which the FOs/FAs operate. Following is the summary of factors which constitute task environments:

(I) Task Environment of Factoring Organisations' Potential Market.

Dimensions	*Factors*
Demand	
	(1) *Size and growth of markets*: Low levels of demand and modest growth rates in different industries constitute threats in a market and will intensify competition. This market has to be monitored by FOs to see whether intense competition results in non-price competition like more credit sales. If it does, it constitutes a potential market for FOs.
	(2) *Number and size of customers to whom companies sell goods on cash as well as credit :* More the number of customers, more is the potential for factoring the debts. Less the number and higher the size of the customers less are the chances for factoring the debts.
	(3) *Terms of sale*: Cash, credit with incentive for cash discount, open account credit, credit with bills. Credit sales, specially open account sales, constitute the potential for factoring services.
	(4) *Geographical distance between different companies in industry/groups and their customers:* More the distance, more are the chances of factoring debts.
	(5) *Characteristics of customers*: More diverse the customer groups, more is the potential for factoring.
	(6) *Physical distribution channels*: More the channels, less the chances of factoring (since the multi-distribution channels are more likely to know their respective customers better because of proximity).

(7) *Nature of competition in the market*: The nature of competition (derived from the nature of product and customer's perception of products) will influence competitors' choices of individual strategy. Firms operating under near perfect competition and having less number of large customers will have low profitability and limited room for strategic manoeuvre. FOs have to analyse this type of companies to know whether or not they constitute the potential market for debt factoring. While limited number of large customers may be a good market for FOs, companies selling to those customers may prefer to collect the debts on their own. But if large number of companies are selling to a few large customers and the latter have strong bargaining power, then this constitutes a potential market for FOs. If there are large number of customers under perfect competition markets, this may constitute the potential business for FOs depending on the terms of sale.

If firms under different industry groups are operating in common markets and are selling highly differentiated products to a large number of small customers, they will experience high levels of profitability. Such firms may or may not constitute potential markets for FOs depending upon the terms of sale. As there is no price competition between firms under such markets, they may resort to non-price competition. It is the presence on the latter which constitutes the potential for FOs.

Market Structure:

(1) *Barriers to entry and exit in the market*: Barriers will afford protection to existing sellers and pose a threat to new entrants. So the latter may be forced to offer incentives like more credit periods

to compete with the existing firms. It is these new entrants which are strategically more important for FOs. Absence of entry and exit barriers will intensify competition (depending upon the nature of industry) which may constitute the potential market for the FOs.

(2) *Number and size distribution of companies and their customers in industry groups*: The potential of this market for FOs will depend on the nature of competition and the terms of sale (discussed above).

(3) *Product characteristics*: Companies selling closely substitutable products normally experience high competition and low levels of profitability. This may constitute potential markets for FOs if there are large number of customers buying on credit. Whereas, companies selling highly differentiated products may experience high levels of profitability. This market may offer the potential for FOs depending on the bargaining power of customers and terms of sales.

The second type of task environment is the environment in which the FOs themselves operate. These are discussed below:

(II) Task Environment in which FOs Operate.

Dimension	*Factors*
Demand	
	(1) *Size and growth of existing markets for credit sales*: Bigger the size and higher the growth, more is the strategic opportunity for expanding the market by FOs/FAs.
	(2) *Number and size of organizations which have factored debts to FOs*: This gives an indication of the type of companies which avail the factoring services. This information vis-a-vis the analysis

of market structure (discussed above) gives information on the strategies to be formulated by FOs to explore the new markets.

(3) *Nature of competition*: Competition among the FOs has not been much in India as only limited number of FOs have been operating. At the international level only Exim bank has been permitted to offer forfaiting services, that too only as an intermediary for a foreign forfaiting agency. With the entry of private FOs in the domestic market competition may develop in the long run.

FOs would do well in their strategy formulation if they consider the competition for trade finance from different sources. Currently there are many alternative avenues for availing the trade finance. These are: Working capital finance from commercial banks, ECGC cover in case of exporters, money market instruments like commercial papers, and debt securitisation. If FOs focus on the relative costs of these alternate avenues for trade finance, they can benefit in formulating their cost structure.

Market Structure:

(1) *Number and distribution of competitors:* Currently there are limited number and the distribution is governed by the RBI directive to set up FOs in each geographical segment. Initially there were clearly demarcated territories for each FO. But this restriction has been relaxed in the recent years. For International trade only Exim bank has been operating. But in the years to come banks like SBI may offer forfaiting services.

(2) *Barriers to entry and exit in the market:* Initially the RBI permitted only four nationalised banks to offer factoring services. So, the entry was virtually banned. But in the recent years some private sector companies have started offering

factoring services. With more financial liberalization measures, foreign forfaiting agencies may set up their subsidiaries in India.

(3) *Characteristics of services offered:* Characteristics of services offered by different FOs is a significant factor in strategy formulation. These include services like sales ledger maintenance, credit intelligence, with or without recourse factoring, invoice factoring and factoring against bills, exchange rate and country risk covers, information to customers about emerging trends in the markets (market intelligence services).

Technology:

(1) *Cost structure:* Service fees charged and the extent of benefits of economies of scale passed on to the customers.

(2) *The MIS base:* The MIS base of FOs/FAs and the benefits of this to customers while selling in the existing as well as new market is important factor to attract business. MNCs would increasingly look for the MIS base of FOs to capture the vast and relatively unfamiliar markets in Asia and Africa. These companies will look for information relating to the potential customers and their expectations in buying a product, marketing skills to be used in the new markets, understanding the basis on which the customers buy various products, the existing manufacturers and their technological expertise etc. So FOs should develop MIS base to capture new markets by offering not just the trade finance but the strategic advantages associated with factoring/forfaiting services.

Government:

(1) *Impact of changes in law on FOs*: Changes in various laws, trade relations between countries, RBI's decision to abandon the territorial boundaries for different FOs, decision to allow private

sector FOs to offer services, and RBI's decision to notify the names of large defaulters to commercial banks (this type of decision may force companies to factor their debts to get immediate cash) will either open new opportunities or pose threats to FOs/FAs.

(2) *Impact of changes in import and export policies*: Government policy to slash import duties on many items resulted in many Indian companies losing markets to imported items. This type of policy changes have to be anticipated by FOs as these are likely to affect the sales growth of companies which may constitute the major customer base for FOs/FAs.

Commerce ministry's decision to focus the short term export strategy on 15 countries and 15 commodities (country-commodity matrix) to boost export volume to about $75-100 billions by the year 2000 from the previous year's (1995-96) target of $31 billions. will open up new avenues for Exim bank as well as the domestic FOs. While the Exim bank may formulate strategy to offer forfaiting services in these country-product groups, the domestic FOs will have to look for industries which are likely to grow because of this specific export strategy. Similarly the signing of 47 new business deals between Indian and Canadian businessmen at the meeting of Indo-Canada Joint Business Council to increase the bilateral trade will also open avenues for FOs as well as Exim bank.

There is evidence to suggest that firms which carry out environmental analysis enjoy higher financial performance than others (Grinyer and Norburn (1974)). Therefore, every firm should use environmental analysis to maximise its competitive advantage vis-a-vis its competitors. Environmental analysis will show how and when a firm should change or adopt its business strategies for anticipatory changes in various variables. The complexity and the number of variables in the environmental analysis will depend on the market conditions in various industries. For example, industries in which production and supply are determined by administered policies of government (like sugar, cement and steel till the recent years), the number of variables is relatively less and the process of estimating the impact of these variables is less complex. Also, these variables are likely to be relatively stable. But in the consumer goods market where production and supply are determined by the market forces, the number of variables is more and it is more complex to estimate the impact of these variables since they change quite fast. Therefore, the biggest question that is to be answered is how to track the changing environment? Although business data bases have been growing in the liberalized economic environment, these have not produced easy methodology for firms of ordinary capabilities. Various methodologies have been developed for capturing developments in different sectors of the economy/ business segments[1]. But very few studies are available for capturing the total environmental impact.[2]

The above process suggests that the process of obtaining strategic information for environmental analysis is "far from being systematic, complete, or even really informative about anything except current developments," (Christensen, Andrews and Bower (1978), p. 250) in a specific industry segments. Therefore, any company undertaking this type of analysis requires vast network of data and a mechanism to scan developments in various fields. This could be achieved partly by using new resources and partly by exploiting the already existing business strengths and resources. This takes us to the question of analysing internal strengths and weaknesses of FOs.

Internal Strengths and Weaknesses

The above discussion makes it clear that merely because the environmental would lead to identification of strategic business opportunities, no firm can afford to ignore the resources and its own strengths in formulating its strategy. So it is important to consider the resources position and the relative strengths of

FOs and the Exim bank in India. Although the discussion on environmental analysis may look uneconomical for small and new FOs, the existing firms have strategic advantage in the Indian context. Since the FOs and Exim bank are quite large in size and have relatively vast untapped market, they can afford this type of environmental analysis. There is also an added advantage to these organizations. Commercial banks which have opened factoring subsidiaries have been operating in India as well as in the international financial markets for a long time. So the parent organisations of factoring subsidiaries already have vast network of information which can be tapped and used by their subsidiaries. Also, these banks have vast network of bank branches which is surely a strategic advantage for factoring services. Same is the case with Exim bank. Being a bank involved in financing import-export trade, it already has information base of domestic as well as international markets. In addition to this, the vast expertise and information base of ECGC can be tapped to the potential advantage of Exim bank. Thus the FOs and the Exim bank in India have distinctive strengths to formulate and embark upon new strategies.

While the above are the strengths, the relatively low growth rate in this market and the introduction of new money market instruments may pose threats to FOs. If FOs and Exim bank focus on offering innovative services (discussed in task environment), they can convert this threat into an opportunity. Even the competitive trade finance of debt securitisation can be used to solve the liquidity problems of FOs/FAs. The movement towards market determined interest rate structure will make the corporate borrowers to scout for cheap sources of finances. The rate at which the prime lending rates are increasing in the Indian capital markets, it may become increasingly difficult for small time borrowers to afford high rates of interest (as prime lending rates are applicable only to highly rated companies). These developments point out that FOs will have to convert these developments into opportunities and tap the potential market. FOs should use the position of their sponsor banks to borrow funds from Euro and US markets where the funds are available at relatively low rates of interest.

Conclusion

The combined analysis of environmental factors and the internal strengths and weaknesses of FOs/FAs should go beyond the listing of consequences of different variables on firms financial targets. It should lead, as discussed above, to the identification of appropriate business strategies for a specific FO/FA. The uniqueness of business strategy is that the way the environmental variables, internal strengths, resources, opportunities, threats, organisational values, etc. are combined will result in different business strategies for each organisation. But identification of some of the factors suggested by Christensen, Andrews and Bower will be useful for all FOs in formulating their business strategy. These are:

> What really is our product? What functions does it serve? To what additional functions might it be extended or adapted?
>
> What is happening to the market for our products? Is it expanding or contracting? Why?
>
> What are our company's major strengths and weaknesses? From what sources do these arise?
>
> Do we have a distinctive or core competence? If so, to what new activities can it be applied?
>
> What, if any, better combinations of market opportunities and distinctive competence can our company effect, within a range of reasonable risk?

If the FOs/FAs seek answers to these questions and undertake environmental analysis on a continuous basis, it will surely put these organizations in advantageous positions. In conclusion it can be said that the large size of factoring and forfaiting organizations and the unique advantage enjoyed by these organizations should induce them to focus on strategic decision-making process in tapping the vast untapped market. Needless to say that there are no readymade strategies which will lead all business organizations to success in all settings. Continuous SWOT analysis can produce better results for this new service industry in the liberalized economic environment.

Notes

FOs: Factoring organizations. FAs: Forfaiting agencies.

1. For a discussion on some of the forecasting techniques see the background papers published in, TAPMI (1989), Workshop on Futurology; and TAPMI (1990), Seminar on Futurology (with special focus on methodologies); T A Pai Management Institute, Manipal.
   Some of the important papers are focusing the forecasting methodologies are:

Seth, S.C., ABC of Futurology, in TAPMI (1989), pp. 1-11.

Rao H.R.S., Futurology & Management, in TAPMI (1989), pp. 22-27.

Mohan S., Technological Forecasting Methodologies, in TAPMI (1989), pp. 28-56.

Jha, L.K., Management of Technology: Today and Tomorrow, in TAPMI (1989), pp. 61-76.

Lillge, W., High Technology for Health Care, in TAPMI (1989), pp. 119-139.

Acharya, G.N., Futurology in Electronics, in TAPMI (1989), pp. 146-170.

Martino, Joseph P., Technological Forecasting—An Overview, in TAPMI (1990), pp. 1-11.

Nayar N.K., An Econometric Approach to Forecasting Demand for Cement Industry during the Sixth Plan, in TAPMI (1990), pp. 12-28.

Mahasheri Fred, Lowell H. Qrren and Fereidoon P. Sioshansi, Scenario Planning at Southern California Edison, in TAPMI (1990), pp. 40-62.

2. The exception to this seems to be John D. Glover's study quoted by Christensen, Andrews and Bower (1978, pp. 250-1). They report that Glover has developed an approach to the total environment of a business firm as an ecological system. Glover's framework consists of four sub-systems— the immediate total community of a company, the culture in which it operates, the flow of goods and services being produced or consumed, the natural and man-made physical setting. Most of his work (as stated by Christensen, Andrews and Bower) is unpublished but has been summarised in "Strategic Decision-Making: Planning, Manning, Organization," in John D. Glover and Gerald A. Simon, *Chief Executives' Handbook* (Homewood, III.: Dow Jones-Irwin, Inc., 1976), pp. 423-41.

References

Bhattacharya, Rajat (1996), Forfaiting Services: The missing link in trade finance, Economic Times, January 4, p. 6.

Bose, S.K. (1990), Factoring: Means to end cash flow problem, Management Accountant, December, pp. 776-7.

Business Line (1995), 15 items to be promoted through brand equity fund: Short-term export strategy unveiled, Business Line, December 28, p. 1.

Christensen, C. Ronald, Kenneth, R Andrews and Joseph, L Bower (1978), Business Policy: Text and Cases, Richard D. Irwin Inc., Homewood, Illinois.

Grinyer, P H and Norburn, D. (1974), Strategic Planning in 21 UK Companies, *Long Range Planning,* August, p. 80; quoted in Howe (1986).

Hindu (1996), Chill in ties gone for good: Chretien, The Hindu, January 14, p. 1.

Hindu (1995), Focus on 15 products to boost exports, The Hindu, December 28, p. 13.

Howe, W. Stewart (1986), Corporate Strategy, Macmillan Education Limited, Hampshire.

Mallikarjunappa, T (1995), Factoring Business—An India perspective, in Financial Management of Developing Economies, G.S. Batra and Narinder Kaur (eds), Anmol Publications Pvt Limited, New Delhi, pp. 133-142.

Mallikarjunappa, T (1992), Factoring Business in India: Need, Dimensions and Implications, an unpublished manuscript, Department of Business Administration, Mangalore University.

Paine, F.T. and C.R. Anderson (1983), Strategic Management, Dryden Press, New York, p. 10; quoted in Howe (1986).

RBI (1988), Report of the study group for introduction of factoring services in India, Reserve Bank of India, Bombay. (Kalyanasundaram committee report).

Sengupta, A K (1992), International Factoring: Framework, Global Scenario and Indian Perspective, Finance India, September, pp. 515-24.

Shetty, J V (1992), Factoring Services in India, Valedictory address at the Top Management Conference on Factoring Services, NIBM (31.10.1992), reprinted in Canbank Quarterly Review, Oct.-Dec., pp. 5-11.

Tandon V G (1996), Forfaiting needs review, Economic Times, January 4, p. 5.

6

Observations on Mode Switching and Environmental Analysis and Diagnosis

Dilip Roy

The continuous interaction of the logistic process of a firm with its environment gives rise to various types of action needs covering, viz., operating, administrative and strategic decisions. According to Ansoff (1968) the strategic decision area is "concerned with establishing relationship between the firm and its environment". Increasing variability and unpredictability of the business environment constrain the functioning of the business managers forcing them to take active interest in environmental analysis for continuously adjusting to environmental changes.

Every firm has its own approach for adjustment which may be explicit or implicit in nature. While explicit process of formulating strategy benefits a firm significantly the implicit process rarely converges to the optimum one. As a result, there is a growing awareness to move away from the traditional system of first generation planning, i.e., evolving a single plan for the most probable future and go for strategic planning or strategic management that focuses on second generation planning by developing several courses of action for several scenarios of the future.

Emergence of the Concept

The subject being complex in nature drew little attention of the academicians at the early stage of its development. Mainly the practitioners felt the need of it and started developing different tools and techniques for their own benefit. But these works were done in isolation without any system approach. Credit goes to the works of Sloan (1964) who during his days in General Motors observed that initially they were not knowing what they were trying to do except sell cars which ultimately took volume from each other of the production divisions of the company. They realised that in the absence of a corporation policy each division was making its own policies and marketing some cars in identical price ranges. While trying to develop competitive strategy for fighting out the then unbeatable Ford they noted that they needed concepts of industry and business. They realized and boldly admitted that their first objective was to ensure satisfactory dividends, preserve and increase capital and not just to manufacture cars. The product policy they developed not only made General Motors a giant industrial house but also laid the foundation of structural analysis of industries for the development of competitive strategy.

Sloan's work was not lone in the line. The need for strategic management got considerable ground from the works of Ansoff (1971) and his associates who closely examined decision-making process of 93 companies that had gone for acquisitions during 1946-65. Their study revealed that planners outperformed the non-planners when measured in financial and sales terms.

Hegarty (1976) in his study of 46 firms for the period 1970 to 1973 observed that successful ones were those who could link strategies to objectives. Schoeffler, Buzzell and Heany (1974)'s study on 57 large corporations, engaged in 620 different product fields, revealed that strategic planning helped them well in achieving high return on investment and high profitability. All these works created awareness among the managers in the USA and European countries about the usefulness of business concept and strategic planning for becoming successful in the long run.

EAD Neglected in the Past

Unlike the western managers many of their Indian counterparts were paying very little attention towards strategic planning during the last decade. The traps of inertia and myopia had caught quite a few giants. Remington Rand is one such example where the firm did not correctly react to environmental changes. It lost its number one position in the field of manual typewriter by forgetting the need for marketing and giving emphasis on sales only. By the time the firm became aware of its deep trouble it became too weak in resources due to past losses to meet the challenges of both manual and electronic typewriter markets. Poor implementation also limited its diversification activities in the field of other office equipments like STD locks, Autodiallers.

The Indian Duplicating Company Limited is another example of stagnant bureaucracy. It was market leader having a near monopoly in early '80s. Its complacent attitude and short-sightedness have forced it to swim up-stream now. But inadequate environmental analysis resulted in unplanned launching of outdated selex copier without any zoom facility and of technologically obsolete Towa electronic typewriter. Of late the company has realized that its business should be in meeting customers' requirement rather than selling a machine it was offering in the past.

Even HMT, the India's largest watch manufacturer, did not care to study the environment and segment the market ignoring thereby the voluminous data available to it. Its over-emphasis given on four basic designs created little excitement in the minds of the customers. Its market dominance prompted it in ignoring the retail trade. In the early '80s when it entered the market of quartz watches the available designs looked no different from the mechanical ones. And all these added together opened up attractive watch-market for the competitors and new entrants. Now HMT is fighting out those challenges by paying more attention on segmenting market, putting up displays, offering better servicing facility and opening up exclusive shops but only as a giant under fire.

We need not go for many such examples because any one is good enough to portray the past scenario where frequently the idea of sales not only cornered the idea of marketing but also drifted away the attention of top executives from the concept of their industries.

While much emphasis has been given in the literature on Environmental Analysis and Diagnosis (EAD) and on defining the organization in respect of its external environment to legitimize its activities in the eyes of the society at large, the actual roles of the decision-makers were not at all satisfactory. With the introduction of the new industrial policy by the Government of India there is a total change in the business environment of our country. While Government has come forward with a package of business opportunities the ease in entry of the transnational companies may convert a part of the opportunities into threats for the existing giants and marginal players in many product fields. To what extent strategists are analysing and diagnosing the changes and rebuilding their strategy making process are yet to be watched in details. We have taken up this task of examining the attitudes and roles of the decision-makers during this transient phase of the Indian economy and for this purpose we have conducted a survey on corporate decision making process covering 426 executives at the top and middle level throughout the country. Though the survey work has a wide coverage the present study will be confined to attitudes of managers on environmental analysis and diagnosis only.

Need for EAD : Strategists' View

We have followed a structured interview method for our survey work giving emphasis on projective technique and inbuilt consistency checks. For example, a direct question of asking an executive about the importance of EAD could have been misleading because of the obvious reason that the answer would always have been affirmative in nature. In our survey work we have avoided this direct question and made an indirect assessment by requesting the respondent to indicate his or her preferred mode of functioning under a stable and turbulent environment. A change in the mode of functioning for a change in the state of the environment has been considered by us as an act of assigning importance to EAD. This approach may lead to overestimation of the proportion of executives ignoring environmental factors in their decision-making process because the planning mode of functioning may remain unaltered under environmental changes. But the conservative estimate we propose for the proportion of pro-EAD executives will definitely portray the situation with minimum number of false alarms.

Following the standard theoretical classification we have identified three pure modes of strategy making as proactive/entrepreneurial mode, reactive/adaptive mode and planning mode. As we are aware the proactive mode is centred around opportunities with an urge for expansion and growth, the reactive mode is centred around remedial activities and planning mode is oriented towards detailed analysis having both proactive and reactive thrusts.

As the mode of functioning of a top executive might depend on this attitude towards risk, we have used their inclinations towards attracting and retaining junior executives of different risk values for sub-dividing the 426 managers into three categories—risk-oriented managers (ROM), risk-aversive managers (RAM) and average risk-taker (ART). We have observed from our survey result that out of 426 managers 254 are risk-oriented i.e. nearly 59.62 percent managers take risk in their strategic planning. Number of risk aversive managers is found out to be 87 i.e. 20.42 percent. Rest of the managers are average risk takers in the sense that they have both risk-oriented and risk-aversive thrusts.

To eliminate the possible mixing up of value system of the top executive with the preferred mode of strategy making under the two extreme states of the environment we have examined through two-way classification (stable and turbulent environment) the mode switching behaviour of executives separately for each risk group. Presented below are three tables depicting the mode switching matrices.

Table 1
Mode Switching Matrix for ROM

		Mode under turbulent environment			
		Proactive	*Reactive*	*Planning*	*Total*
Mode	Proactive	7	24	37	68
under	Reactive	4	2	6	12
stable	Planning	47	102	25	174
environment.	Total	58	128	68	254

Table 2
Mode Switching Matrix for RAM

		Mode under turbulent environment			
		Proactive	*Reactive*	*Planning*	*Total*
Mode	Proactive	2	7	8	17
under	Reactive	1	0	2	3
stable	Planning	17	33	17	67
environment.	Total	20	40	27	87

Table 3
Mode Switching Matrix for ART

		Mode under turbulent environment			
		Proactive	*Reactive*	*Planning*	*Total*
Mode	Proactive	0	4	13	17
under	Reactive	1	3	5	9
stable	Planning	25	23	11	59
environment.	Total	26	30	29	85

Now to estimate the groupwise mode loyalty we calculate the proportion of mode loyals (i.e. proactive to proactive, reactive to reactive and planning to planning modes) to the total number of executives covered under a specific group. For managers falling under ROM group, mode loyalty is obtained as 13.386%. Same for RAM and ART group are 21.839% and 16.471% respectively. Thus conservative estimates for percentage of pro-EAD executives workout as 86.614%, 78.161% and 83.529% respectively for ROM, RAM and ART groups.

The general belief that risk-oriented managers pay less attention on EAD is not at all tenable from our survey results. Rather it is observed that they give more weightage on environmental analysis and do not act on impulses. The main reason behind this may be for locating opportunities much ahead of others. Risk-aversive managers are at the other end of the continuum with average risk-takers paying more attention on EAD than risk-aversive managers and less attention on EAD than risk-oriented managers. However, the differences among these three groups may not be significant enough.

Risk and Strategy Making

To critically examine the differences, if any, among the ROM, RAM and ART groups we next construct two contingency tables corresponding to two extreme states of the environment. In Table 4 we examine the significance of association between risk taking propensity and mode of strategy planning under a stable environment and in Table 5 we examine the significance of association between risk taking propensity and mode of strategy planning under a turbulent environment.

Table 4

A cross classification of managers by mode of strategy planning and the risk-taking attitude under a stable environment.

Mode \ Risk	*Risk Oriented*	*Average Risk Taker*	*Risk Aversive*	*Total*
Proactive	68	17	17	102
Reactive	12	9	3	24
Planning	174	59	67	300
Total	254	85	87	426

From the above classification we can easily examine the null hypothesis that risk propensity and mode of strategy planning are not associated against the alternative that they are associated. The standard χ^2 test reveals that the observed value of χ^2 test statistic is 7.60040 against a tabulated value of 9.488 for 4 degrees of freedom and for a size of the test as 5%. As the observed value is less than the tabulated value we conclude that these two attributes are not associated under a stable environment. Thus propensity to take risk need not be taken into consideration for cross classifying the mode of strategy planning.

Similarly if we examine the situation under a turbulent environment the corresponding derived table of importance will be the following.

Table 5

A cross classification table of managers by mode of strategy planning and risk taking attitude under a turbulent environment.

Risk / *Mode*	*Risk Oriented*	*Average Risk-Taker*	*Risk Aversive*	*Total*
Proactive	28	26	20	104
Reactive	128	30	40	198
Planning	68	29	27	124
Total	254	85	87	426

The null hypothesis that the propensity to take risk and the mode of strategy making are not associated is found to be tenable here also as the observed value of the χ^2 test statistic is 6.10884 against the critical value of 9.488 as pointed out earlier at a 5% size of the test.

Thus we are in a position to draw a major conclusion that irrespective of whether the environment is stable or turbulent mode of strategy planning does not significantly depend on the risk taking attitudes of the managers.

Environmental Turbulency and Strategy Making

It may, however, be noted that working under a stable situation decision makers mostly prefer the planning mode of functioning; the percentage of such executives being as high as 70.422%. The next best mode of strategy making is proactive mode covering 23.944% of the executives. The reactive mode is followed by only 5.634% managers. The situation becomes completely different under a dynamic environment. More and more the environment becomes turbulent, more and more decision-makers switch-over to reactive mode of functioning. An estimated percentage of 46.479 executives prefer reactive mode of strategy planning under unpredictable situation. Percentages of entrepreneurs preferring proactive and planning modes are 24.413 and 29.108 in that order. Thus the major switch-over is from planning mode to reactive mode and this may be due to the fact that planning becomes increasingly difficult under uncertainty induced by the environmental changes. That the idea of fishing in troubled water is not very appealing to managers at least in case of making policy decision is clear from the fact that nearly same proportion of proactors is observed under the two extreme states of the environment. Our observations are different from what has been suggested by Khandwalla (1977). In his study on some top management styles he suggested that under maximum turbulency of the environment entrepreneurial, i.e., proactive mode and neoscientific mode are preferable, and under minimum turbulency of the environment conservative, i.e., reactive mode is preferable.

In the light of inferential statistics we may observe a significant structural change in the decision-making process if we compare the χ^2 measure on equality of proportions with that of its critical value.

The following table depicts the proportion of managers preferring different modes of strategy making under the stable and turbulent nature of the environment.

Table 6

Proportion of managers preferring proactive, reactive and planning modes under stable and turbulent environment.

Mode / *Environment*	*Proactive*	*Reactive*	*Planning*	*No. of observation*
Stable	.23944	.05634	.70422	426
Turbulent	.24413	.46473	.29108	426

The observed value of the χ^2 measure for closeness among these two sets of proportions works out as 104.7272. The corresponding critical value at 5% level of significance with two degrees of freedom is 5.991 only. Thus the difference is not at all insignificant, i.e., the two sets of proportions describe two different approaches observed to be widely apart.

Mode Switching Pattern

Since mode of strategy planning does not depend significantly on risk taking attitude of a manager, we may combine the mode switching matrices presented under Tables 1-3 to obtain the managers' overall mode switching matrix.

Table 7

Mode Switching Matrix for all Types of Managers.

From	*To*	*Mode under turbulent environment*			
		Proactive	*Reactive*	*Planning*	*Total*
Mode under stable environment	Proactive	9	35	58	102
	Reactive	6	5	13	24
	Planning	89	158	53	300
	Total	104	198	124	426

From the above table we estimate the overall mode loyalty as (9+5+53)/426 = 15.728% and the total mode switching coefficient as 84.272%. Thus the conservative proportion of pro-EAD managers work out as high as. 84272 and is probably one of the most significant impact of the new industrial policy of the Government of India on business executives.

Making an appeal to the standard theory of brand switching [see Fitz Roy (1976)] we may now obtain the transition matrix for mode switching from stable to turbulent state, as the Indian business environment is moving in the same direction.

Table 8
Transition Matrix for Mode Switching

From \ To		Mode under turbulent environment		
		Proactive	*Reactive*	*Planning*
Mode under stable environment	Proactive	.08823	.34314	.56863
	Reactive	.25000	.20833	.54167
	Planning	.29667	.52667	.17666

This transition matrix can be used for obtaining steady state solution through Markovian analysis. One may also examine the dynamicity of this transition by applying SBS, Hendry and entropy models on the above data set. Further the degree of turbulency can be estimated by observing changes in the transition matrix, if any.

Thus, if we summarise our observations made so far we may conclude that the mode of strategy planning is closely associated with the state of environment and is rarely dependent upon the risk-taking attitude of the strategist. It has also been observed that the planning mode is highly preferred under a stable environment; this may be true because a meticulously drawn complex plan works with reasonable certainty under a stable environment. The major shift in mode takes place from planning to reactive one, when the environment changes from stable to transient state. It has also been observed that proportion of pro-EAD managers is highly significant.

Since environmental turbulency has a significant impact on strategy planning and managers assign high weightage on environmental analysis one should examine the environmental factors in details and try to assign ranks to those factors for arriving at a combined measure of environmental impact on a firm. Remaining part of our study deals with these issues and makes a comparison with earlier works on factor ranking.

Choice of Environmental Factors

It has been observed by many researchers that firms which perform EAD properly become successful in the long run. Failing archetypes are those which either do not perform EAD or do it in an inadequate and a cursory way. According to Miller and Friesen (1977) impulsive and stagnant bureaucratic managers do not adequately study the environment. Also firms with weak leadership or with weak financial base may not be in a position to make use of any environmental change and remain a captive in the hands of the external forces.

The business environment is so wide, heterogeneous and complex in nature that one has to divide and select a few major parts of it for the purpose of gathering information. According to Porter (1980) the key aspect of a firm's environment is the industry or industries in which it competes and the competition in an industry has its origin in the basic economic structure. The five fundamental forces driving industry competition have been identified by Porter as rivalry among existing firms, bargaining power of buyers, threat of new entrants, bargaining power of suppliers and threat of substitute products or services. To cope up successfully with these forces Porter has suggested three generic strategies as cost leadership, product differentiation and focusing on a particular buyer group. Glueck (1980), on the other hand, has given emphasis on supplier/technological factor, market/competitive factor, Government/legal factor, economic factor, geographic factor and social factor. The coverage of Glueck's classification is more than that of Porter and has a wider emphasis as may be noted from the discussion that follows.

If we start from Porter's competitive forces and combine the bargaining power of suppliers and threat of substitute products or services along with the technological changes in the field of processing activities, facilities and input materials we may obtain an environmental factor termed by Glueck as supplier/technological factor. Similarly, the rivalry among the existing firms, threat of new entrants, and a part of threat of substitute products or services may be placed under a common umbrella of market/competitive factor. Further, the bargaining power of buyers in particular and society at large, the changes in the life-style and demand for quality products, the emerging values and ethos may get intermingled with each other and develop a broader expectation from and role of the society giving rise to a wider concept of social factor much wider than what Porter thought as sufficient.

According to us, Porter's basic economic structure is not only the root of industries competition but also the generator of business concepts. Most of the past studies on EAD have attached utmost importance on economic factor. If we consider the inflationary or deflationary forces acting on prices of goods and services, we see that they affect both ends of the logistic process of a firm. The management process is also tied up with the stages of the business cycle. For depression, recession, recovery or prosperity action needs differ in nature and magnitudes and as a result action instructions start varying. Our study, therefore, wants to attach due weightage on economic factor during our survey analysis.

While Porter was mainly concerned with firms operating in the U.S.A. we are concerned with firms operating in India and that too under the new industrial policy of the Government of India. Infact we feel that in India the Government and legal factors increasingly affect business operation in a significant way. It plays many a role—the role of a regulator of marketing forces, the role of a bulk purchaser of goods and services, the role of a promoter of many industries, the role of a subsidiser and a protector of firms operating in different vulnerable sectors of the economy and the most important role is the role of a tax-setter. Our study therefore keeps in its fold the government and legal factor as a major sub-division of the business environment and wants to portray the present perception of the decision-makers about it and match the same with past reactions.

Truly speaking we do not have much to reason for the geographic factor and defend its inclusion in our study. We know that the emerging concept of global village and slow but steady development of the infrastructural facilities for production and transhipment of goods for almost all the business centres in our country and abroad may in due course reduce the geographic factor to a non-entity. But for the present study we have included this factor mostly to retain the compatibility with the classification of other research studies.

During the course of analysis and diagnosis of the business environment a decision-maker may not attach equal weightage, on all the six factors enlisted above and studied by us. Collection of information being a costly affair, managers assign different priorities on different factors. Various research studies have been conducted on this crucial issue and the most important environmental factor has been identified in different places at different points of time. But none eliminated the effect of risk in their analysis. We feel that there is every possibility of getting a distorted picture if we do not consider the role of risk on assignment of highest priority to an environmental factor. In our study on environmental factors we have therefore tried to first examine this association between the risk-taking attitude of a decision-maker and his assignment of highest priority to an environmental factor. Though we have already seen that the propensity to assume risk does not affect the mode of strategy planning yet it is quite probable that the most important factor for a business executive may be dependent on his risk-taking attitude. The other aspect of our study is to assign rank/weightage to environmental factors for a possible use in the development of environmental threat and opportunity profile, commonly known as ETOP.

Priority Assignment and Risk

In the following table we present the frequency of occurrences of different environmental factors considered by managers as most important under various risk-taking propensities. The total number of managers covered here is 422 as 4-answer slips were found to be incomplete in respect of this particular item of interest.

To examine the equality of proportions amongst ROM, ART and RAM in respect of their assigning highest importance to different environmental factors, we observe that under the standard χ^2 test the observed value of the test statistics works out as 26.86874. The critical value at 5% level of significance for 10 degrees of freedom being 18.307 we reject the null hypothesis of equality of proportions. Thus there are significant differences among risk-oriented, risk-aversive and average risk-taking managers in respect of their views about the most important environmental factor. This non-uniformity among the three risk groups automatically calls for further sub-division of the table 9 for pairwise comparisons.

Table 9

Frequency table for most important environmental factor with stratification by risk-taking attitude.

Most Important Environmental Factors	*As viewed by*							
	ROM		*ART*		*RAM*		*Total*	
	Frequency	*Proportion*	*Frequency*	*Proportion*	*Frequency*	*Proportion*	*Frequency*	*Proportion*
Economic	85	.33865	19	.22619	21	.24138	125	.29621
Government/ legal	24	.09562	20	.23810	11	.12644	55	.13033
Supplier/ Technological	13	.05179	5	.05952	2	.02299	20	.04739
Market/ Competitive	83	.33068	16	.19048	26	.29885	125	.29621
Geographic	23	.09163	9	.10714	10	.11494	42	.09953
Social	23	.09163	15	.17857	17	.19540	55	.13033
Total	251	1.00000	84	1.00000	87	1.00000	422	1.0000

A close look at figures on proportions indicates that there may not be much difference between ART and RAM and hence we first examine these two groups of managers for equality of proportions among themselves. The χ^2 measure of closeness between these two groups works out as 6.5066, while the critical value at 5% level of significance for 5 degrees of freedom is 11.070. We thus note that in respect of assigning highest priority to an environmental factor risk-aversive and average risk-taking managers behave in an identical fashion. Combining ART and RAM groups under one fold and comparing the same with ROM group we recalculate the χ^2 measure and observe that its value now comes out as 19.73599 against a tabulated χ^2 value at 5% level of significance for 5 degrees of freedom as 11.070. Thus we arrive at a conclusion that the type of environmental analysis carried out by a risk-oriented manager is markedly different from that of the rest. Because of this inherent heterogeneity among the groups, factor ranking should be done separately for ROM group and for the combined ART and RAM group.

Factor Ranking

Since rank is measured on an ordinal scale the usual calculation of average rank score for the environmental factors and re-ranking them based on those average values may not be technically sound. We consider a different approach which may be termed as Elimination and Combination approach for factor ranking. This approach is based on recalculation of cumulative frequencies, at multiple stages. For example, to pick up the factor of r-th rank we calculate cumulative frequencies for those factors which are yet to be ranked and select the factor with highest cumulative frequency. The factor so selected at the stage of r-th ranking will be eliminated from the factor list for all the subsequent rankings.

The following table presents rank frequency matrix for risk oriented managers covering all the environmental factors.

Table 10

Rank Frequency Matrix for Environmental Factors for ROM.

	Environmental Factors						
Rank	*Economic*	*Govt./ Legal*	*Supplier/ Techno- logical*	*Market Compe- titive*	*Geo- gra- phic*	*Social*	*Total*
1	85	24	13	83	23	23	251
2	64	47	33	62	18	27	251
3	54	54	64	28	28	23	251
4	25	64	68	30	31	33	251
5	19	36	47	30	55	64	251
6	04	26	26	18	96	81	251
Total	251	251	251	251	251	251	—

For assigning the highest rank i.e. rank 1 to an environmental factor we examine the highest frequency corresponding to that rank. The highest frequency is 85 corresponding to economic factor. Hence economic factor is assigned rank 1. Now eliminating the economic factor from the list we calculate the cumulative frequencies for all the remaining factors, cumulation being upto rank 2. The cumulative frequencies for Government/Legal,

Suppliers/Technological, Market/Competitive, Geographic and Social factors are respectively 71, 46, 145, 41 and 50. The highest cumulative frequency 145 corresponds to market/ competitive factors. Hence rank 2 is assigned to market/competitive factor. Proceeding in this fashion we get the final ranking as follows:

Rank	*Factor*
1	Economic
2	Market/Competitive
3	Government/Legal
4	Supplier/Technological
5	Social
6	Geographic

The rank frequency matrix for the combined groups RAM and ART is given in Table-11 followed by the final ranking table.

Table 11

Rank Frequency Matrix for Environmental Factors for the Combined RAM and ART Groups:

RANK	*Economic*	*Environmental Factors*					
		Environ-mental Govt./ Legal	*Factors Supplier/ Techno-logical*	*Market Compe-titive*	*Geo-gra-phic*	*Social*	*Total*
1	40	31	7	42	19	32	171
2	45	30	31	29	20	16	171
3	42	27	28	39	22	13	171
4	30	44	33	23	23	18	171
5	11	27	44	23	33	33	171
6	3	12	28	15	54	59	171
Total	171	171	171	171	171	171	

Rank	Factor
1	Market/Competitive
2	Economic
3	Government/Legal
4	Supplier/Technological
5	Geographic
6	Social

Thus, views of risk-oriented managers differ from risk-aversive and average risk-taking managers in respect of market/competitive and economic factors on one hand and geographic and social factors on the other. In respect of government / legal and supplier/ technological factors all the managers assign same ranks. Probably the risk-oriented managers feel that they can take care of the competitive forces if the overall economic condition is good and hence assign highest weightage to economic factor. Risk-aversive and average risk-taking managers being more defensive in nature want to know the competitive situation and market condition first and then to depend on economic condition. Similarly a risk-oriented manager may be more interested in noting social changes while offering a new product concept or a modified version of the existing product. Risk-aversive and average risk-taking managers on the other hand may assign least weightage on it as they do not prefer to lead the market. However, if one combines economic factor with government/legal factor and social factor with Geographic factor one may arrive at identical factor ranking for all the groups.

In this context let us refer to the work of Glueck (1980) covering 358 large corporations. He observed that economic and government factors were most important. The next important factor according to his study was market challenges. Supplier's challenges were noticed to be far behind. Similar observation was also made by Bibault (1982). Our study on risk-oriented managers is again comparable with that of Glueck. Further division of economic and government factor in our study is of course giving a better insight indicating that economic factor is the most important one. The study of Collings (1969) also confirmed that the most important environmental factor for scanning by managers was market/competitive factor. However, in case of Collings study the next important factor was social/geographical factor. According to Aguilar (1967) and Wall (1974), the most important factor was market/competitive factor followed by supplier/ technological factor. While our study on risk-aversive and average risk-taking managers confirm that market/competitive factor has been considered as the most important factor by the risk-avoiders, supplier/technological factor has been found to be far behind the economic and governmental factors.

In the Indian context Wadhva (1974) made a detailed study on environmental planning. Analysing the input-output structure over a ten-year period, Wadhva observed that economic and regulatory conditions were the two most important environmental factors. Our study, however, reveals that the economic factor is still one of the most important factors but the regulatory factor holds the third position now. This may be due to withdrawal of many regulatory measures in the recent past and creation of a comparatively free environment.

The following table gives a summary of different studies made in the past along with the one we have presented here.

Factors	*Wall*	*Agu-ilar*	*Coll-ings*	*Bibault*	*Glueck*	*Wadhva*	*Roy*
Economic/ Governmental	-	8%	5%	67%	Most	Most	Most
Supplier/ Technological	Next Most	10%	15%	7%	Least	-	Next Least
Market/ Competitive	Most	75%	60%	26%	Next Most	-	Next Most
Social/ Geographical.	Least	7%	20%	-	-	-	Least

Study on Internal Environmental Factors

Our discussion may remain incomplete if we do not examine factor ranking for internal environment and the effect of risk-taking attitude of the top executives on the same. Unlike external environment for which different researchers have proposed different classifications internal environment can be divided into major functional areas, i.e. Finance, Marketing, Production, personnel and corporate resources without raising any controversy.

We have already seen that in respect of external environmental factors priority assignment is highly related with risk taking attitude of top managers. If similar such relationship exists for internal environmental factors also may need to be examined. For this purpose we present the following table where the frequency of occurrences of different internal factors considered by managers as most important under various risk-taking propensities are given. The total number of managers covered here is 420 as 6 answer-slips were found to be incomplete in respect of this particular item of interest.

Table 12

Frequency table for most Important Internal Factor with Stratification by Risk—Taking Attitude.

Most important internal factor	*As viewed by*						*Total*
	ROM		*ART*		*RAM*		
	Frequency	*Proportion*	*Frequency*	*Proportion*	*Frequency*	*Proportion*	*Frequency*
Finance	45	.18072	17	.20000	16	.18605	78
Marketing	44	.17671	16	.18824	7	.08140	67
Production	54	.21687	27	.31765	22	.25581	103
Personnel	14	.05622	9	.10588	8	.09302	31
Corporate resources	92	.36948	16	.18824	33	.38372	141
Total	249		85		86		420

To examine the equality among the three sets of proportions corresponding to three stratum ROM, ART and RAM we apply the χ^2 test for closeness and observe that the value of the test statistic is 16.5921. The corresponding critical value at 5% level of significance for 8 degrees of freedom is 15.507. As the observed value is greater than the critical value we reject the null hypothesis of equality of proportions among the three risk groups. For both external and internal environmental factors managers of different risk values attach different priorities to different factors.

If we make a pairwise comparison we observe that the χ^2 measure of closeness between ROM and RAM is 5.66447 while the corresponding critical value at 5% level of significance and 4 degrees of freedom is 9.488. This leads to a rather surprising conclusion that both risk-oriented and risk-aversive managers behave in an identical fashion for picking up the most important internal factor. The measure of closeness between ART and RAM is 10.01352 against the critical value 9.488 as noted earlier. Thus,

ART group is the odd group, so far as internal environmental analysis is concerned. In fact all the risk-oriented and risk-aversive managers prefer corporate resources as the most important internal strength. On the other hand, average risk-taking managers give the highest weightage on production capabilities.

When we go for factor ranking for ART group and the combined RAM and ROM group using tables 13 and 14 respectively and follow the earlier stated Elimination and Combination approach we get completely different pictures.

Table 13

Rank Frequency Matrix for Internal Factors for the ART Group.

			Internal factors			
Rank	*Finance*	*Marketing*	*Production*	*Personnel*	*Corp.-reso.*	*Total*
1	17	16	27	9	16	85
2	19	18	24	13	11	85
3	21	31	13	18	2	85
4	15	16	9	30	15	85
5	13	4	12	15	41	85

Table 14

Rank frequency matrix for internal factors for the combined RAM and ROM Group.

			Internal factors			
Rank	*Finance*	*Marketing*	*Production*	*Personnel*	*Corp.-reso.*	*Total*
1	61	51	76	22	125	335
2	62	92	86	56	39	335
3	68	95	66	75	31	335
4	65	71	55	104	40	335
5	79	26	52	78	100	335

The comparative study is given in the following abridged display.

Ranking by ART	*Internal Factors*	*Ranking by RAM and ROM*
2	Finance	5
3	Marketing	3
1	Production	2
4	Personnel	4
5	Corporate resources	1

A close look at table 14 reveals that for RAM and ROM groups importance of corporate resources as perceived by the managers has a heavy-ends distribution. As the elimination and combination approach is weak towards heavy-ends distribution we are not very sure about the sensitivity of the ranking of corporate resources for the RAM and ROM groups. This rank could have been 5th rank in place of 1st rank if we would have used this ranking procedure in a reverse direction.

A close examination of the above display reveals another interesting fact that a firm's strength in marketing attracts average attention of the managers and is against the general belief that a firm's strategy making process mostly depends on its strength in marketing and sales. If we avoid the controversy that arises out of the ranking of corporate resources then we may note that the strength of a firm mostly emanates out of its strength in production and operation activities as perceived by the managers irrespective of their risk-taking attitudes.

References

Aguilar, F.J. (1967) : *Scanning the Business Environment,* MocMillian, New York.

Ansoff, H.I. (1968) : Towards a strategic theory of the firm, *Economies et Societes,* vol. 2, no. 3.

Ansoff, H.I. (1971) : *Acquisition behaviour of U.S. manufacturing firms, 1946-65,* Nastiville, Tenn, Vanderbilt.

Bibault, D.B. (1982) : *Corporate turnaround,* McGraw Hill, New York.

Collings, R. (1969) : *Scanning the environment for strategic information,* Ph.D. Thesis, Harvard Business School.

Fitz Roy, P.T. (1976) : *Analytical Methods for Marketing Management,* International Student Edition, McGraw Hill.

Glueck, W.F. (1980) : *Business Policy and Strategic Management,* International Student Edition, McGraw Hill.

Hegarty, W.H. (1976) : The role of strategy formulation on corporate performance, *Proceedings of the Midwest American Institute of Decision Sciences.*

Khandwalla, P.N. (1977) : Some top management styles : Their control and performance, *Organization and Administrative Science,* vol. 7, p. 32.

Miller, D. and Friesen, P. (1977) : Strategy making in context : Ten enterprise archetypes, *Journal of Management Studies,* vol. 14 pp. 253-280.

Porter, M.E. (1980) : *Competitive Strategy,* The Free Press, A Division of McMillian Inc., New York.

Schoeffler, S. Buzzel,
R. and Heany, D. (1974) : Impact of strategic planning on profit performances, *Harvard Business Review,* pp. 137-145.

Sloan, A.P. Jr. (1964) : *My Years with General Motors,* Matson, New York.

Wadhva, C.D. (1974) : Environmental Planning for Corporate Planning, *Economic and Political Weekly,* vol. 9, March issue.

7

Strategic Repositioning of RBOs : Alliance and Offensive in Respect of Multinational Invasion

Mrinmoy K. Sarma

It is a well-known fact that a large number of profitable business organizations operate region-wise. These organizations have already created niches for themselves in various industries. For these areas or regions they are the specialists; these units have developed their own distribution channels, service networks, production facilities, etc. and are operating profitably. These organizations may be termed as Regional Business Organization (RBO). Some of the small scale sector units as well as cottage industries may be defined as RBO as long as their efforts are co-operative and organized. In that respect the *Bhujia* (saltish dish) manufacturers of Bikaner can be termed as RBO even though they have a set of cottage industries. But all such organizations cannot be termed as RBO because a majority of them are not possessing the following characteristics phenomenal to the ordinary RBO.

General Characteristics of RBO:

(a) Limited area of operation. For example, within a particular geographical region.

(b) Creates niches for profitable operation.

(c) Small entity.

(d) Basically private limited company or State P.S.U.

(e) Strong and effective presence in the region.

(f) Own network for physical distribution (in some of the cases no exclusive network is needed).

(g) Service network is also exclusive and very efficient.

(h) Reluctant to allow any entry to its region by competitors.

(i) Very little or no promotional expenses like advertising etc.

(j) Low product pricing.

(k) Quick accessibility by the target customers.

(l) Specialist in target customers' behaviour and psychology.

Normally the RBOs are small to medium sized organizations having a paid-up capital between Rs. 1 crore to 5 crore.

Not much research and deliberations have been done on the working of these organizations. Also not much attention has been paid by the business world as a whole on these organizations because of the fact that they always keep a low profile, publicity shy, and of course neglected by the media.

It has been observed that RBOs are effectively thwarting national business giants in their area of operation. Even if the national level competing firms are able to enter the respective geographical territories, because of stiff resistance by the local RBOs they are having limited success. Despite the fact that these organizations are having very limited or no access (due to obvious resource crisis) to mass advertising and publicity, they are enjoying complete customer confidence. The brands floated by the RBOs having ready acceptability among the target customers may be due to following reasons :

1. RBOs are local organizations and hence enjoy more accessibility in Pre-Purchase and Post-Purchase decision making by the customers.

2. Targeting to medium and low end markets with lower prices than that of the national level organizations.

3. Supplementing the point at (1) above—the RBOs are having effective, efficient and quick service network.

4. The customers are thoroughly known by the RBO and hence acquainted with their psychology, preference, etc.

With these strategic advantages RBOs have been effectively putting a barrier of entry for other competing firms from outside. Writer's personal experience of Marketing in Electronics industry shows that the points mentioned above play vital role in entry of other firms into the region. Specially, the attachment with the target group of customers by way of understanding behaviour from the part of the organization through friendly pricing (which may also be flexible) helps the RBO for a long term in winning customer confidence. For example, a state-run PSU Assam Electronics Development Corporation Ltd. (AEDCL) has been negating the presence of strong national brands like Tata Telecom, BPL, L & T etc. in the Electronic Exchange (Small capacity) market in the north-east region of India. But with the emergence of new economic era and the challenge put forward by the MNCs, RBOs are now open to more cut-throat and cruel competition than ever before. The MNCs with their highly motivated and aggressive forefront personnel and abundant resources are challenging the very existence of the RBOs. Faithful customers for long period are now taking new look at the offerings of the RBOs comparing the alternative products offered by the MNCs which are trying to woo these customers with their high profile image and strong product quality. Customers get crazy at the fact that the most heard about brands are available at their doorsteps. At this situation one should always be ready to accept any circumstances—like a drastic change in their sales figure.

SWOT analysis of both types of organizations would help us in analysing the situation and to determine how the RBOs can convert the so-called *threat* into *opportunity*.

The Analysis

The SWOT table for both types of the organisations will be as follows.

SWOT of RBOs

Strengths	*Weaknesses*
Easy accessibility to the target market Low end and medium end target market Own and experienced distribution channel. Expertise in the geographical area Better understanding of the target market.	Little or no advertising. No corporate image outside the region Old technology. Medium or low quality product. Low price and hence loss adaptability in the up end market—the most profit able segment.

Threats	*Opportunities*
Presence of MNC with great fanfare in the home region of RBO with high quality, high corporate image and aggressive marketing. Employees with low moral with the entry of MNCs	Divert the MNC offensive to a different position of the market. Use MNC's expertise in RBO's favour* Use extensive product awareness campaign by the MNCs in favour of RBO

SWOT of MNCs are discussed below.

SWOT of MNCs

Strengths	*Weaknesses*
High corporate image. High quality product. Aggressive marketing programmes like high level of advertising. Aggressive entry. High brand awareness from earlier media advertisements Experience in versatile geographical area around the world.	High or premium price. New entry into the area. Little or no first hand knowledge of the area and the market therein. Upper end position.

* This is discussed in detail in other parts of the study.

Threats	*Opportunities*
Presence of already flourishing RBOs in the area. Direct offensive by the RBO.	Weaknesses of the RBO like low quality obsolete technology, etc.

Though we find lot to include the points tabulated above are more distinct and important for SWOT analysis. After careful scrutiny of the points in the table above we find that RBO should adopt the following five alternatives to counter the *Multinational Invasion*.

Fight for the Same Market Segment and Position

This alternative suggests that the RBO should fight the MNC which is targeting the same market segment. The RBO should not allow the competitors to consolidate their position in the home ground. It would be a very tough job for the RBO considering the SWOT analysis above. There remains an inherent risk of loosing out the race due to the fact that any tactless move would be destroyed by the powerful MNC with its so many advantages.

Therefore, this alternative is not suggested wihout any strategic change in tactics. These are elaborated below with the other alternatives.

Reposition the Product and Fight for Maintenance of Earlier Niche or for a New One

In continuation of the alternative (1) it would be wise for the RBO if it repositions its products to a different segment of the market away from that of the competing MNC. It can be maintained here that most of the MNCs are maintaining high quality products at a premium price. For example, Motorola offers zero defect rugged telecommunication product at a premium price which is much higher than its Indian counterparts. Therefore, it is very natural that Motorola will be targeting the up end of the market who can pay a premium price for quality.

Also the MNCs are not covering the whole of India as its territory. They would be looking at among host of other factors profitability of the region with respect to prospective customers disposable income and their buying capacity. Also they might restrict their movement within urban and semi-urban areas only. Hence lot of areas untouched by the MNC will still remain open. Like in north-east region, MNCs are not expected barring Assam. Also the MNC would avoid the rural market in most of the cases except that of a few rich states.

Keeping the above situation in consideration the RBO may reposition its product(s) to target at low and medium end market and also towards the geographical areas where the MNCs are not expected. From the SWOT analysis it is clear that the RBOs are operating within their respective regions with host of advantages which the MNCs do not possess. Like strong presence in the region, high awareness about the market, geographical network for logistic, already established service network and customer confidence. In this circumstances repositioning would mean ready acceptance of RBO products by the prospective customers. This would in turn consolidate the position of the RBO in the market as well as within the region.

Let us discuss a related case of Assam Electronics Development Corporation Ltd. (AEDCL) which is engaged in manufacturing and marketing of electronic exchanges besides other products with its Head quarter at Guwahati and having a strong presence in the north-east region. In fact, AEDCL was the market leader for EPABX in 1990-93. AEDCL is a RBO operating in north-east region of India. It has its own service team, full-fledged laboratory and a strong sales force. It aimed at low and upper end market initially. In 1993-94, it faced stiff competition from national level electronics exchange manufacturers like Tata Telecom, Crompton Greaves, BPL, L & T, etc., who were entering the north-east region aggressively. Facing such a situation the RBO repositions its products into the low and medium end market which could not afford the high initial investment and post purchase cost like Annual Maintenance Charges of the national companies. It was seen at the end of 1994 that AEDCL's total turnover from Telematics Division touched on all time high. The customers who went for its competitors also were not happy with the post sales attention provided by other companies. For these companies were covering the whole of north-east region with only two-three service personnel compared to AEDCL's more than 12 highly-trained engineers. Moreover, one or two companies did not have offices at Guwahati and were operating from Calcutta instead because they did not find it profitable to set up a office at Guwahati. This situation made AEDCL to emerge more strongly than ever before. Reputed and upmarket buyers like North Eastern Power Corporation Ltd. Power, Grid Corporation of India Ltd. were happy with the performance of AEDCL's exchanges that they started placing repeat orders for the same without even considering the national giants. That is why it may be maintained that the *corporate buyers who are very organized in their purchase procedures are not quickly adaptable to the change in technology or to availability of reputed brand names.* They are comfortable with their old partner only.

Analysis of the situation described above shows that the MNCs will also have to face a tough time in fighting the RBOs present in the respective regions. And with the unique advantages they are enjoying RBOs can make the life of MNCs difficult. In such a favourable situation the RBO's strategic plan of action should be as follows:

(1) Observe and determine the target market segment of the competing MNC. This would not be difficult as the MNCs are unlikely to change their target market region-wise; for that is not cost effective in terms of product manufacturing, quality control and advertising programme. Here the RBO can determine without much difficulty the target group of the competing MNC. For example, if Motorola enters north-east region for its telecommunication equipment it would target the quality conscious customers who are obviously in the up market end. Likewise if AT&T enters Assam in electronics exchange market (small capacity) it would eye only for the upper end of the market who are looking for more advanced features and facilities at a higher price.

2. Also determine the area untouched or unlikely to be touched in the near future by the MNC within the home region. The qualities of products, distribution network, service channels would speak themselves about the MNC's intended geographical area of operation.

3. Reposition of the product(s) quickly into these consumer segments and geographical area.

Preferably keep the price low and ideally aim at low and medium end markets.

Revamp and if need be reorganize the already experienced distribution and service channels to provide maximum exposure to these geographical areas.

Use the service network more aggressively than ever before and help the prospective customers in pre-purchase decision making and post-purchase satisfaction. The yardstick for performance of the service network should be to leave *none* of the customers unsatisfied. After all, quality of service is the standard of responsibility you are taking on behalf of the customers to satisfy their needs. This is needed because of one dissatisfied customer tends to spread bad word-of-mouth 11 times (Kotler, Principle of Management, '94) whereas, a satisfied customer may never tell others about the RBOs performance.

Use local newspapers and local radio centre as media for building a strong corporate image around the region as these mediums are very cost effective. Also try to utilize local media for free publicity—as such publicity is more effective in building corporate image than only through advertising. It is worth mentioning here that detailed product advertising may not be possible from the RBO's end because of resource crunch. However, if can be arranged extensive product advertising would help the RBO in a long way.

4. Try to improve overall quality of the product to a high standard without increasing the selling price.

5. Start aggressive marketing activity with all the components discussed above. With improvised products, marketing and service the RBO would distinctly gain a strategic advantage over the MNC in question. The increasing reputation which will follow such steps would challenge the MNC and open up avenues of guerrilla warfare.

Also try aggressively to increase the employee moral. Prepare them in a warfooting for the intending offensive. This is needed because a clever MNC would always look for key personnel from the successful competitors. And a work force with low moral and lesser sense of belongingness would easily fall into the dragnet of MNC.

This is also needed to prepare the employee specially from the forefront like people from personnel, from sales and service for the intending aggressiveness.

If possible try to offer more incentives for these personnel. Train them up with better methods of operation in the field and show them that the organisation cares for them.

Reposition the Organization as a Whole : Have Truce with the M.N.C.

The RBO may adopt another alternative of repositioning the organization as a whole and thereby establishing a truce with the MNC. In this strategy the RBO in question would try to make a truce with the MNC regarding the operation in the home region before the later's entry. This is possible if the RBO act in close collaboration with the *competing* MNC. For this the RBO will have to try to work as a *representative* of the MNC. If successfully done the RBO will be able to convert the threats arisen out of the presence of the MNC to its most profitable opportunity.

The RBO may lend out the servicing or physical distribution or the marketing network to the MNC. Also the MNC can utilize the benefit from the longstanding experience of the *collaborating* RBO in marketing their products in the region. This would help both the sides in following ways :

(a) RBO will not have to reposition its product which involves lot of expenses and uncertainty.

(b) RBO will retain its own presence in the field and at the same time could continue its products without any hindrance.

(c) Corporate image of RBO increases as customer would relate the RBO with the MNC's image.

(d) MNC would gain from borrowed physical distribution and service network. Now it does not have to extend own PD and service network into this new region. It saves considerable resources like money and time.

(e) MNC can reap the benefit from the RBO's expertise of this region and its manpower.

Thus the cooperation will create a synergy of benefits which would be available for both the sides. But in real field it is very difficult to arrive at such a treaty as the MNCs are very selective in choosing a partner. However, the collaboration may be effected the following ways:

(i) Make sales and service tie-up; i.e. the RBO would assist the MNC in setting and providing other related services like pre-sales counselling, installation, post-sales attention, etc.

(ii) Both the organizations can arrive at a production alliance, if possible, for sale in that particular region. Or this may be extended upto a national level tie-up for production of MNC branded products for sale even outside the region. For this generally, following conditions should be satisfied.

- Expertise in production field.
- Production by the RBO should be profitable for both the sides.
- The natural and political environment around the RBO should be suitable for such production and so on.

Or the RBO may work as a franchise and/or ancillary unit of the MNC in marketing and/or production sectors. Also the RBO may try to work as a vendor to the MNC by producing the raw materials for them. But all these alternatives must be profitable and workable from both the sides.

(iii) The RBO becomes only a service agent of the MNC in that region for providing installation after sales attention and pre-sales counselling, if needed. This will help the RBO in the long run as their personnel will get training and exposure to new technology generally used by the MNC. This would help the RBO afterwards if they choose to pull out.

AEDCL has successfully collaborated with Wipro Gee for sales and service of its whole range of medical equipment. Though Wipro Gee is a indigenously promoted company it has a strong national level presence and AEDCL with this strategic move have been able to thwart other competing firms like L & T.

Let us cite another strategic mistake committed by AEDCL. When the Telerama brand of TV was taken over by the Peerless Group, the later approached AEDCL for a tie-up in production. AEDCL refused the offer and thereby lost a long-term cash cow. Now AEDCL make TVs are pulling along somehow, whereas the Telerama brand TVs are doing well.

However, from this single example it is not safe to conclude MNCs would also behave likely. But if the RBO can meet the MNC parameters there should not be any problem in having a profitable production tie-up. Meanwhile lot of MNCs are having tie-ups with national business organizations. Like General Electric is having a tie-up with Godrej, IBM is having with Tatas etc. And this is a very common practice as far as Indian manufacturers are concerned. Like in consumer goods very few companies produce all the products they market.

However again, as MNCs are very quality conscious RBOs must rise to the occasion to have a tie-up with them.

Synergy by Collaboration among R.B.Os.

In view of the threats the MNCs are putting forward the RBOs may have better tie-up among themselves within a broad area of operation and become stronger to counter the entry of MNCs. This would help in thwarting the entry of MNCs in the following ways :

(a) This would increase the financial base among the RBOs and facilitate the following:

- High level of advertising would be possible,
- Acquisition of latest technology would be possible,
- Offerings with better quality would be possible *and like.*

(b) This would increase technical and marketing bases and thereby improve in quality.

Diversify Profitably and/or Retrench

If the presence of MNCs is very strong and cannot be negated by any one of the above or if it is not possible to adopt any of them, RBO should diversify profitably to the related fields or to a nearby geographical area. However, this is very difficult to adopt and should always be used as the last resort. It is difficult because the RBOs normally depend upon three or four related products and they are not spread out to diverse fields. Hence it is very difficult and time consuming for the RBOs to diversify. However, if need arises they must do the same and try to enter into the present field in the next possible opportunity.

The alternatives discussed above are not mutually exclusive. Because the RBO must consider the alternatives from the point of view of the individual product. If it is profitable to reposition in respect of one product the other product may require an alliance with another MNC or retrenchment.

It can be aptly concluded from the discussions above that the RBO must not allow the MNCs to enter their territory easily and exploit the market developed by them over the years. The RBOs can easily find their plan of action with the model shown in the next page.

References

1. Lawrance R. Jauch, William F. Glueck: Business Policy and Strategic Management : 5th Ed., McGraw Hill.
2. S.V. Ramaswami, S. Namakumary: Strategic Planning for Corporate Success—McMillan, 19'91.
3. Rohinton D. Aga: Changing the Mindset : Tata McGraw Hill, 1994.

RBO Vs. MNC : ACTION PLAN FOR R.B.O.

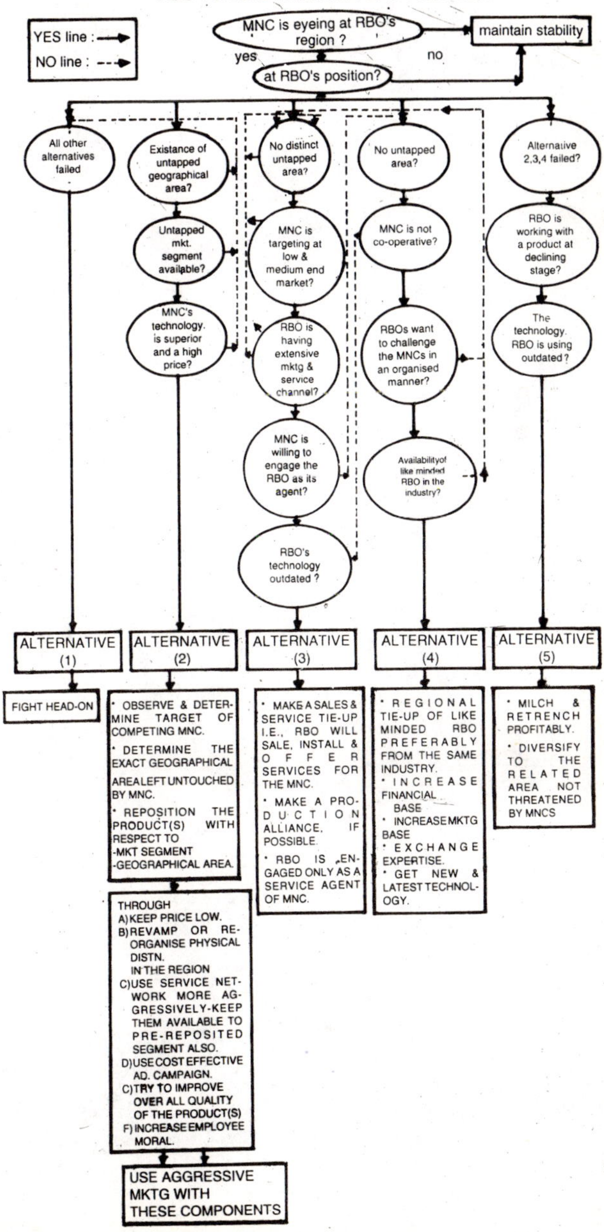

8

Warfare

Anjan Raichadhuri

War or Business: Same Strategies

During the last decade, there have been many publications comparing business strategies to military warfare by authors like Barrie James, Philip Kotler, Al Ries, Jack Trout, and so on. This study explores some of the salient ideas on the subject with the help of a few Indian and international cases.

Defence and business are two major preoccupations for every nation. There are obvious differences between the two, but there are also uncanny similarities. Defence forces protect or acquire territories to achieve national advantages, companies protect or acquire market share for their own profits There are many similarities in structures, systems functions, procedures and training. Armies fight enemies in the battlefield suiting strategies to the terrain, supported by weaponry, intelligence, communication and logistics. Companies fight competitors suiting strategies to the business environment, supported by resources (technological, production, financial and marketing), information system and material inflow and outflow systems (Table-1).

Table 1
Similarities between Military Warfare and Business Warfare

Military Warfare	Business Warfare
1. Enemy	1. Competitor
2. Acquire/Protect territories	2. Acquire/Protect market share
3. Battlefield	3. Market
4. Weaponry	4. Technological, Production, Financial, Marketing Resources
5. Terrain	5. Business Environment
6. Intelligence	6. Internal/External Information Systems
7. Logistics	7. Material Inflow and Outbound Systems

Table 2
Frontal Strategy

Airbus	*Boeing Lockheed*
Multi-country funding	Company funding
Captive markets in Europe	No captive markets
Advanced cost-effective technology	Standard technology
Easy credit/penetration pricing	Standard pricing/credit

Once in a while, however, companies become complacent, and tend to forget the harsh realities of warfare. They end up paying a heavy price for it.

•GM remained comfortable for years as the world's largest automobile company. Unfortunately, it ignored the slow and systematic US market penetration by Japanese car manufacturers. The resultant disaster in the market left the company badly scarred, from which it has taken several years to recover.

•During the '70s and '80s, many well-known Indian companies such as Metal Box were leaders in their own business. They failed to adapt to the changing environment and emerging competition. Today they are in shambles.

•Indian Airlines, long used to a sheltered monopoly, finds

itself steadily losing market to the offensive by private operators in an open market combat.

As economic, political, social and technological developments increasingly change the business world, old markets become narrower, competition intensifies and growth becomes synonymous with new opportunities or newer ways of doing business. Companies must be prepared to fight—either to defend their own markets or attack new markets and opportunities. In mature or stagnant markets, success comes from taking market share from rivals. In growth markets, success results from acquiring and protecting market shares from newer entrants. Clearly, business can gain significantly by remaining 'fighting fit'; and centuries of research on military warfare has a lot to tell in this context.

There are broadly six types of military strategies which have also been used in business. They are not necessarily used alone—sometimes combinations are also used.

Direct Strategy

Direct strategies are the most common form of military strategy and consist of deployment of direct forces. They can be used for both offence and defence. Military history indicates that in direct frontal attack, a weapon superiority of around 3:1 ratio is normally necessary.

• Airbus Industries used a successful frontal attack against Boeing and Lockheed in the passenger airplane market. Airbus was formed as a consortium including France, Germany, Spain and UK. It utilised advanced technology which resulted in lower noise levels, better fuel efficiency and lower operating cost. The European partners provided a captive market for Airbus, which helped them offer easy credit terms and penetration pricing to enter the world market. In five years between 1976 and 1981, Airbus increased its market share from 3 to 33 per cent of the world market.

Direct frontal attacks are quite often unsuccessful because of the massive resource requirement. In such situations, flanking attacks which focus on weaker points of the enemy have been widely used throughout military history.

•In the mid '70s, the Japanese chemical industry was fragmented with chlorine and caustic soda being produced in 53 small plants, leading to high raw materials and energy costs. Since a regulation was passed to convert the technology (existing technology used mercury which caused an environmental problem), the leading American supplier Dow Chemicals felt that many units would close down because they would not be able to afford the costly conversion. Dow had substantially higher capacity units with significant cost advantages, and was therefore able to penetrate the Japanese market through bulk supplies.

•A classic example of flanking strategy is provided by Michelin's entry into the US tyre market. The major US manufacturers—Goodricks, Goodyear, Firestone and Uniroyal focused on the OEM market with traditional cross-ply tyres. Michelin focused on the replacement market with the newly developed radial tyres, which decreased fuel consumption by 5%. Very soon, the major US car manufacturers switched to radial tyres. While the US tyre manufacturers were busy in developing and perfecting radial tyre technology. Michelin was able to build up market share of almost 25% in the huge US market.

•Y.K.K.s dominance in the world zip fastener market is another interesting example. When Y.K.K. entered into the US market, the largest chunk in the world market was dominated by Talon. Who sold the product as a commodity and used the traditional distribution system through the wholesaler network. Y. K. K. started selling direct to fashion design houses, bypassing the conventional distribution network. Within a few years, Y.K.K. acquired one-third of the US market. It successfully repeated this strategy in Europe and built-up world market leadership through local manufacturing plants and offices in 40 countries.

Alliance Strategy

Sometimes different armies join hands to fight common enemies—the World War II and the Gulf War of Feb. 1991 are the famous examples of the strategy. The Japanese manufacturer, Fujitsu is a strong believer in this concept. It formed alliances in Europe with ICL and Siemens, and in the US with Amdahl. Its entry into India shows a similar pattern through an alliance with a leading Indian player, ICIM. Many Indian groups have been following this strategy to help them consolidate their position in existing markets, as well as for exploring new avenues. Some of the technology-oriented business groups in the South have followed similar strategies.

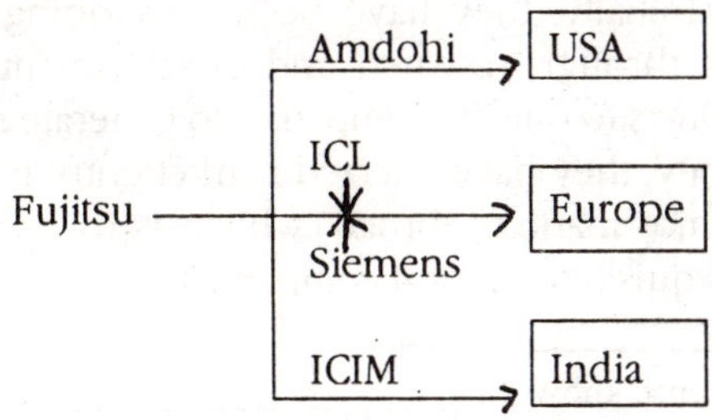

Fig. 1 : Alliance Strategy.

*The IT market in India indicates a large number of companies following the alliance strategy—IBM/TATA, BULL/PSI, MODI/OLIVETTI, and so on.

Wipro Infotech strengthened its position in different segments of the IT industry through alliances : with Seiko Epson (printers), Sun Microsystems (workstations), and Tandem Computers (Online Transaction Processing or OLTP.)

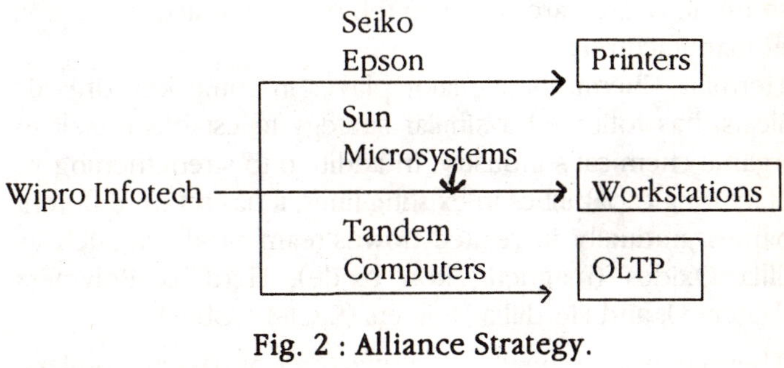

Fig. 2 : Alliance Strategy.

Sequential Strategy

This strategy consists of a series of actions, each building up on the former, finally leading to the overall objective. In the Falkland Island's war against Argentina in 1982, the British started by controlling the sea route, then established air superiority through raids and bombardment blocked communication and material supply before successfully landing and reoccupying.

* Japanese pharmaceuticals and speciality chemical companies have been using sequential strategies to achieve leadership in the world market. Initially, they have been developing new/ improved products through research and development, then licensing these products to outside companies to generate royalty income. Subsequently, they have effected market entry through joint-ventures in major markets abroad, which is followed up with the selective acquisition of local companies.

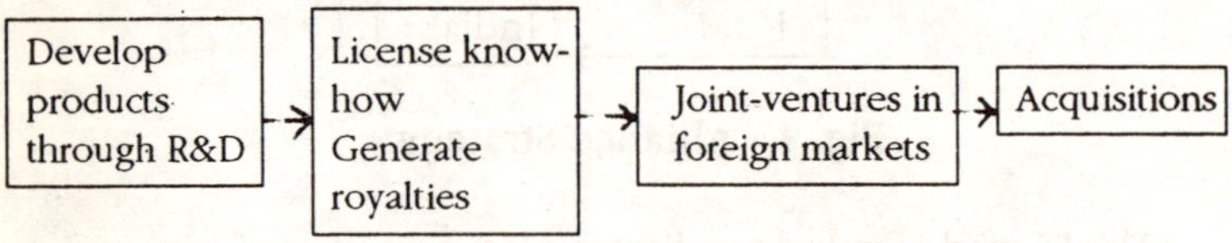

Fig. 3 : Sequential Strategy (as practised by Japanese companies).

ABB's strategy for the power sector business in India is somewhat similar. It has clubbed together different sister organizations under one umbrella. It has formed joint-ventures like Tailor Instruments, Integra Hind Controls, Gujarat Primemovers and so on, in related areas. It is in the process of acquiring ABL (boiler manufacturer).

*Herdillia Chemicals, a major player in some key organic chemicals, has followed a similar strategy to establish itself in the organic chemical's industry. In addition to strengthening its manufacturing capabilities in existing lines, it has set up different companies gradually in related downstream products such as Herdillia Oxides (magnetic iron oxide), Herdillia Polymers (polybutenes), and Herdillia Unimers (EPDM rubber).

*Thermax was originally a manufacturer of package boilers. Its experience in the boiler industry led to an entry into water treatment plants, followed by water treatment chemicals. Problems with usage of polluting and costly fuels in boilers offered opportunities for entry into energy conservation, followed by pollution control.

Today, Thermax has 12 such divisions set up in a sequential manner.

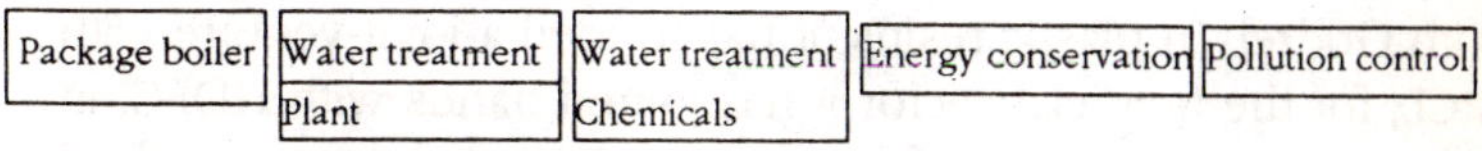

Fig. 4 : Sequential Strategy (as followed by Thermax boilers).

Cumulative Strategy

Cumulative strategy consists of apparently unrelated activities, which put together, ultimately create a tremendous impact. Cumulative strategies quite often are a combination of other strategies such as alliances and flanking. Between 1945 and 1948, Russians occupied different European countries which individually posed little threat to West European security. However, the combined effect of nine Soviet-occupied East European countries resulted in changing the world's political equation for almost five decades.

•The domination of the European car market by Japanese manufacturers followed a similar pattern. Initially, the Japanese entered markets without indigenous car production, such as Finland and Switzerland. This was followed by gradual penetration into Scandinavia and UK, which was then followed by entering France and Germany. Within two decades, the Japanese were able to build up market share from scratch to around 10 %.

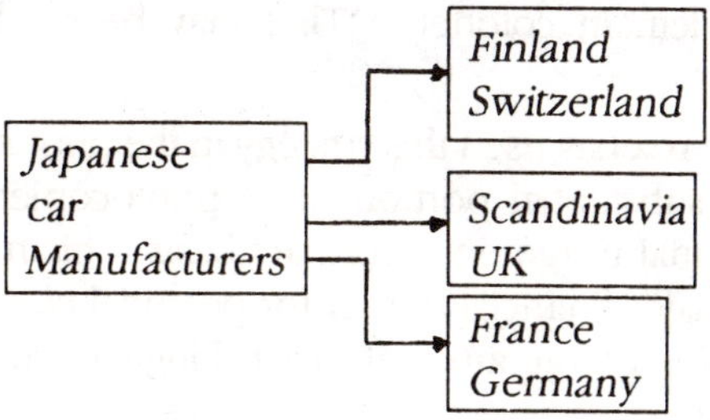

Fig. 5 : **Cumulative Strategy.**

*GE's strategy to be a major player in the Indian market shows a similar pattern. It has systematically built joint-ventures in different business sectors of interest which, taken together, make it a major corporation in India.

In the home appliance market, GE has formed a joint-venture with Godrej. In plastic resins, it has formed a joint-venture with IPCL, for the financial sector it has joined hands with HDFC, in lighting systems it has formed GE-APAR, while in medical equipment it has tied up with Wipro.

*In the tourism business, the Welcome Group established itself in a short-time period to compete with the long established Oberoi's and the Taj Group. The Group followed a strategy of joint-ventures, acquiring and franchising a wide network of hotels all over the country.

Big business houses such as Reliance, Essar, Mittal's and Jindal are following cumulative strategies to build up their dominant positions in business sectors of their choice—petrochemicals, steel, and so on.

Indirect Strategy

Indirect strategies avoid physical conflict and use psychological pressure to defeat an enemy. North Vietnam used pressure of world opinion to stop the US attack which subsequently led to US disengagement in 1972. It is interesting recalling a conversation which took place between Colonel Harry Summers of the US army, and a North Vietnamese colonel in Hanoi.

Summers : "You know, you never did beat us on the battlefield."

North Vietnam colonel : "That may be so, but it is also irrelevant."

*Modi Xerox has used this strategy in the photocopier market in India. A substantial portion of its photocopier is leased or given in annual usage on a contract basis. This has resulted in building a major financial barrier for potential competitors, who would require a large amount of working capital if they are to match this offer.

*SSI units in different industrial sectors have used indirect pressure to provide protective barriers through government subsidies and tax relief. The jute industry has used this strategy for several years to fight competition from plastic bags—through successful lobbying has been able to get mandatory usage norm in user industries.

Counterforce or Countervalue Strategies

These strategies are to destroy/neutralize select enemy capabilities or infrastructure, population centres, and so on. In wars, precision bombing is used to destroy armament plants, communication centres or industrial plants and transport infrastructure. In the business context, this implies challenging patents, copyright, advertising claims or neutralising access to raw material or markets.

*Standard Batteries is using this strategy through a catchy advertising campaign, undermining the leading brand's product performance. Questioning advertising claims is a common strategy employed by prominent consumer product brands.

In the office automation market, this has been a regular pattern of attack on established leaders by new entrants.

*Pearl Pet's entry into PET resin manufacture, with consequent control over raw material, indicates a similar strategy.

*Blocking retail shelf space to limit the competitors' access to the market is a common strategy followed by consumer product manufacturers.

In the years to come, conflicts in the market are going to intensify—in the sense that mature or declining markets will have too many players. On the other hand, emerging markets will have large global corporations or alternatively, they will have several new players all of whom will be highly skilled.

Success then will depend on out-manoeuvring or defeating competition, not through blind use of theoretical plans or models, but by examining proven strategies and making innovative use of them.

9

Winning Business Strategies : In the Light of Global Competitiveness

Sanjib Raj

The present global corporate environment has become increasingly unstable, accelerative and revolutionary. The international economy has witnessed the meteoric rise of Japan as a major player followed suit by South Korea, Taiwan, Singapore and Hong Kong. Meanwhile, technological breakthroughs, radical social changes, radically different organizational styles have created a novel environment for business. It is within this environment that Indian industries are expected not only to survive but also to create a niche for themselves. However, certain ground realities that currently exist in the country have to be taken into consideration when we talk of any strategies by Indian companies.

"By the end of this decade, India's population will have reached one billion. By then, we will need approximately 90 million tonnes of crude oil and 46 trillion cubic metres of gas;

400 million tonnes of coal; 1,60,000 MW of electric power, 19 million telephone and telex lines; 460 billion tonnes-kms of railways, 160 billion tonnes-kms of road transport, 22 million tonnes of steel; 8 million tonnes of petrochemicals; 16 million tonnes of fertilizers; 75 million tonnes of cement, 240 million tonnes of foodgrains to mention only a few"—Bellare, M.V. 'The Indian Challenge, Indian Management, May 1989, p. 5.

The above statistics provides a view of the huge requirements needed by the Indian market; which comes across both as a challenge as well as an opportunity for the industries of our country to rise up and meet these requirements in the near future. If, even now, Indian companies are not geared up to meet this challenge, then as a fallout of the liberalization process in India, foreign multinational companies will enter the Indian market to fulfil these requirements, apart from the Indian government. Hence, Indian companies will lose the opportunity to serve their own society and will lose the battle to foreign companies, even in the domestic market, leave alone trying to compete globally.

Thus, the Indian companies are no longer in a position where they have the option of whether to grow or not to grow. A stagnant firm will not only be unable to meet the expectation of its investors, but will also lose vital market share and thereby lose customers' confidence. At the micro-level growth means increase in volume first, followed by market share leading to higher profitability. Moreover, growth is vitally necessary to sustain the motivation and loyalty of employees, especially executives and skilled operators with outside job opportunities, growth is required for career progression. Growth is also necessary to meet the increasing aspirations for job challenge and quality of work life. Moreover, growth helps to reduce human and physical obsolescence and inefficiency of the firm.

It is indeed a great tragedy that though growth and self-reliance formed the backbone of our national plans, since independence, India has never been able to overcome the 5.8% growth barrier. It is even more depressing when we compare the growth rates of the four Asian Tigers—South Korea, Taiwan, Singapore and Hong Kong. At the present level, India is way behind these nations. As such it becomes worthwhile to draw lessons from these countries in developing winning strategies for business growth. Giving due considerations to the imperatives of the times, it must still be said that since our independence the focuses of our economic planners on one hand has been self-reliance and on the other, social equality. In the name of self-reliance, the government became progressively involved in the promotion and management of businesses. In the name of social justice, there was wasteful distribution of wealth. At a time when capital was (it still is and is becoming dearer), wealth generation should have been given the highest priority. Our government companies have become a dumping ground for non-performers. As a matter of fact, in many a Public Sector company, its manpower has become the greatest liability rather than its most valuable resource. It is important to realize that the fundamental requirement for an industry at the early stages of development is surplus generation across all operational levels. In other words, the industry as a whole should commit itself to those economic activities where surplus could be earned by Indian industries from such nations where resides. It is the wealth earned which would be used to invest in further progressive activities which would produce gainful employment for the industry as well as the country. Gainful employment would in turn increase the purchasing power of the individuals which would directly boost domestic demand. Domestic demand essentially gives impetus to the process of growth as domestic demand increases savings rate which in turn stimulates further profitable investments for the industries.

The Asian Experience

As mentioned earlier, the ground realities being different for India, the solutions for India would also be quite different and a copy of the strategies developed by these Asian countries could spell disaster for our nation. It is worth mentioning that management styles and organizational patterns are culturally bound. The management styles developed in the United States were not found to be effective in rebuilding the economy of battered Europe. As such a blindfolded approach to following the path of the Asian countries could well be a classic case of jumping from the frying pan to the fire.

However, there are some aspects of these Asian countries which seems innovative and nearly identical to Indian conditions. At a time when India was planning to celebrate its first independence, Japan was gearing itself up for her 'tryst with quality'. In 1946, the Japanese Union of Scientists and Engineers (JUSE) was founded, to popularise the concepts of 'Total Quality Control', 'Statistical Quality Control', etc. In Japan, the responsibility for quality lies from the top management down to shop floor workers. Within a decade Dr. V.A. Feigenbaum's concept of total quality control, controlling product design and development, production, sales and after-sales servicing was implemented. The method used by JUSE was most innovative, which could well be thought over by our business houses. JUSE used the mass media to educate foreman and group leaders on quality control and began correspondence courses for them in quality control through the Japan Shortwave Broadcasting Corporation. Indian business houses can also use the mass media like Doordarshan and the Satellite television network in India for a similar purpose. Japan's ideas on management were translated into Japanese under the title *The Secret of Saving Lost Motion*, and other such books were distributed to workers of factories of Mutsubishi and Kawasaka Shipbuilding Yard. It is pertinent to note that new management ideas were taken to the workers in their own language. Needless to say this contributed to the reputation Japan possesses today. In business terms the goodwill to Japanese products are so high that even the American customers, so proud of their domestic products, have turned to Japanese products. The flooding of Japanese automobiles in the late eighties in the US market is a case in point.

'Catch up' Mentality

Another thought provoking aspect of the Japanese and also the other Asian countries was their basic desire to 'catch up' with the west. It is indeed this basic desire of 'catching up' with the west that has become one of the most potent forces to push these industries so hard that now they have left behind many western multinational companies. This catching up mentality of these companies essentially became the mission of the nations themselves. From the standpoint of developing winning business strategies, identifying the mission of the corporate is the first stage. This 'catch up' mentality in essence provided the top management of these industries a very clear mission and immediately provided a stage where appraisal of their present situation could be taken objectively. Comparing that mental state of those companies some four decades back with our present mental state in India provides a really pathetic picture. In the Indian context, one finds a lack of readiness to compete even in the domestic market. Liberalization in India has created more contradictions in terms of what the different sectors of the industry want for themselves and their customers. Even at the current junction of the economic liberalization process we are witnessing an absence of close cooperation where the industry and government find each other symbiotic. It is for this reason strategies have to be formulated where a synergy of the existing forces and strengths of the country have to be attained. In other words, as a very first step the Indian Corporate Sector as a whole should actually look into the prevailing situation in a more comprehensive manner rather than adopting *ad hoc* or stop gap arrangements. The problem besetting the nation must be taken into consideration during the strategic decision-making process.

This strategic decision-making process should take place in stages. At the first stage, the individual company must decide once and for all what is its mission in terms of what it intends to accomplish and for whom. For this we need to state a mission which the company can identify even at the operational level.

The second stage in the formulating winning business strategies for growth, would involve appraisal of current and future global environment of business, global market opportunities and threats. Opportunities for business growth could be new market areas into which existing products can be sold or new markets and new demands which would match the unique strength existing in the particular industry. Threats could be decline of the market demand on which the business is dependent. Such an analysis would essentially mean a SWOT analysis at the mega level. No doubt such an exercise would indicate greater importance and stress to some operations of the industry. However, if we look at other developed nations it is seen that most nations have built their economic policies around a few key industries, carefully keeping in line with their own strengths and weaknesses. The growth of Singapore is an apt example. Singapore started off initially as a successful air-traffic hub. At the next phase it made efforts and developed as an international clearing house and a shopping and leisure centre. By early eighties, it provided manufacturing facilities and base to companies of US, Europe and Japan. Since then it has progressively developed itself as a location for Regional Headquarters RHQ and International Purchasing Organisations (IPO). To provide full satisfaction to her clients, individual business houses continuously upgraded their services so as to remain one of the best in the field.

Japan too, had placed stress to different specific industries at different stages of her development. During the '50s, reconstruction was the dominant theme with emphasis on industries like ship-building, steel, cement, textiles. By the '60s, 'income doubling' became the dominant theme and industries like automobiles, petrochemicals were given top priority. By that time they were in a position to consider global economic leadership.

The next stage in the formulation of strategy could be a SWOT analysis at the corporate level. Such analysis could reveal weaknesses that should be remedied for continued existence. A corporate house may have strengths arising from its positive image through maintenance of high quality standards or through prompt and reliable after sales service or it may have acquired considerable financial resources accumulated over years of profitable ventures. However, its productivity could be a weakness as because of outdated technology. Thus, in choosing a strategic option a company would like to capitalise on its strengths and minimise its weaknesses.

The next stage could be determining corporate objectives in quantifiable terms over the next five to ten years. These objectives can be in broad terms along the dimensions of quality, profitability, growth, etc. By the early '70s, there was tremendous change in the industrial scenario of the US. Having completed the transition from agriculture to industrialization, the US was rapidly moving into the new stage of development : Super-Industrialization based on more advanced technology, radical organizational styles, new and radical sexual and social values. This new environment necessiated strategic changes of the individual organizations in the US. In such a situation corporations like AT&T of US had to undergo a similar analysis. It became essential for AT&T managers to recognize new goals for the next 10-20 years period ahead. It required to transform its present industrial form into a form more adapted to the emerging Super Industrial System. On top of that it was necessary for them to achieve this transformation with the least internal upheaval possible while continuing to provide basic communication services to the society at large.

It is important to realize that such big multinational companies' effect of changes transcend national borders. The economic and intellectual power, their geographical reach even at the grass root level is so immense that many a time such companies overshadow the intellectual and information power of the national government. Even today such changes are taking place and more rapidly, we have seen mergers of not only multinational company but large national companies whose effect is felt beyond the corporate barriers. Individual corporate houses should take into considerations those changes and decisions in fixing their own corporate goals and objectives.

The next stage would result in the formulation of strategy after careful analysis of options available to the corporate house. An organization should attempt to seek a match between goals and objectives reached at the preceding stages with the results obtained from earlier stages of internal analysis of the organization and the external environment analysis.

Formulating of strategies of individual firms becomes extremely difficult if the relevant environment cannot be identified. For example, a firm may have a diversified product mix which could include products like Electromedical equipment, computer peripherals and so on. Each product line belongs to a specific industry employing many micro-environments, one for each specific industrial group. However, due to limitations of range and specification, the entire micro-environment of an industry may not be relevant for each of its specific product lines. Micro-environment is essentially the industry environment which has a substantial impact on the organization's current business. Similarly at the 'mega' level in spite of the company being an engineering company, it may find only a limited portion of the mega environment relevant to it as compared to another engineering company. Mega environment refers to the global environment of business. Every Indian company, therefore, has to commit itself to the objective formulation of winning business strategies in tune with its internal strengths and weaknesses within this relevant environment.

Some of the broad winning strategies for growth implementable by Indian industries are stated below. It must, however, be emphasised at this stage that the intention of the author is not to give innovative foolproof strategies. The following strategies are only meant to be indicative and an eyeopener for enlightened Indian industries to consider. However, as has already been mentioned repeatedly before, the industries have to adapt and mould these guidelines to strategies to suit their relevant external environment and their internal strengths and weaknesses. It is hoped that these strategies would serve as examples to Indian industries to formulate their own winning business strategies for growth as well as be a framework for introspection of their own internal performance till date.

1. **Commitment towards quality**. The corporate houses must give highest priority to quality. Quality at all operational levels must become the key word in the company's strategy for becoming globally competitive. Top management of corporate houses would do well to educate and involve every individual involved so as to maintain highest level of quality within the organization. A clear and objective reward and punishment procedure may be adopted by the industrial houses, to develop an obsession for perfection for products, meant even for the domestic market.

2. Human resource development. The country has the third largest reservoir of technically skilled personnel in the world. It would be the greatest mistake strategically if this reserve is used by multinationals to further their own interests. As such Indian industries should make efforts to attract and preserve this precious resource and try to prevent these resources from being used by their competitors. As of today, we find a rapid flow of this resource from Indian industries to foreign multinational companies. This has got to be stopped before it is too late.

3. Think globally. Industrial enterprises in India should try to develop and grow in that sector of the industry where the country as a whole has a natural competitive advantage. Detailed knowledge of its costs, capacity, position and quality standards of the top ten global players of the industry has to be attained. On top of that Indian corporate houses should try to find out their source of competitive advantage and the possibility of the Indian company to also gain access to similar source of advantage.

Indian companies should look for global partners to build global competitiveness in the segment of business where the Indian company seeks to grow.

Indian companies should look beyond the national frontiers for marketing their products. This is true for all companies irrespective of whether they are big or small. Small Malaysian companies thrive on supplying electronic components to the global market. In India, some companies are tying up with foreign multinational companies to flood the domestic market. In the process we are allowing foreign companies to enter into the domestic market without gaining any competitive advantage in the international market. In the Indian scenario Wipro of India has successfully tied up with General Electric of US to market Wipro GE Medical systems globally, which is the correct approach.

4. Stress on critical mass. The success of a company depends largely on the organization's ability to fully understand all the necessary requirements for success from manpower to machinery. Companies should never compromise in this critical requirement at any cost.

5. Preserving identity and values. Indian companies should never give up its own identity and the basic values it stands for. Japanese companies have proven to be masters at managing their identity and values, both internal and external to the organization. Indian corporate houses should devote considerable time and effort to monitor and tailor its corporate image. Profit maximization at the cost of identity and social values would prove counter productive in the long run. A good example in the Indian scenario of growth with preservation of identity is the TATA conglomerate.

A tremendous change is sweeping over the country. The post-liberalization era has opened new vistas for Indian businesses to grow. Every company in India, should plan to grow in real terms, net of inflation, of at least 10% and also try to achieve a minimum of 8% overall average growth. If current business do not have the potential, the company should diversify seeking higher rates of growth.

The time has come for Indian industries to wake up to the fact that, given the present scenario of our dismal performance, we may be losing even the domestic market, leave alone competiting globally. We have achieved political independence from the British after 200 years of dominance. Let us not lose our economic independence now, so soon after gaining our political freedom. Let us not forget that the British also came to do trade with India at the beginning. Let us usher in our real freedom and independence by producing globally competitive Indian multinational companies who operate winningly at all levels of the globe.

10

Trading Area Analysis for Marketing Strategy

Gautam Chakroborty

Modern business environment is becoming increasingly sophisticated and complex. The state of affairs is demanding increased use of strategic management.

Managing the internal activities of an organization is a part of today's managers' responsibilities. The ever-changing external environment is always a challenge to the manager.

To deal effectively with all these executives design strategic management processes which they feel facilitate the optimal positioning of the firm in its competitive environment.

Let us discuss the relation between marketing and strategic planning. Philip Kotler who needs very little introduction has shown the relation between marketing and strategic planning in the figure given in exhibit.

It is noted that the marketing department supplies information and strategic recommendation (Step 1) to the strategic planners for the latters' analysis and evaluation (Step 2). The strategic planners then negotiate goals and resources (Step 3). Marketing department then formulates marketing plans based on these goals (Step 4) and carries them out (Step 5). The results are evaluated by the strategic planners and the process recycles.

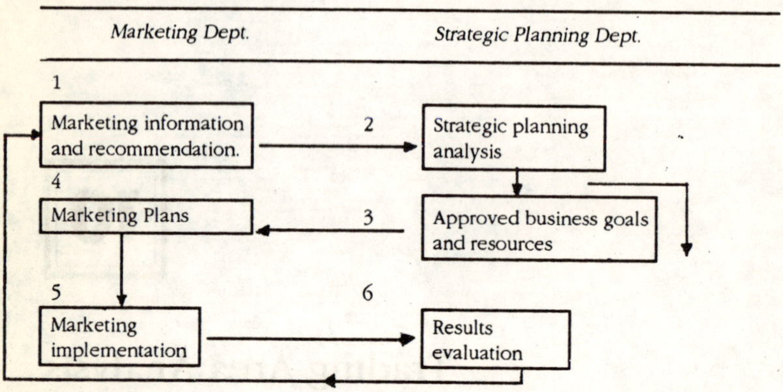

On the other hand the marketing process may be diagrammatically shown as exhibit :

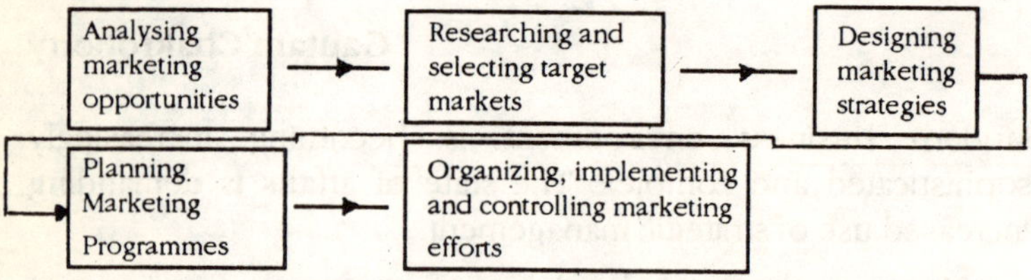

Source : *Marketing Management* Philip Kotlar, 8th Edition, page 95.

On the background of our preceding discussions the importance of marketing strategy on the overall strategic planning need not be overemphasized. Now we shall try to throw some light on the strategic planning aspects of a middle level manager. In most of the Indian companies the role of a middle level manager is transitional. While leading and controlling of the subordinates are important tasks, planning and organizing to achieve the designed goals also are often important for him. With increased use of strategic planning, suggestions for improved planning are very often asked by corporate level executives from the middle level ones.

Trading Area Analysis and Characteristic Study

Before planning it is very important to demarcate the domain where the plan is envisaged to perform. In Indian market condition, varieties of consumer's—characteristics make the job of marketing manager extremely difficult to plan a unique marketing manager extremely difficult to plan a unique marketing strategy. In recent times, when emphasis is laid on satisfying a customer in every possible way the relationship between a customer's acceptance of a product and the marketing mix of the product has to be studied in detail. Therefore, for the middle management, the characteristics of a consumer are not merely the traditional features of demography and lifestyle only but a concerted study of a consumer's perception of the company's marketing mix. The weightage that consumers are assigning to the various constituents of the marketing mix has to be studied to find out where the marketing plan of a company lies and what can be its future. As it is well understood that with difference of consumer characteristics and difference in company's marketing plans in different geographical regions, the relationship pattern between the consumers' characteristics and their perception on the P's of marketing shall vary. Hence different patterns will be obtained which can be similar, or contradictory and overlapping or isolated. The question is how to study the patterns—pattern of consumers' perception of a product or service on the basis of the marketing mix? Marketing research is undoubtedly the best tool in identifying the consumer's characteristics and preferences, provided the methodology is well designed. Problem lies on how to transcribe the marketing research findings to a pattern. Before we move to various factors of research, design and pattern construction, enumerating the various functions of a marketing manager is necessary.

Key functional strategies	*Typical question that should be answered by the functional strategy.*
Product (or Service)	(1) Which products do we emphasize?
	(2) Which products/services contribute to profitability?
	(3) What is the product/service image we seek to project?

	(4) What consumer needs does the product/service seek to meet?
	(5) What changes should be influencing our customer orientation?
	(6) Are the package and product mix ideally suited?
Price	(1) Are we primarily competing on price?
	(2) Can we offer discounts or other pricing modifications?
	(3) Are the pricing policies standard naturally or is there regional control?
	(4) What price segments are we targeting?
	(5) What is the gross profit margin?
	(6) Do we emphasize cost, demand or competition oriented pricing?
Place	(1) What level of market coverage is necessary?
	(2) Are there priority geographic areas?
	(3) What are the key channels of distribution?
	(4) What are the channel objectives, structure and management?
	(5) Should the marketing managers change their degree of reliance on distributors, sales representatives and direct selling?
	(6) What sales organizations do we want?
	(7) Is the sales force organized around territory or product?
Promotion	(1) What are the key promotion priorities and approaches?

(2) Which advertising/communication priorities and approaches are linked to different products, markets and territories?

(3) Which media would be most consistant with the total marketing strategy?

It can be seen from the important strategy issues mentioned above that very few issues related to product and fewer issues related to pricing can be decided by marketing manager because they are corporate level issues, especially the issues relating to price, as it directly influences demand and supply, profitability, consumer perception and response. Hence except discount related issue which partly falls under the promotion function, the price function is beyond the purview of the middle level managers.

Therefore for operational reasons price is being put outside the strategic decision-making domain of a middle level manager.

Our next stage is to study the research design in brief to outline the bases for coming into a domain to identify the perception of a consumer. If we study the table below we may get an idea of the design of research to arrive on a numerical data of a consumer's perception about the product, promotion and place function of the product/service.

	Factors related to	*Weightage assigned by manager*	*Rating assigned by consumers*	*Value*
	Question related to		(–5)	
Product	Product variety	.20	4	.8
	Quality	.15	5	.75
	Design	.15	4	.60
	Features	.10	3	.3
	Brand Name	.10	2	.2
	Packaging	.10	2	.2
	Sizes	.05	1	.05

	Services	.05	1	.05
	Warranties	.05	2	.1
	Returns	.05	2	.1
		1.0		3.15
Place	Channels	.20	2	.4
	Coverage	.20	4	.8
	Assessment	.15	5	.75
	Locations	.15	4	.6
	Inventory	.15	1	.15
	Transport	15	1	.15
		1.0		2.85
Promotion	Sales Promotion	.20	2	.4
	Advertising	.15	4	.6
	Sales force	.15	4	.6
	Public relations	.10	2	.2
	Direct Mktg.	.05	2	.1
	Discounts	.05	2	.1
	Credit terms	.15	4	.6
	Other Promotional efforts	.15	5	.75
		1.0		3.35

Therefore, if we calculate the per cent value of product, place and promotion on the total value we shall get :

(1) % value/product $= \dfrac{3.15}{3.15 + 2.85 + 3.35} = \dfrac{3.15}{9.35} = 33.7\%$

(2) % value/place $= \dfrac{2.85}{9.35} = 30.5\%$

(3) % value/promotion $= \dfrac{3.35}{9.35} = 35.8\%$

We find that $V_{Product} + V_{Place} + V_{Promotion} = 100$

and (i) the emphasis is highest on promotion

i.e. $V_{Promotion} = 35.8$

(ii) the difference between the highest and the lowest value is 35.8 – 30.5 = 5.3 denoting dispersion.

V = value

Hence it can be concluded that a consumer has placed more or less equal emphasis on his perception of the product with reference to the Ps.

Pattern Formation

It is generally found that graphical or illustrated version of a statistical study is simple and more revealing. The salient features are easier to be noted in a graphical representation rather than in long mathematical deductions. A triangular plotting of the figure is ideal in this case as there are three constituents in the plot, i.e., value product, value promotion and value place.

Before actually plotting the result let us briefly describe the rules and procedures of a triangular plot.Let the $V_{Product}$, V_{Place} and $V_{Promotion}$ represent the corners of an equilateral triangle.

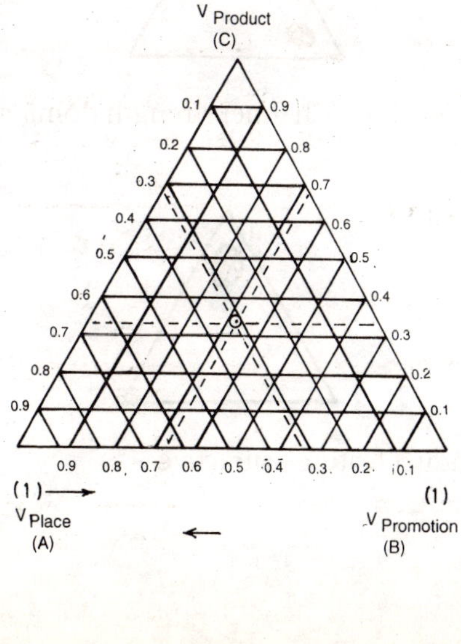

then the sides of the triangle represent the various proportions of the Binary systems $V_{Product}$ $V_{Place,}$ of $V_{Place} - V_{Promotion}$ & $V_{Product} - V_{Promotion}$. A point within the triangle represents a definite proportion of each of the three components. The length of each side is made equal to 100 per cent of each constituent as indicated. The amount of each constituent in a response x is determined by drawing a line through x parallel to the side of the triangle opposite the constituent. The point of intersection of that line with the side of the triangle indicating that constituent is its percentage composition. Thus, the percentage x is determined by the intersection of the line $V_{Promotion} = 35.8$ parallel to CB and is equal to $V_{Product} = 33.7$, $V_{Place} = 30.5$, and which is the composition of our response which can be plotted by the procedure described above.

If the consumers' response in a geographical area is studied various types of pattern of plotting may emerge depending upon the consumers' perception of the company's product in that area.

A few probable examples are given below.

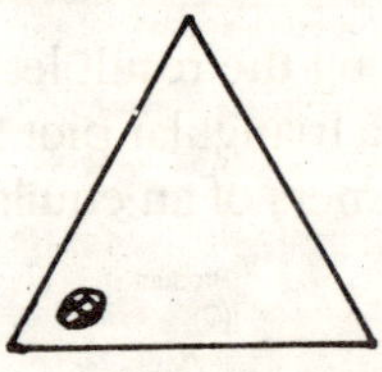

(1) Distributors/Channel strength dominant.

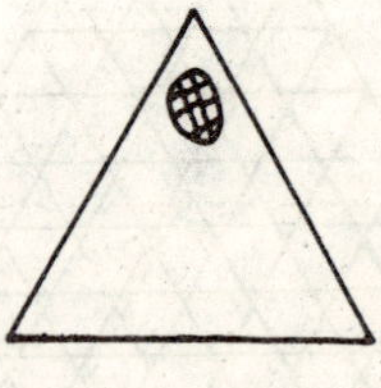

(2) Product features attractive

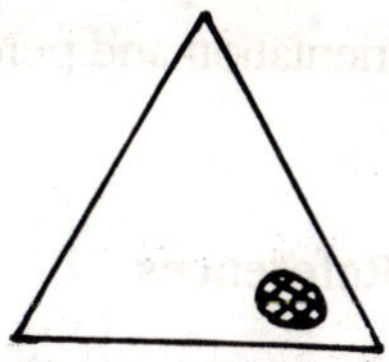

(3) Promotion dependent.

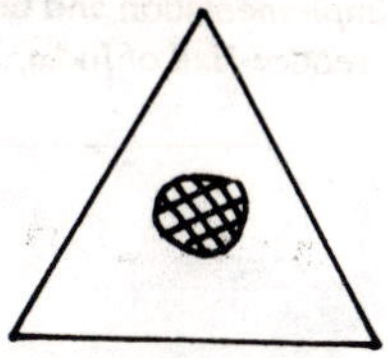

(4) Equal impetus of the factors.

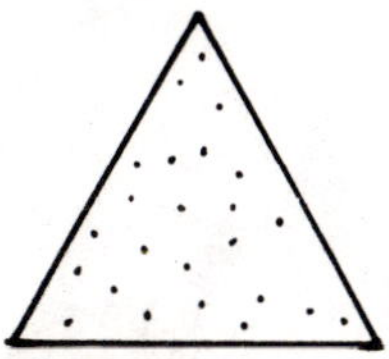

(5) Directionless state of affairs.

Depending upon the competition, growth of the industry, stage in product life cycle, relative market share of the firm and different entry barriers and bargaining power of vendors/suppliers is suggested that a stable, equal impetus oriented marketing strategy is ideal (Fig. 4).

Therefore, the tasks of the marketing managers are to concert the efforts so that all the functions are equally perceived by the customers. This should be done on an absolute basis rather than by shifting the importance from one function to other.

No solution is unique in marketing, experience and experimentation are an integral part to take a decision at a point of time.

In near future with increase of liberalization and consumer awareness the geographical or product based organizational networks shall be getting less importance. Trading area based on similarity of consumers orientation and perception shall become important.

References

Glueck F. William and L.K. Jauch : *Business Policy and Strategic Management* (1988) McGraw-Hill, Singapore).

Kotler Philip : *Marketing Management : Analysis, Planning, Implementation and Control, Prentice Hall of India, 1994*

11

Role of Consultancy in Integrating Human Resource Planning with Strategic Planning

Rituparna Chowdhary Raj

In the post liberalization scenario in India, a vital issue that has emerged is that of strategic management of industries, with a view to withstanding the winds of change, sweeping all across the country, in the form of the recent economic reforms. Every company in today's modern industrial world is trapped in a whirlpool of change. 'Change', irrespective of its pace, nature and impact is the only certainty in a turbulent environment, unsettling every individual organization. However, when this change becomes adverse, one thing becomes conspicuous and glaringly visible, and that is the difference between a well managed organization, which can withstand the adverse effects of the change taking place and a poorly managed one which places itself at the mercy of the strong currents of the change. How well a company gears up and adopts to the change teaches us a few lessons about planning, directing and controlling organizational activities. According to Prof. Y. Saran, "If an institution wants to survive and remain credible, it must change with the times by being 'pro-active' rather than being a helpless witness to the process of change. The changing here implies that people within the organization and the relation between them must also change according to changing functions, environment and expected performance standards". Hence it becomes invariable that the essential business and character of an enterprise be changed according to changing circumstances. Otherwise, changing circumstances become the determining factor and the function of the organization remains no longer within the control of the management.

In an era of rapid change and intense inter-industry and inter-company competition, improvisation, however brilliant, cannot suffice as a company's sole weapon against the negative effects of change. The range of activities planned in advance is generally much wider than that determinable on the spur of the moment. Many moves, because they require long preparation, cannot be made at all without forward planning. When new product development requires years and a new distribution network may cost millions of rupees, purpose must necessarily be considered in details well in advance of investment.

Planned purpose can affect and change the character of future development which otherwise might endanger even the healthiest of organizations. Reliance upon adaptation alone leaves the company at the mercy of strong currents. Innovation and the creativity which supports it can enable a company to carve out its own future rather than simply to depend on favourable circumstances. But, such a course requires predetermination of what must be done to minimise the adverse effects of change or to capitalise on a change to its own advantage. New opportunities, unexpected innovations, sudden emergencies, competitive pressures and changing regulations compel a company to change its course of planning and action so as to remain firm in the market place.

Thus, it is inevitable that since we live and operate under highly turbulent and dynamic work environment, companies have to plan ahead their course of action in order to achieve any degree of certainty in their activities. Hence, planning has become the foundation, and is no longer considered the first step of all corporate moves. Moreover, this planning has to be strategic, and not merely routine and cosmetic, in order to affect the character of future development. The importance of strategic planning is that it provides a direction to achieve the ultimate goals for the organization. Strategic planning results in very specific actions that can be easily implemented to ensure long-term success. After the Second World War, the world has witnessed a complete revolution in the sphere of business and technology, with an enormous expansion of industrial activity, unprecedented in the history of industrial revolution of the world. Hence, from the mid-sixties, i.e., from the time when the world changed the way in which businesses manage themselves, corporate managements have resorted to strategic planning as a major tool to keep the company in league with its changing environment—ensuring its continued survival and growth, and hence its earning potential in the market. The most neglected aspects of strategic planning is human resources which is common in many Indian companies. Human resource planning, although often recognized and admitted as a vital aspect for the success of the organization, is rarely considered systematically as a part of strategic management planning. Human resource needs are usually limited to Annual Budgeting and planning. In most Indian companies, the need for human resources is limited only for staffing planned operations, essential for achieving business objectives. Organizations are often confident of meeting their manpower requirements from the outside environment as and when necessary, because of the highly educated and trained but unemployed manpower market in India. Hence, Human Resource Planning is considered subordinate to the general strategic planning process of the company.

Attitude of our Business Houses

This attitude of Indian companies has mainly stemmed from two factors. First, of course, is because of the easily available workforce in India. Indian companies tend to believe that necessary qualified personnel can always be recruited from the market place to meet any manpower needs in the future, should the internal manpower supply prove inadequate. Secondly, management planners themselves often over-emphasise the financial, marketing, technological and production aspects of planning, undermining the relative importance of human resource as a planning issue. They often overlook the fact that the real appreciating resource of a company is its human resource, most other resources having a depreciating value. Human resource planning, thus, often fails to establish its integration with strategic business planning of the company. The risk of neglecting this integration is very great, because, ultimately, the success of all other functional planning of the company depends on its human resource to carry them out efficiently. The success of even the most well thoughtout strategic business planning of a company requires correct implementation of the plans by the human resource of the company. For example, as a company adds more and new products and production facilities and expands the existing plants to meet future demands, it must, for ensuring the success of the above, also plan for effective recruitment and training of managers to manage these expansions. Otherwise, even the most well-designed and meticulously planned programmes may go off-track, due to the lack of experience and ability of the key personnel of the company.

Waterman et al., in the famous McKinsey 7-S Framework has defined organizational changes in terms of a complex relationship between Strategy, Structure, Systems, Style, Skills, Staff and Super-Ordinate goals.

Source : *Thomas J. Peters and Robert H. Waterman, Jr., In Search of Excellence: Lessons from America's Best Run Companies', p. 10.*

This framework suggests that there is a multiplicity of factors that influence an organization's ability to change, while adopting a particular strategy, and the proper mode of change. Because of the interconnectedness of the variables mentioned above, it would be difficult to make significant progress in one area without making progress in the others as well. If one were to consider all these factors as critical in formulating a business strategy, the integration between strategic planning and human resource planning becomes self-evident. Among these seven factors—Strategy, Structure, Systems and Super Ordinate goals form part of strategic planning, while the rest, i.e., Style, Skills and Staff are part of human resource planning. It is only when all these seven critical factors are integrated together that a firm can hope to diagnose the causes of organizational problems and to formulate programmes for improvement.

Validity and Ability of Mckinsey Framework

There has been some doubt about the validity of the McKinsey Framework and its ability to integrate human resource planning with the strategic planning of the organization. In this context, it must be remembered that the very concept of this integration is a most recent one and a still unexplored area. Hence, there does not exist any foolproof model or technique with which to start the experimentation of this integration. In the absence of any other guideline to show us the way towards this integration the McKinsey Framework at least provides us with the direction in which to proceed in order to achieve this absolutely unknown and all-important integration of human resource planning with the strategic planning process of the organization. More research is needed on this new subject to find out more relevant and effective methods and techniques and better models have to be developed than the McKinsey Framework, to achieve this integration. However, till this is achieved, we have to depend on the McKinsey Framework to guide us in our efforts.

(The aim of all seminars and workshops to open up new areas for debate is to discuss new subject matters, to accept and appreciate novel ideas and not to dwell on well-researched, well-known and age-old concepts and subjects. Hence the aim of this study is to open up a new subject area for discussion and to come up with better solutions through debates. This study only seeks to set up a new trend of thought in a till unexplored area of Personnel Management and suggests the use of the McKinsey framework for the purpose. However, the use of this framework is not conclusive and prescriptive, but only suggestive. Moreover, the writer firmly believes that the McKinsey Framework is best suited to our needs at present.)

According to the components of the McKinsey Framework, super-ordinate goals refer to 'a set of values and aspirations that goes beyond the conventional formal statement of corporate objectives. Super-ordinate goals are the fundamental ideas around which a business is built. They are its main values. They are the broad notions of future direction. Examples of this would include Hewlett-Packard's objectives to have "innovative people at all levels in the organisation".

Even in the case of organization structure, it is easy to see the integration of human resource planning with the strategic planning of the organization. Organization structure prescribes the formal relationship among various positions and activities. Arrangements about reporting relations, how an organizational member should communicate with the other members of the organization, what roles he should perform and what rules and procedures exist to guide the various activities performed by the organizational members are all part of the organization structure. This structure helps to reduce internal uncertainty arising out of variable, unpredictable, random human behaviour within the organization and also helps human resource development through functional specialization, division of labour, etc. Incidentally, this is precisely what is required in human resource planning. Hence, integration between strategic planning and human resource planning becomes automatic, if this framework is adopted. In case of 'systems' also, we have production planning and control systems, cost accounting procedures, capital budgeting systems along with recruitment, training and development systems, performance evaluation systems, etc. The integration of human resource planning with strategic planning hardly needs any explanation in this context.

'Style', often called the 'soft' S of the McKinsey Framework is one of the levers which top management use to bring about organizational changes. Organizations differ from each other in their styles of working. The style of an organization, becomes evident through the patterns of actions taken by members of the top management team over a period of time. The aspects of business most emphasized by top management tend to be given more attention by people down in the organization. The McKinsey Framework considers 'Style' as more than the style of top management. The failure to make an acquired company successful, even after thorough analysis, could be the mismatch of the corporate culture of the acquired organization with that of the parent company. Time and again, strategic possibilities are blocked out, or slowed down, by cultural constraints. Organizational culture provides a way to bring in the people dimension in macro organizational analysis without using psychological models of human behaviour. Moreover, the concept of culture describes organizational realities that are difficult to define but are accepted by managers as relevant to running organizations. Human beings can be warm, aggressive, friendly, open, innovative, conservative and so forth. So can organizations. Organizational culture is expressed in a variety of ways—unwritten rules and traditions, shared norms, prejudices, standards for social etiquette and demeanour, established ways of relating with peers, subordinates and superiors, etc. These aspects of culture, which form a part of organizational style, which in turn has its impact on human resource planning, must be taken into consideration during the process of strategic planning.

'Staffing', the process of acquiring human resources for the organization and assuring that they have the potential to contribute to the achievement of the organization's goals, cuts across all organizational levels, functions and operations. In human resource planning, the planning process basically relates to selecting the right person for the right job in specific organizational positions and developing in them the ability and skills that they would need to be effective in those and subsequent assignments. Moreover, it takes into consideration the ability of the organization to motivate and keep motivated, the employees of the organization. To integrate this aspect of human resource planning with the strategic planning of the organization, it is needed to be planned ahead, how to introduce young recruits into the mainstream of the organizational activities and the manner in which they manage their careers as the new entrants develop into future managers on whose shoulders will lie future strategic planning and implementation of the company. Superbly performing companies pay particular attention to the development of managers who are ultimately responsible for formulating strategic planning for the company in the future. That way, the company can be sure, not only of its current security, but its future growth and development as well. Of the Western companies, examples can be cited of IBM, Texas Instruments, Proctor & Gamble, Hewlett-Packard & City Bank, whose top managers took extraordinary care in moulding young executives into future managers. On the Indian scene, examples can be cited of Larsen & Toubro Limited, TATA, Hindustan Lever, companies who consider money spent on human resource development as a future investment and not an expenditure.

Integration of this aspect of human resource planning with strategic planning is an absolute necessity for the future growth and development, and in fact, the very survival of the firm. 'Skills' is one of the most crucial attributes on capabilities of an organization. For example, Hindustan Lever is known for its marketing skills, Larsen & Toubro and TELCO are known for their engineering skills, IBM is known for its marketing orientation, customer service and market power, Du Pont for its research skills and Sony for new product development. Whatever be the skill of the organization, yet, its key strength is the skills and their upgradation of its human resource of the company. These skills of the organisation are meaningless without the development of these corresponding skills in their manpower. These skills in the human resource are developed over a period of time and are a result of the interaction of a number of factors, performing certain tasks successfully over a period of time, the kind of people in the organization, the top management style, the organization structure, the management systems, the external environmental influence, etc. Hence, when organizations make a strategic shift, it becomes necessary to consciously build new skills in the workforce.

The McKinsey Consultants call 'Strategy', 'Structure' and 'Systems' the hardware of the organization and calls the other four Ss i.e.,—Style, Staff, Skills and Super-ordinate goals as the software of the organization, because they are often ignored by corporate strategists. These are, however, the human resource planning factors which needs to be integrated with the other Ss of the framework. While Strategy and Structure are important to the organization, they by themselves cannot assure success which comes about by corporate commitment. It is the other 'Software'

Ss which play an important role in creating a climate of commitment. The better alignment between and among all the 7 Ss of the organization, the better are likely to be the results of strategic planning. Hence the need for integration of human resource planning with the strategic planning of the company.

The Importance of 7-S Framework

The 7-S Framework illustrates, in a simple way, this process of integrating, and bringing all the 7-Ss into harmony. When the 7-Ss are in good harmony the organization is poised and energised to execute its strategies to the best of its ability. The McKinsey model provides a convenient checklist for judging whether the organization is well-equipped for implementing the strategy or not. It also helps in diagnosing why the results emanating from the implementation of a strategy fell short of expectations and therefore what new 'fits' would be required. The framework helps strategists in evaluating their organizations along each of the seven dimensions, thereby identifying organizational strengths and weaknesses. The importance of this framework in the process of integrating human resource planning with the strategic planning of the organization, lies in cautioning professional managers by telling them that the factors which they have been dismissing for so long as the intractable, irrational, intuitive, informal organization can in fact be as much a part of strategic planning as Marketing, Finance or Production. It emphasises that the organization's human component is likely to have effects on all the other formal factors of strategic planning.

As a company expands its business or diversifies its areas of operations, systematic manpower planning becomes almost indispensible for the effective implementation of its strategic business plans. Lack of proper manpower resources may be the single major constraint on the otherwise virile and high growth potential company in its ability to sustain future expansions and diversifications.

It is apparent that when the organization requires manpower to implement all its future plans, as in the case of expansion plans, it can draw manpower from the current pool of its existing human resources. However, for new areas of activity, recruitment of needed personnel with specific skills have to be done from the outside environment. Whether such skilled personnel are readily available in the existing market is what such organizations have to ponder over. If such skills are not readily available in the nearby vicinity, how the process of procurement of such skilled personnel can be carried out, has also to be planned ahead. Moreover, when an organization affects major technological changes in its current mode of operations, many of the existing manpower may become redundant. What to do with this redundant workforce, how to absorb them productively elsewhere is what enlightened companies will have to plan ahead. Thus, the manpower plan forms an integral part of the strategic plan of the organization.

Strategic Manpower Planning : A Significant Factor

This strategic manpower planning will have to focus on and address itself to diverse needs of the workforce. Training is one such need. New technology, expansion of the market place, changing work culture, added responsibilities tend to make an employee bewildered with the rapid changes going on all around him, making him face unknown and undiscovered situations, while he sees his familiar and secure world fading from his sight. In such a situation, not only does the employee need to learn new skills and activities, but he also has to be trained on how to readjust himself psychologically in the face of changed surroundings so that he can go on contributing significantly as a productive member of the company's workforce. Strategic manpower planning has not only to design such training programmes, but also to anticipate when such a training need may be required.

Another significant factor of strategic manpower planning is compensation. For the wide and diverse categories of employees staffing an industrial organization, implementing an uniform compensation structure becomes a very difficult and unworkable proposition. However, a very diverse compensation range may cause dissatisfaction and low morale among the employees, besides being non-feasible. Hence the manpower plan of the company has to give due importance to this factor. However, designing the compensation structure of the company will be based on a policy and this policy should form a part of the overall strategic planning of the company.

Moreover, the human resource plan of the company has to take cognizance of the internal personnel structure of the company. This will require identifying the individuals who are high performers and hence the star personnel of the company; those who show promise and can be developed through training and exposure and hence are the high potential personnel of the company; and those who lag behind irrespective of the support and incentives given to them, and hence are the Dead Weights of the company. After this identification, individual career planning of the employees in the organization has to be done. It is in this context that it becomes essential to involve the HRD department in the strategic planning of the organization.

In the traditional human resource planning process, usually companies in India, prepare an annual forecast of manpower needs for the coming one year for the company. This forecasting is done as a basis for future recruitment from external sources, annual training, personnel reassignments, promotions, retirements and resignations. However, for strategic planning, this one year time horizon becomes too narrow, as it fails to take into consideration the long-range business plans and goals, and its future impact on expansion, new product addition, diversification, addition of new facilities, retrenchment of workers, etc. of the company. Strategic planning of the company deals with a long-term perspective and is then sub-divided into operational planning and annual planning. The integration of human resource planning with the strategic planning of the organization is shown in the following diagram:

Integration of Human Resource Planning with Strategic Planning

	Long-term Perspective	*Operational Planning*	*Annual Planning*
	Corporate Vision Corporate Mission New Opportunities	Programmes Resources- Required	Annual Target Annual Budget Project-Imple-

STRATEGIC	Added Threats	Product-	mentation
	Internal Strengths	Launch	Monitoring of
	Internal Weaknesses	Market-	Results
PLANNING	Long-term Objectives	Entry	Programme-
	and goals	New Techno-	Scheduling
		logy needed	Availability
		New Skills-	of Resources
		needed	on Time
		Finance from	Performance
		Public	Appraisal
	Analysis of Manpower	Recruitment	Recruitment
	Requirement based on	Levels	Process
	Strategies planned	Job Analysis	Training
	above	Job Description,	
		Job Information,	Promotion
		Job Design	Transfers
HUMAN	Internal Existing	Types of Skills	Job Re-
	Supply	reqd/available	assignment
RESOURCE		Recruitment Time,	Performance
	External Requirement	methods	Appraisal
PLANNING			Motivation
	Management Implications		Morale.

The critical issues that arises from such an integration is:

What are the human resource implications of the proposed business strategy adopted by the company?

Are the existing manpower resources geared up to take advantage of any new opportunities in the market place and to offset the external threats?

What are the strengths and weaknesses of the human resources of the company? In which areas skill upgradation through training has to be done to implement the strategies adopted by the company?

What are the human resource constraints in the achievement of planned goals and objectives of the business?

What activities are implied in the short-term to meet the long-term perspective of the company?

Consultant's

It is to solve these critical questions that the role of a consultant becomes helpful. It has been stated before that the first step in strategic planning is an external environment scan to locate opportunities which the company may exploit to its advantage and to anticipate threats which might rock the business at a later date. This, then has to be matched with the existing strengths and weaknesses of the company. However, scanning the external environment requires wide up-to-date information and a correct perspective of the environmental events all over the world; which busy and mostly overburdened managers and executives may not have. Similarly, in the analysis of the company's strengths and weaknesses also, an unbiased and detached view is most essential, which may not be possible in case of an internal member of the workforce, and if done in-house. Integration of human resource planning with strategic planning, is not easy, and to do it effectively, managers need professional help and expertise.

It is in this context that a consultant's help can be taken. A consultant's role in strategic planning process begins with assisting the planning team in conducting a meaningful and honest scanning of the external environment. The consultant usually have the advantage of a possibly broader perspective of environmental events as well as the opportunities and threats present therein, and also objectivity regarding the company's strengths and weaknesses. Once this is achieved, the company has to define its long-term objectives and goals. Here, an experienced consultant can guide the development of challenging yet achievable objectives covering all important areas of the business.

After this, at the operational level, the strategies for meeting the long-term goals and objectives of the company has to be defined. At this stage also, the consultant can help to provide the basic framework and a checklist of all the issues to be tackled in implementing the strategies can be provided. This will help the operating managers to carry out the task of strategic planning at their end in a most systematic manner.

Then comes the task of annual planning, wherein the consultant can provide the framework and methodology to carry out the functional operations of the company. The comparative advantages of companies are continuing to move further away from the availability of cheap labour to upgradation of skills and knowledge, while knowledge itself is becoming increasingly perishable and continuously obsolete. Therefore, the role of the consultant as change-agents in the organisation becomes more and more dependent upon education and retraining in new technology. As part of the company's competitive strategy, the consultant can prepare the workforce for life-long training, to continuously undergo cycles of 'learning-unlearning-relearning'.

Moreover the consultant can help to design a carefully and rationally conceived plan and a systematically implemented strategy built on excellence, currency and appropriateness. For a consultant, people are the most important asset. They facilitate the unleashing of creative energies of the people whom they serve. Under a consultant, people generally are provided with the opportunity to achieve their full potential.

However, people generally have the misconception that the services of a consultant is very expensive and beyond the means of small corporate firms and SSI units. It is to be emphasised here that the role of a consultant does not limit itself to only providing expensive consultancy to big business houses, but every consultancy firm worth the name has many schemes tailored and targeted for small businesses, suited to their needs and easily affordable by them. Moreover, an organizational expense should always be viewed, not in isolation, but in relation to the returns it brings. Consultancy service is such an expense. The returns from using a consultancy service is so great that ironically it is the small corporate houses that benefits more from the services of a consultancy than the big business houses. Whenever, a business firm faces life-threatening crises from the environment, that its very survival is at stake, the big business houses manage to survive such crises by their sheer size and the huge resources at their disposal, but the small business houses get wiped off from the marketplace trying to fight off the crises. Hence the only option available to these small firms is not to allow such crises to occur and hit them at all or even if such crises do happen, these firms are made so strong internally that threats from the external environment cannot wipe them off and they can fight with external threats successfully. And this can be done only if the personnel of these small firms are experienced, competent, dynamic and highly motivated so that by their own efforts, they are able to reduce the severity of these crises and the adverse impact of these threats upon the organization. This is a very challenging task and can be possible only if correct recruitment and selection of personnel is done and personnel turnover is reduced in the organization. This in turn is possible only if human resource planning of these firms are correct and this human resource planning is integrated with the strategic planning process of the organization. This again brings one to the basic question of how this integration is to be carried out. Because this integration requires expertise in the relevant area, which only a specialist and an outside non-biased, experienced agency having wide knowledge of the outside environment like a consultancy service can provide, the importance of using consultancy by the small business firms can hardly be over-emphasized. Thus the returns from using consultancy services by these small firms is enormous. When the returns from an expense far exceeds its cost, then this expenditure ceases to be an expense and becomes an investment. And this investment has to be made by these firms, if they want to survive and competitively operate in today's dynamic, ever-changing and turbulent environment. In trying to save this cost, let them not make even more costly mistake of compromising with their future and their survival in the market place.

This is precisely the reason why there has been a tremendous increase and multiplication of consultancy services in the country since the beginning of the 1990s, in all possible sectors of business and industry. The scope and importance of consultancy services will only increase with the expansion of the liberalization process. Not using a consultancy service because it is expensive, cannot, in any way, justify the failure of a firm in the market-place.

Whenever any changes are introduced in an organization, the first instinct of human behaviour is resistance to change. This is not so much a resistance to the change itself, but an instinctive fear for the unknown. Behavioural and attitudinal barriers have always been major factors to be taken cognizance of in any management process. In this connection, an outside consultant, who, in the opinion of the employees facing the impact of the change, has no reason to be biased, can help to tackle the following major forces delicately but firmly—

Information sharing-explaining to those concerned, the need

and impact of the change required by the adopted strategy, their role in the process of the change, etc.

Fear of making too many commitments, specially among the operation managers, and that too over an extended period of time.

Fear of admitting weaknesses and being retrained—employees may be tempted, if left on their own, to overstress their strengths and play-down their weaknesses, which would hamper rather than facilitate an honest planning exercise.

However, the most important role that a consultant can play for the client company is to impress upon all levels of personnel of the company the passion about the future and the need to anticipate and manage it efficiently. Then the company will find itself equipped with its manpower who have the kind of attitude and mindset as examplified in the quotation given below.

"It must be borne in mind that the tragedy of life doesn't lie in not reaching your goal. The tragedy lies in having no goal to reach. It isn't a calamity to die with dreams unfulfilled, but it is a calamity not to dream. It is not a disaster to be unable to capture your ideal; but it is a disaster to have no ideal to capture. It is not a disgrace not to reach the stars, but it is a disgrace to have no stars to reach for. Not failure but low aim is the sin."—Dr. Benjamin Mays. If the consultant can imbibe this attitude and dynamic foresight on the part of the workforce of the client company, then truly, it would have played its true role for the company.

With the overwhelming complexity of relations emerging among people, organizations and technologies as a result of some strategic changes in the organization, management consultants as change-agents have a responsibility to approach these changing times more knowledgeably and guide the organisation more deterministically, by integrating the needed human resource changes of the organization with the strategic changes. The purpose of consultancy in bringing about this integration is to usher in a planned change through collective concern and participation, which the in-house management may fail to do so. It is with this belief that management consultants can make the strategic changes of the organisation more effective, the operations more productive and at the same time make the work more interesting and satisfying to employees, that their role is suggested in integrating human resource planning with the strategic planning of the company.

12

Merchandising: A Functional Marketing Strategy

Sajal Kumar Das

In simple terms, merchandising is nothing but the attractive display of a product at a shop in a manner that is consistent with the brand image. It reminds the consumer about the brand at the point of sale when the final buying decision is made. Merchandising resources the consumer about the brand when it is seen prominently displayed by the retailer, the sole objective being to rise above the 'Point of Purchase' (POP) clutter.

Theoretical Backdrop

Consumers are continuously confronting and reacting to a great variety of specific situations: seeing of an advertisement, learning of new product or experiencing dissatisfaction. In fact there is a large number of variables influencing the consumer while making a purchase decision.

By means of factor analysis we can develop three envelope type variables which are very instrumental in studying consumer behaviour.

Stimulus Variables

The variables that exist in the consumers' external environment fall into this group.

Response Variables

These are the resulting activities of the consumers who are initiated by stimulus variables to do something.

Intervening Variables

At least some stimulus-variables do not directly affect responses but their effects are modified by the influences of intervening variables.

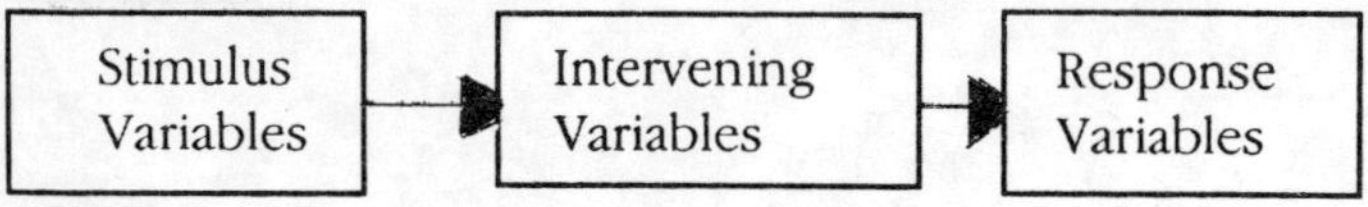

The Interaction Process

For our present purpose the intervening variables are of most importance. Merchandising being a very indirect type of advertisement campaign naturally falls under the 'intervening variables' group. The objective is to stimulate the consumer's attitude towards a particular brand of a particular product. It is a very cognitive process of attitude formation. Fishbein, Martin (1967) is of the opinion that to understand consumer's attitude adequately we must determine the beliefs that form the basis of these attitudes. A recent study by Onida (*Business India*, January 15-28, 1996, p. 122) reveals that consumers believe mostly in credibility while choosing a retail outlet. Merchandisers try to form the belief regarding the credibility—indeed the company's go, quite literally, to any length to catch the buyer's eye. For example, earlier the last year, Bombay's leading departmental store Shopper's Stop displayed a 221.5 ft. tie sponsored by Zodiac just to snare at the customers.

Merchandising is just like the silent salesman of the company. Here, by no means the customers are pulled to the product but the product is pushed towards a consumer.

The process which a prospective consumer goes through before he either buys or does not buy a particular brand of a particular product is a most complex system to model. Outside stimuli, e.g., price, quality, novelty and reputation aren't too difficult to measure. The individual also has measurable characteristics, e.g., social class, family position and regional influence. But the process which turns such stimuli into a purchase, or even into an attitude towards a product is not surprisingly difficult.

Stochastic models are most appropriate where major element of the choice process involves uncertainty (vs. rational choice), as in the low-involvement case.

Ehrengberg (1972) noted that the data on the number of purchases of a product over a given period of time for a sample of households exhibited consistent properties. Clearly the distribution would be skewed. Remarkably, the skewness tended, in most cases, to be of a form fitted by the Negative Binomial Distribution (NBD). There are a number of possible explanations for this phenomenon.

Here we consider that the number of purchases of an individual household is Poisson distributed. Over the population of households the mean of the above mentioned distribution may be considered as a random variable with a gamma distribution. From this we get sample proportion making no purchases.

The underlying assumption for purchase rate to be characterized by a Poisson process are:

1. The likelihood of purchase in any period of short duration is independent of time when the last purchase was made.
2. The likelihood of purchase does not change over time.

Admittedly, this does not allow us to move freely to estimate the human purchase behaviour stimulated by merchandising.

This is one of the most difficult portion of behavioural science—to model the cognitive process of decision-making. For this reason we can make use of the artificial intelligence using fuzzy logic.

Using historical data a market-like condition can be simulated with formal forecasting techniques giving values of input variables as well as that of output. Assigning random weights to each of input variables and minimising the error by changing the random weights with the help of an artificial neutral network. We can develop one model-free estimation technique. The advantage here is that we can consider as many input variables as we can which we consider influencing the purchase behaviour. Now changing the decision variables (input variables) and keeping the networking system intact we can obtain the changed value of output giving the actual effect of merchandising. What's more, this system is capable of forecasting the effect on sales if the decision variables are changed as per the capability of the company.

Why Merchandising

Under the structurally adjusted set-up there can be no doubt that a consumerist India is on the make. This changing psychology asks for the 'consumer oriented policies' of the companies. On the other hand, we cannot deny that the competition is increasing.

Now the normally price conscious Indian customers are taking notice of the smart displays. As a result, the first 4 P's are becoming crude, overused tools more and more.

There has been some interesting developments in recent retailing business. While the durables sector is booming the channels, the customers have not been growing fast. All the many new brands and models, both Indian and foreign being launched jostling for space at retailers' end.

At the beginning of the nervous '90s there has been a shift from zero level to multiple level channels. Yet, the minimum number of exclusive showrooms are there just to show the whole range of products. Under the circumstances the concept of 'shop within a shop' is upcoming. Revlon and Lakme have already adopted this policy. Lakme keeps a 'computer beautician' in six selected outlets in Delhi. It is a specially designed software for instant counselling. Whenever the customer keys in the details of her complexion and texture of skin, the computer suggests the shade specification. Revlon also has a specialized beauty-advisor posted at every Revlon counter.

Exploratory type study reveals that there may be some correlation between the attractive shop arrangements and the customer-purchase. This hypothesis can very easily be tested by a χ^2 test for association (independence). But the problem arises when we go in for studying whether alternative shop arrangements make an appeal to the customer or not. The orthodox procedure is to develop some Likert type questions or to carry out motivation research. But some recent techniques like Perception Analyser System (PAS) have made this process more scientific and accurate.

Real-life Exposure

Merchandising is increasingly becoming a critical marketing tool for consumer goods where impulse determines purchases at the point of sale. These include soft drinks, snack-foods, and cosmetics. It is not just low-priced items like cigarettes, beverages and chewing gums that are registering brisk sales as a result of merchandising. Even the expensive lipsticks, tyres, contact lenses, sunglasses and costly home appliances are seeing a higher off-take. What is more, an increasing number of global labels jostle for attention in precisely these categories, foreign companies setting up shops in our country are bringing their years of experience in merchandising.

With parity products inundating the market place; instore visibility (the other name of merchandising) has gained crucial importance. It alone may not be able to pave the way to brand success. But what it can certainly do is that it can lend an edge in a scenario where all the brands are busy devising strategies to sharply elbow the competitors out.

To tell the truth, achieving this is more difficult today. Everyone is a party to this rat race to have a sales boost up POP danglers, banners, posters are now very common. An edge can only come through the pace above parity.

The Danish Company CO-RO-FOODS took up a merchandising exercise two years ago (organized by the advertising agency Rediffusion—DY 2R's customer insights cell) just before Diwali. The company sells Sunquick in India. Over four days, almost 5000 people sampled the juice in seven outlets in Delhi and the trial sales were very significant.

The Italian chewing gum manufacturer Perfetti India distributed specially designed three-tier racks. In one rack eight boxes of Perfetti chewing gum can be arranged. The company carried out its merchandising strategy in 80,000 outlets all over the country. For small kiosks, it has designed a 4" × 4" minirack. The result proved to be satisfactory.

Pepsi Foods' snack food division decided to take up a merchandising exercise. Soon after, special baskets, chip station stands hit the shelves in the shops.

Simultaneously the colour on the packaging was changed from red and yellow mix to bright blue. The focus was on any gimmick which would appeal to the children.

In Bombay, where space is scarce, this snack foods multinational introduced what's called "in the air" merchandising two years ago.

Pepsi has special merchandising teams. They fan out time to time and clean bottles, racks, put up new posters and rearrange bottles in such a way that the brandname faces the customers.

A division of Pepsi Foods Limited, which just deals with on promise selling, hit upon a novel idea in 1993. It introduced 'visi-coolers-slim refrigerators with look through door'—that did not only provide added cooling infrastructure in the retail outlets, but also totally redefined storage norms and visibility. Though this type of visicoolers can be seen in 12,000 to 15,000 outlets (out of a gigantic total number of 2,50,000 outlets) it has certainly jacked up sales by 30 to 40 %.

The chocolate giant Cadbury revealed that as much as 35 % of all chocolate sales are really impulse driven with no prepurchase intention. To capitalise this opportunity the company came out with box-shaped, glass-tapped dispensers placed near the cash counters.

Nestle could well understand the importance of merchandising while launching its chocolate bars. Its promotional campaign was talk of the town and won many awards. But the company insisted that the chocolates be stored inside the refrigerators; otherwise they would melt. The ruling out of merchandising gave a heavy blow to the company and the product did not move.

Britannia Industries Ltd. (BIL) also took the advantage of in-store-visibility while launching 'Little Heart' biscuits.

Strategist's Paradise

Merchandising becoming necessary and widespread a relevant question arises: what type of self-arrangement is most effective—which brand or product itself to come just beside a particular product?

Three types of self-arrangements may be suggested which are most general in nature

Types of Self-arrangements

* Competitive

In the 'competitive' case we see that there may be a number of attributes which provide competition among brands. This would be in accordance with consumer's perception. Three factors, giving rise to competition, e.g., price, quality and outer facilities may be specified.

Neutrality

'Neutrality' means that a particular brand has got nothing to do with the brand just beside, i.e., there exists no perceptual context. Here it may be seen that neutrality arises out of three factors:

- same brand but different service
- competitive brand but different service
- neither competitive brand nor same service.

Complementary

'Complementary' brands theoretically mean 'made for each other', i.e., while buying one item the consumer has to keep in mind that he or she has to buy the item just at the side of it. Complementarity, thus arises out of

- same brand but complementary service
- competitive brand but complementary service
- neutral brand but complementary service

Now by changing these alternative self-arrangements a Latin Square Design (LSD) can be developed and can easily be tested whether the consumer can be effected by any of the alternative self-arrangements.

The underlying assumption here is that the consumers are more or less homogeneous in nature. The heterogeneity among consumers is excluded ex-hypothese as we are believing in a kind of Markorian ideology. But basically there are three types of customers :

Types of Customers

In an impulse-stimulated purchasing behaviour the type of customers is important.

- *Decided customers* are those who come to purchase being decided about the brand.
- *Undecided customers* come without being sure which brand to buy. They are of most importance for the merchandisers. Here the shop display has got tremendous potential to form their attitude towards a particular brand.
- *Lookers* only look through the shopping windows. They can also be fairly effected by the merchandising activity as they may be made prospective customers in near future.

This model will be more consumer specific if three LSD's can be framed for the three types of customers.

Here, wilfully the time factor is not taken into consideration as the treatments are considered independent of time.

The exploratory type research reveals the fact that the consumers are attracted by the competitive self-arrangement rather than any other. The basic reason behind this as may be pointed out that under competitive self-arrangement consumers are having a wide range of choice.

Now, merchandising being an important marketing strategy the strategists' role becomes instrumental. They will be trying to condition the consumers' attitude. The strategic focus under the circumstances is on changing the consumers' attitude in such a way that the consumer is practically hypnotised by the attractive display. But, fortunately or unfortunately, the strategic options will be different for the low-involvement and high-involvement items.

Strategies for low-involvement goods
* Linking of the product to an involving issue * Linking of the product to a presently involving personal situation * Changing of importance of product benefits * Introduction of important product characteristics

Strategies for high-involvement goods
* Changing of existing beliefs about the consequences of behaviour * Changing of consumers' evaluation of the consequences of a particular action * Introduction of new belief/evaluation combinations * Changing of existing normative beliefs * Changing of motivations to comply with subjective norms * Introduction of new normative concepts

References

1. Della Bitta, Albert J. and Loudon, David L. *Consumer Behaviour: Concepts and Applications,* McGraw—Hill Book Company (1988), New York, pp. 30-32, 531-35.
2. Kotlar, P., *Marketing Decision—Making: A Model Building Approach,* McGraw—Hill Book Company (1986), New York.
3. Parsegian, V.L., *This Cybernatic World of Men, Machines and Earth Systems,* Doubleday and Company, Inc. (1972), New York, pp. 103-50.
4. Pessemier, Edgar A., *Product Management: Strategy and Organisation,* Second Edition, Robert E. Krieger Publishing Company (1986), pp. 156-75.
5. Srivastava, Nitin:, *Simulating The Market,* Strategist Quarterly, January-March, 1996.

13

Strategic Issues on Mines Safety Management

S. Mallick and K. Mukherjee

Mines safety management covers under its scope all issues relating to safety, health and welfare of mineworkers. It is guided by the basic principle that all mineworkers, during their working hours, are entitled to a reasonable standard of safety, health and welfare. More recently, the traditional outlook has been expanded to responsibility of mines safety management towards society in general, and issues of environment degradation/pollution are receiving greater attention.

Management of hazards of personal injuries has always received the maximum attention, because it not only affects the production process more adversely than anything else, but also degrades quality of workforce, and also makes management incur losses due to compensation, rehabilitation, etc. Mine accidents, which are an undesirable and almost inevitable byproduct of the production process, is the basic loss-producing event leading to personal injuries.

Role of Accident Prevention

The role of accident prevention in mines safety management is best illustrated in the following excerpt taken from the English translation of the classical text 'The Art of War" written by the Chinese philosopher Sun Tzu, where he discusses principles of strategy in competition and conflict:

"A lord of ancient China once asked his physician, a member of a family of healers, which of them was most skilled in the art. The physician, whose reputation was such that his name became synonymous with medical science in China replied, 'My eldest brother sees the spirit of sickness and removes it before it takes shape, so his name does not get out of the house. My elder brother cures sickness when it is still extremely minute, so his name does not get out of the neighbourhood. As for me, I puncture veins, prescribe potions, and massage skin, so from time to time, my name gets out and is heard among the lords."

The art of healing and the art of safety may be distinctly different professions, but as this story implies, they are basically the same as both require strategies to deal with disharmony (lack of control); both suggest that the less effort, energy or contact the better; and both emphasize that knowledge of the problem (loss exposure, control weakness) is critical to the solution.

Three Control Strategies

As illustrated above, while describing or modelling the cause/effect sequence of a loss-producing event such as mine accident, it is helpful to differentiate three stages where interventions can be made to control the outcome—either by preventing it or by minimizing the downgrading effects when it occurs. The following diagram shows these as Pre-Event, Event and Post-Event.

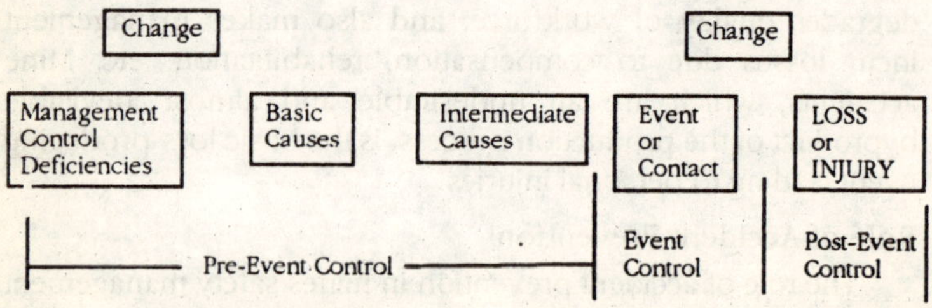

Pre-Event Control

Accident prevention in mines safety management is nothing but a pre-event control strategy. It is the most productive and proactive of all other alternatives. Here we develop not a safety programme, but rather a safety management system. From these efforts come optimum performance standards, effective communications, meaningful measurements and performance evaluations, and a desired compliance level through regular performance feedback.

Therefore, safety managers should concentrate their efforts on strategic planning and identification of potential loss-producing events at the earliest stages, before they become great or actual losses requiring intervention occur. Success in safety management (greatness) comes from a strategy of loss (injury) avoidance or control; attacking loss sources when they are potential (easy). This would require (i) a full, open and accurate description of the workprocess; (ii) a comprehensive description of problems/symptoms that impede process performance; and (iii) a continuing stream of new ideas for process improvement.

Table 1

Common Pre-Event Control Instruments

Management Leadership and Administration
Employee Participation
Management Training
General and Special Inspections
Emergency Preparedness
Task Observation
Work Rules and Permit Procedures
Standard Operating Procedures
Employee Training
Hiring and Placement Practices
Contractor Safety Controls

Engineering Controls
Purchasing Controls
Security
Communications
Environmental Protection
Occupational Health and Hygiene
Safety Promotion
Off-the-Job Safety

Event Control

The next best alternative strategy is to make intervention when the sickness (system deficiency) has manifested itself (an event or contact has occurred), but can be controlled at its earliest stages so that loss is avoided. The exposure has not exceeded the threshold limit of the body or structure. At this stage, chance also plays its hand, and abundant near miss events appear and other warnings of impending accidents may be noticed.

Several control interventions are typically called upon to reduce the harmful contact or the amount of energy transferred to the body or structure (Table 2). These represent the visible side of safety; guards and barriers, enclosures, manual material handling devices, ground fault interrupters, low-voltage equipment, double-insulated tools, personal protective equipment, wellness programmes, etc. This side of safety management, according to the tale of the physicians, "does not get out of the neighbourhood"—the company or industry.

Table 2
Common Event Control Instruments

Substitute Alternate Forms of Energy
Use Less Harmful Substance
Reduce Energy Used or Released
Guards or Barricades
Strengthen the Body Structure
Personal Protective Equipments

These measures do not, by themselves, prevent the contacts or events, but they can prevent the loss and do significantly contribute to control efforts. Safety programmes utilizing these interventions can be characterized as having a more enlightened, proactive approach than pre-event control strategy.

Post-event Control

When an accident or some form of disaster occurs, there is a significant marshalling of human, material and financial resources. This process is very visible, with much attention directed to the accident scene; the victims, the fire or inundation or explosion, the emergency services, the damage. Headlines and statistics are generated. Regrettably, it is these accidents or disasters that stimulate change in the battle against injuries, illness and other loss-producing events.

Post-Event Controls also do not directly prevent accidents; however, they do minimize the effects of losses. As Table 3 illustrates, these and similar activities can mean the difference between minor injury and death, between an ordinary accident and a disaster, between temporary work-stoppage and closing down a mine. Hence these measures have their importance when situation comes to such a pass. But by no means they represent the best strategy for mines safety management.

Table 3
Common Post-Event Control Instruments

First-Aid/Medical Care
Emergency Response/Rescue Operations
Accident and Incident Investigation
Damage Control
Salvage Operations
Claims Handling
Rehabilitation
Communications to the Press/Public
Legal Defence
Citation Abatement Efforts

It is obvious in principle, but not always in practice, that success comes from a balanced approach utilizing all three strategies. The challenge for line managers, therefore, is to collectively develop a strategy that will result in an acceptable level of control for a particular system and its inherent risks.

Mine accidents are basically the results of a flawed production process. Therefore, accident prevention strategy must be based on a set of principles that address to all-round improvement of the quality of the production process.

In the manufacturing industry, quality has traditionally been viewed in terms of improvement of production process and reduction of defects. Inspection of product to check its conformance to specifications used to be the control strategy. This technical view has largely been a failure. In mining industry also limited success can be achieved through exercising regulatory controls based on technical/legislative specifications. Quality experts like Deming, Crosby and Juran have developed the basic principles of Total Quality Management (TQM), which provide a simple and direct method for addressing process quality in any organization. TQM is a management issue, not a technical one. Its principles can be translated into the context of mining industry to formulate strategies for accident prevention.

TQM is defined as "a customer-focused, strategic and systematic approach to continuous performance improvement". In the context of mines safety management the definition may be interpreted as follows:

Any organized effort towards improvement of safety in mines has to be total, that is, it requires commitment to the ultimate goal, on the part of mine management, government, mineworkers, labour unions, contractors and suppliers.

Quality refers to the satisfaction of the customers, internal as well as external, regarding standard of safety. The external customers are government, labour unions, etc. The internal customers are mineworkers and management. It is very much important to identify all customers and proper classification of their needs. Purposeful communication with the customers are required to determine their needs of workplace safety.

It is basically a management issue. Just like any other commercial business, accident prevention programmes are also to be managed via mission, goals, policies, objectives, process improvement, financial support, measurement, communication, participative supervision, training and education.

It has to be customer-focused. Reasonable standard of safety and the need for improvement to the existing standard should be suggested by the customers.

Contrary to the earlier belief that safety standards are counter-productive for a mine, the strategy for better productivity is one which has accident prevention as one of its major components.

The accident prevention programme has to be systematic, that is, it should have perfect compatibility with production, information, financial and personnel systems. Moreover, it has to be well-defined and well-organised, not a peacemeal or ad-hoc attempt.

It has to be continuous, in the sense that mineworkers and supervisors should be empowered to routinely identify and solve problems, help improve workprocesses, and make improvement in safety standard a matter of habit.

The thrust should be on performance, that is, on *prevention* of the events that impede production, rather than their *detection*. The safety problems should be solved upstream, rather than inspecting for defects downstream.

There should be a constant effort directed towards improvement of safety standards. The tools are gathering of safety-related information, encouragement for innovation and better workstep design, remove barriers to effective performance, etc.

While recognizing that accident prevention programme can be managed as a quality improvement programme, we should not forget that fundamentals of mines safety management remain unchanged. Regardless of the organizational change that may occur, the heart of the matter is still unsafe human behaviour and inherently hazardous environment. Existing skills and techniques to control these two factors from technical viewpoints are sought to be brought together under a disciplined structure as defined by TQM.

Deming emphasizes both statistical process control techniques for a proper understanding of the production process, and fundamental management changes to bring in quality improvement in all stages of production process. These are the two basic steps of TQM, which are applicable in the context of accident prevention also.

Juran's view regarding implementation strategy is that quality improvement should be driven from the top, where selected quality problem areas are documented through use of a Pareto chart. Then there is need to identify people who should serve on short-lived quality improvement teams on a project basis to address to the problems. This idea suggests that there is a need for designing an objective method of selection of problematic mines, and also their specific safety problems.

The other part of the implementation strategy is how to bring about the desired improvement in quality of workprocess for solving the identified safety problems. Here the principles of TQM provide the answer.

Selective Approach

In the Indian context, all coalmines and non-coalmines of all important minerals including oil, operate under the management of a number of Public Sector Undertakings. Over 90% of the mining workforce are employed in these mines. Apart from these there are a large number of small mines of other minerals which belong to private ownerships.

Under the Constitution of India, "Regulation of Labour and Safety in Mines and Oilfields" is a Central Subject (entry 55 of the Seventh Schedule of Article 246). The matter is regulated by the Mines Act, 1952 and the Rules and Regulations framed thereunder. These statutes are administered by Directorate-General of Mines Safety (DGMS) under the Union Ministry of Labour. According to provisions of the statute, everyone in the production chain—the owner, the agent(s), the hierarchy of management supervisory team as also the workpersons to be ever vigilant throughout the operations, in detecting and responding to anomalous conditions and any signs of imminent danger. Thus, while the onus, both moral and legal, of continuously monitoring and removing the anomalous conditions rests on the management; role of government is essentially one of defining what minimum safety performance is acceptable and promoting compliance with the requirements so established.

The instruments used under the statute are: (a) periodic inspection in mine workings, (b) investigation into accidents/ occurrence and awarding punishment to persons held responsible for accident, (c) grant of permission for mine workings, (d) approval of mines safety equipments/materials, (e) development of new safety legislation, and (f) grant of certificate of competency, etc.

Under the Public Sector Mining Companies, individual mines operate as a single production unit, and not as separate business units. The safety management policies are also framed by the corporate management for all mines under its ownership. Hence there is a problem of allocating scarce safety resources of the company over its mines.

It is an accepted fact that resources and organization of the government to closely monitor all aspects of mines safety in such a vastly spread mining industry, is far from adequate. A large proportion of mines of minor minerals go almost uninspected every year. With such limited resources, it is difficult to be effective. The much-coveted standard of "Zero-Accident Potential" (ZAP) demands a more intimate involvement of the safety inspectors with the safety problems of a mine, so that no hazard elements are left unaccounted and unguarded. This sets the background for a selective approach.

One common challenge in safety management is the problem of quantification of targets and achievements in financial terms. This is necessary to establish the economic justifiability of a safety programme. Mines safety is a profession where failures are more easily highlighted than success. The accident statistics and counts of injuries, however, are not the end-results. It is often difficult for the safety professional to demonstrate that the cost of resources to be used in a safety programme are justified by the numerous hidden costs related to accident reduction. Especially when the scope of activity is spread over a large group of mines, the problem of objective quantification becomes all the more difficult. Hence, there is a need of selecting a few, distinct target areas, where the ultimate success can be neatly quantified and achieved.

According to a recent study, about 27% of all fatalities in mines accidents occur in a few coalmines which contribute only about 6% to total coal production, and have a share of only 7% in total employment. This 'vital few—trivial many' type of distribution justifies the demand for priority action on a few selected mines.

The strategy is, therefore, simple: 'catch the most notorious ones and crack them'. On the selected few, launch an all-out effort. Let these be the testing ground of the 'total approach' that is required to break the barrier of a stagnant fatality rate. Once the first set of 'accident-prone' mines are thus tackled, a fresh set can be selected, and the process can be continued to cover all the deserving mines. This not only leads to efficient resource utilization, but a stagewise approach reduces the complexity and quantum of problems in implementing the countermeasures.

Sophisticated statistical models can be employed to select the 'accident-prone' mines, based on their past accident experiences and other safety-related characteristics. These models make appropriate assumptions about the stochastic nature of variation in accident count, and also regarding variation in the levels of adversities that the mines inherently possess. Such models have been widely used in identifying 'accident blackspots' in the context of road accidents, process industries, etc. They help objective quantification of 'observed level of unsafety of a mine', 'expected level of unsafety of a mine given its safety characteristics', 'potential of accident reduction of a mine', 'effectiveness of countermeasures', etc.

After identifying the 'accident-prone' mines, an indepth analysis to spot out the sources of trouble is called for. Here the models of accident causation may be of great help.

Typically, accidents are results of complex interaction between one or more of the three factors, (a) Man-machine interface (b) Environment (c) Human behaviour. However, accidents are sought to be defined in a number of ways depending on the perspective and focus of analysis. Each definition is embodied in a separate accident causation model. These models represent, classify and organize a large amount of safety related knowledge. Furthermore, a large number of techniques of analysis have been developed which are based upon these models. Among the models, there are 'process-oriented' models, models of 'human error/unsafe behaviour', and models of 'mechanics of human injuries/ ergonomics'. Among the tools of analysis, there are fault-tree analysis, event-tree analysis, failure mode and effect analysis, causal tree analysis, hazard and operability studies, management oversight and risk tree, etc. Given below are three different definitions of accident based on three different views, viz., chain of events, result of unsafe act, and exposure to uncontrolled energy flow.

(1) An accident is a natural culmination of a chain of events that may lead to injury, property damage of both.

(2) An accident is an unplanned and sometimes injurious or damaging event that interrupts the normal progress of an activity and is invariably preceded by an unsafe act or condition, or some combination thereof.

(3) An accident is a potentially harmful energy flow or environmental condition that is preceded by planning or operational oversights or omissions, resulting in conditions or actions that trigger the incident, which, in the absence of adequate barriers or controls, cause losses—injury, damage or degraded performance—to the persons or objects in the path of the energy flow or exposed to the environmental condition.

Other methods which should supplement are intensified inspection of worksites, study of accident investigation reports, interviews with the accident victims, etc. Results of such analysis/ efforts would be a list of the deviating elements of environment, operation, machineries, organisation and human act/behaviour, along with an analysis of the role played by them in the occurrence of the accidents.

Knowledges and skills of mining technology and other disciplines of engineering, R&D, technical specification of materials/equipment, etc., can be called upon at this stage to devise appropriate countermeasures for each of these deviations. All these technical issues are to be solved at this part of accident prevention programme.

The benefit of selective approach is that here a few problematic cases can be taken up for indepth analysis on a special project basis. Consequently, many minute details of safety problems, which are normally not detected or ignored, can be captured and solved. Moreover, evaluation of effectiveness of countermeasures for improving them, if necessary, becomes a lot more easier.

The other part of implementation strategy chiefly addresses the management issues concerning the subject.

Participative Approach

It has long been recognized by safety professionals that inspections and punitive actions may be essential parts, but not the cutting edge of the instrument of accident prevention programme. It is often a part of production strategy of the mine management to take care of only those aspects of mines safety so as not to attract a contravention of the statute. Many of the safety professionals employed by the mine management are engaged with doing this particular job only. Hence it is clear that the change has to be made in the process and it has to come from within.

But the hard truth is that 'positive action' and not 'reluctant or mindless obedience' to the safety statute on the part of mine management is the sole requisite to achieving overall safety success. Accidents are undesirable byproducts of production process, which is designed, operated and owned by management. Yet, when accidents occur, they are mostly attributed to 'fault of careless mine workers'. It is poor management practices that cause wrong employer attitudes. This conflict is embedded deep in the conventional style of safety management. This can be removed if accident prevention programmes are given the orientation of a quality improvement programme.

Safety rules, however comprehensive they may be, can never adequately address hazard elements in a vast and dynamic industry like mining. Even accident investigations rarely identify critical facts which are embedded deep within the organization. Therefore, recurrence of accidents cannot be completely avoided by enacting rules and regulations on the basis of findings of investigation. Detection of hazards and suggestions for solutions to remove them has to come through an open channel of communication based on participative approach.

In the evolution of theoretical models of accident causation and analysis, increasing attention is being paid to the role of human factor in accident causation. Conventional style of safety management fails to address to this problem adequately. It simply ends up classifying a large majority of accidents as 'fault of co-workers or victims'.

For implementation of accident prevention programme as a quality improvement programme, the major change in management style would be required in terms of (a) supportive culture environment, (b) participative management, (c) team development and (d) training.

(a) Establishing a supportive culture within a mining organization allows mineworkers to achieve their highest potential and permits opportunities for their self-improvement, encourage teamwork, and reward important contribution to the cause of safety.

All mineworkers should be encouraged to make ethical decisions and conduct themselves in an ethical fashion, that is they should be permitted to do what is right than what is expedient.

Consistent and forthright communication regarding all kinds of safety problems is another important element. Effective lines of communication must be established and maintained between different levels of mine management and staff. Any barrier restricting such communication should be removed. Such information sharing helps mineworkers understand priorities, trusting management decisions, and involving themselves in whole-hearted participation.

The other element is discipline. It requires that everyone follows approved policies and procedures in every process, even when it may be expedient to cut corners. Unless discipline is adhered to, changes for improvement will result into organizational chaos.

(b) Mineworkers who perform the hazardous tasks are often best qualified to suggest improvements. All levels of mine safety management should be linked with participative management. Managers should solicit opinions from mineworkers, supervisors, suppliers, and other concerned groups before making final decisions.

Empowerment of workers and supervisors is both a management style and an attitude. As a management style, it provides authority, responsibility and accountability for required decisions, based upon expertise. Expertise in mineworkers must be accurately identified and appropriate boundaries for empowerment must be accurately defined by the management. Through the use of empowerment, the mineworkers have an opportunity to increase individual contribution to the final goal.

As an attitude, empowerment is the feeling of confidence that develops when one becomes comfortable in decision- making responsibilities. Empowering individuals to make decisions at the lowest possible level in the organization reinforces this attitude in a positive and productive way.

Acting on the principle of empowerment, Workmen's Inspectors have been created in Indian mines. This institution has been given necessary statutory recognition.

(c) Another principal element is formation of quality improvement teams. In Indian mines, Pit Safety Committees were formed under this principle, and is now a requirement under the statute. 'Process oriented teams' should include people involved in or affected by a particular process. The team should focus on daily improvements and activities related to a process. The team assignment should match individual skills to the task/ process under the jurisdiction of the team. Team members should be responsible for the results of the process and for continuous improvement of the process. This responsibility is a delicate balance between maintaining discipline and managing change.

Partnership is the other principle to be practised. For a successful implementation of any accident prevention programme, effective partnership between management and mineworkers must be based on a long-term mutual interest in the achievement of goal, mutual involvement, trust and respect. Blaming each other for occurrence of accidents must be stopped. Inter-department partnership in large organization is also essential. In fact, mines safety problems are always multi-disciplinary in nature. Good partnership among department avoid duplication of work and leverage corporate resources.

(d) Quality improvement programme place great importance to training of workpersons. Once it is understood that all injuries are preventable, training provides the means for making injuries predictable. Training enables workers to recognize hazards and unsafe acts, and understand their consequences. These skills are not inborn, they are learned through training.

Since the mining workforce is very large, an effective strategy could be to train the trainers. The results of safety analysis on the accident-prone mines, the experience of successful implementation of the accident prevention programme in those mines, and the various safety features of the latest technologies, all should be systematic documented for downward transmission to the mineworkers through training.

System of imparting vocational training for mineworkers are already in force in Indian mining industry. They need to be given more analytical/behavioural orientation.

Conclusion

When the conventional style of mines safety management has started showing its limitations, it is high time for a shift in the strategy. Accident prevention is the best among all loss-minimising strategies. It is clearly understood that accident prevention programme can be implemented as a quality improvement programme. Philosophies and principles TQM of can be translated into the context of mining industry to show the pathway for change. Keeping in view the size of the mining industry, scarcity of safety resources and role of the various agencies involved in mines safety management in our country, the implementation strategy has to be tailored, so that best results can be achieved.

Table 1

Growth of Mining Activities in India

No. of reporting mines				Value of minerals (in Million Rs.)		Aggregate H.P. (in 1000s)			Explosives used (in 1000 tonnes)		
Year	*Coal*	*Metal*	*Oil*	*Coal*	*Metal*	*Oil*	*Coal*	*Metal*	*Oil*	*Coal*	*Non-coal*
1951	893	1810	—	505	235	N.A.	188	83	N.A.	1.5	1.0
1961	848	2323	—	1141	487	N.A.	438	159	N.A.	4.5	3.8
1971	781	1995	13	2543	1080	756	732	282	25	12.2	9.4
1981	496	1768	8	18114	3620	2748	1841	925	35	46.3	15.3
1991	561	1787	24	79794	19076	18533	4292	1519	507	124.2	40.3
1992	567	1810	27	96377	21700	23104	4653	1644	583	140.0	44.1
1993	570	1845	27	107467	23392	31777	3942	1853	541	155.6	44.1

Table 2

Trend in Fatal Accidents and Fatality Rates per 1000 Persons Employed (Ten Yearly Average)

	Coalmines				*Non-Coalmines*			
Year	*Acc.*	*A.F.R.*	*Fat.*	*F.R.*	*Acc.*	*A.F.R.*	*Fat.*	*F.R.*
1901-10	74	0.77	92	0.94	16	0.52	23	0.76
1911-20	38	0.94	176	1.29	29	0.57	37	0.73
1921-30	174	0.99	219	1.24	42	0.54	50	0.66
1931-40	172	0.98	228	1.33	35	0.41	43	0.51
1941-50	236	0.87	273	1.01	26	0.24	31	0.29
1951-60	222	0.61	295	0.82	64	0.27	81	0.34
1961-70	202	0.48	260	0.62	72	0.28	85	0.33
1971-80	187	0.46	264	0.55	66	0.27	74	0.30
1981-90	162	0.30	244	0.34	65	0.27	73	0.31
1991-94	153	0.28	187	0.34	68	0.32	90	0.37

Data of 1993-94 are provisional.

N.B. : Acc. Accident. A.F.R. Accident Frequency Rate.
Fat. Fatality, F.R. Fatality Rate.

NA - Not Available

References

1. Guha, R., Mallick S., & Rudra A.K., Analysis of Injury Experience in Coal mines—An Approach", Proceedings of seminar on "Mines Productivity and Technology", by MGMI, Calcutta, 1994.

2. Vincoli, J.W., Total Quality Management and Safety and Health Professionals", Professional Safety, June, 1991.

3. Motante, W.M., The Ancient Art of Safety Management", Professional Safety, August, 1991.

4. Directorate General of Mines Safety, Government of India—
   (a) Report of the Working Group on Safety, Health and Welfare of Employees in mines, factories and docks etc.: Eighth Five Year Plan, Vol. I, September, 1989.
   (b) Standard note on DGMS, 1995.

5. Bhattacharjee, B. "Workers' Participation in Safety Management with Particular reference to Workmen's Inspectors and Safety Committees, The Indian Mining & Engineering Journal, August, 1994.

6. Lehto, M. and Salvendy G., Models of Accident Causation and their Appraisal, Journal of Engineering & Technology Management, 8 (1991), pp. 173-205.

7. Wright, C.C., Abbess C.R. & Jarrett D.F., Estimating the Regression to Mean Effect Associated with Road Accident Blackspot Treatment—Towards a more Realistic Approach, Accident Analysis and Prevention, Vol. 20, No. 3, 1988.

14

Strategic Planning and Organizational Performance: Executives' Viewpoint

A.M. Shah

From the very beginning planning has come to be recognized as an important element of management. The empirical research overwhelmingly supports the contention that companies have been going in for planning because of various benefits flowing from it. The activity has become an integral part of the firms' decision process. However, in the face of the rapidly changing market place and environment, companies can no longer rely on traditional planning systems and on simple growth projections in planning their production, sales and profits. The traditional planning systems are often being criticized for their lack of sensitivity and inability to deal with the discontinuities and crises that arise in a dynamic and turbulent environment. Moreover, it has the undesirable effect of reducing a company's flexibility, resulting in missed opportunities. Besides, the environment of the 1990s promises to be full of potential surprises posing significant challenges for strategic planners. Therefore, conventional long-range planning is needed to be converted into strategic planning.

Having survived its original design flaws, strategic planning has evolved into a viable system of strategic management. It deals effectively with all that affects the ability of a company to grow profitably and facilitates the optimal positioning of the firm in its competitive environment. Steiner et al (1989) defined strategic planning, "as a process that begins with the development of objectives, defines strategies and policies to achieve objectives, and develops detailed plans to make sure that the strategies are carried out to achieve the objectives". Strategic planning focusses on strategy as the central theme. Its aim is to shape and reshape the company's businesses and products so that they yield target profits and growth. To Steiner (1967) strategic planning is a tool to achieve strategic management objectives and is a useful instrument to ensure long-term success of firms. While the design of the strategic planning systems adopted by organizations vary there is a basic commonality of factors and a typical, stylized strategic planning system framework would consist of the following activities (Camillus and Datta, 1991):

* Environmental Analysis
* Defining Goals and Objectives
* Internal Analysis (Evaluating strengths and weaknesses)
* Formulation and Evaluation of Alternative Strategies
* Strategy Selection
* Operational Plans and Implementation
* Performance Evaluation and Feedback.

Quite a number of studies in the area of strategic planning and management report that strategic planning is associated with better performance and is highly useful to the companies. One of the first major studies was conducted by Ansoff et al in 1970. In a study of 93 US manufacturing firms, the authors found that formal planners who took a strategic management approach outperfomed non-planners in terms of financial criteria that measures sales assets, sales price, earnings per share, and earnings growth. Thune and House (1970) who studies 36 firms in six different industries found that formal planners in the petroleum, food, drug, steel, chemical and machinery industries significantly outperformed non-planners in the same fields. Fulmer and Rue (1974) made a survey of strategic management practices of 386 companies over a three-year period and concluded that durable goods manufacturing firms with strategic management were more successful than those without. Karger and Malik (1975) surveyed 90 US companies in five industries and concluded that strategic long-range planners significantly outperformed non-formal planners in terms of generally accepted financial measures. Armstrong (1991) a quantitative critique of 28 studies concludes that formal planning is valuable for firms. He reports that out of 28 studies 20 were found of high performance with formal planning, 5 were found with no difference and 3 were found with formal planning to be detrimental. Strategic planning has not only been considered important to large firms, but its usefulness to small firms has also been found. Gibb and Scott (1985) and De Kluyver and McNally (1992) have found it to be of considerable importance to small scale enterprises. Robinson (1982) conducted a survey of 101 small retail, service and manufacturing firms over a three-year period. He finds a significant improvement in sales, profitability and productivity among those businesses engaged in strategic planning when compared to firms without systematic planning activities.

When strategic planning arrived on the scene in the mid 1960s corporate leaders embraced it as "the one best way to devise and implement strategies that would enhance the competitiveness of each business unit" (Mintzberg: 1994). It enjoyed a heyday of almost unquestioning corporate popularity. Large number of organizations engaged in strategic planning exercises, because of its promised benefits. Huge amounts were expanded for training managers in the methods of strategic planning, for compiling and analyzing the mountains of information which lie below the business plans sitting on desk tops like the tips of ice bergs and for writing, reviewing and monitoring the business plans (Marx: 1991) Entirely new organizations (strategic business units) were created to develop the plans and entirely new staff (corporate strategic planning) were created to lead them through this process. However, by the early 1980s there was widespread disenchantment with the planning activities of the previous decade (Wilson: 1994). The reasons varied from company to company, but focused mainly on the failure to achieve results. Paul et al (1978) quoting some examples come to the conclusion that "as one examines the growing list of companies that have become entangled in financial misfortunes because of decisions apparently made in accordance with the principles of strategic planning, it seems that strategic planning may not always produce expected results".

Many American companies which were at the forefront of strategic business planning only a few years ago have now substantially reduced the scope of their planning activities or abandoned it altogether. Some management experts have been sounding the death-knell of planning since the early 1980s, especially after major corporations such as GE, BP and ICI drastically reduced and de-emphasized their formal planning activities (Lorenz: 1990). Keeping in view the failure of strategic planning in some companies, several studies attempted to explore the reasons for this failure. The results suggest that all the inter-related activities of strategic planning needs to be given due attention for making the planning more effective. Murphy (1989) argues that perhaps strategic planning has failed in some cases not because of inherent weaknesses but because of inadequate scanning of environmental changes. Environmental scanning is a major component of strategic planning. Thomas G. Marx (1991) observes that strategic planning has fallen victim to a number of formidable bureaucratic obstacles. He concludes that unless these obstacles are removed and the promised financial returns from strategic business planning realized the decline of strategic planning will continue.

Despite the fact that the importance and practice of strategic planning has declined across American Industry, where it was 'the hot thing' nearly two decades ago, it is interesting to note that in India, strategic planning has acquired new importance in the post liberalization era. Large number of Indian companies have been engaging in strategic planning exercises. Some companies seek help from outside by hiring the services of management consultants, others have set up their own think tanks or strategic business units for effective planning. The rapid spreading of strategic planning in Indian companies bears an eloquent testimony to its growing acceptance by their management as a new managerial approach to ensure future survival and growth of the organizations. It is being argued that the companies using strategic planning often tend to significantly out-perform their own past results and the results of those companies not using strategic planning. This needs to be studied in detail for ascertaining the association between the strategic planning and organizational performance. This study is an attempt in this direction with the following specific objectives:

- To examine the nature of strategic planning in Indian companies.
- To assess the need of strategic planning to Indian companies; and
- To ascertain the relationship between strategic planning and organizational performance.

Methodology

The data was collected with the help of structured questionnaire which was mailed to 95 companies selected purposively to cover a wide cross-section of organizations practising strategic planning. Questionnaire was enclosed to a covering letter requesting the companies that it may be completed by the executives/chief executives heading the strategic business unit/strategic planning cell in their companies. In some cases it was directly mailed to executives of strategic business units. However, only 57 executives returned the completed questionnaire.

The questionnaire comprised 24 Likert type statements pertaining to need and potential benefits of strategic planning. Respondents were asked to indicate their degree of agreement towards these statements on a five-point rating scale in which alternatives were 'strongly agree', 'agree', 'uncertain', 'disagree' and 'strongly disagree'. Means were computed by assigning the values of 1, 2, 3, 4 and 5 to the scale position of strongly agree, agree, uncertain, disagree and strongly disagree. Besides, the technique of choice scoring was also used to assess the degree of importance/popularity of a particular objective/benefit/planning characteristics in the companies. Ranks were assigned on the basis of the percentage of maximum possible score.

Results and Discussion

The results of the study are summarized in Tables 1 to 5. Table 1 presents the nature of strategic planning in Indian companies. Table 2 indicates the objectives pursued through strategic planning. Tables 3 and 4 present the reports of executives' responses to 24 Likert type statements pertaining to need and benefits of strategic planning and Table 5 shows the benefits derived from strategic planning.

Table 1
Nature of Strategic Planning (SP)

(N = 57)

Nature of SP	*Total score (No. of mentions)*	*Percentage of maximum possible score*
SP is our regular feature	47	82.46
SP is need based in our company	18	31.58
SP is based on rough estimates in our company	17	29.82
SP is based on planning techniques in our company	41	71.93
SP is responsibility of our planning Deptt./Cell/SBU	49	85.96
We consult consultants for SP	30	52.63
SP is exclusively carried out by consultants in our company	15	26.32
SP started in our company after liberalization of Indian economy in 1991	41	71.93
SP started in our company before 1991	16	28.07

Table 1 reveals that 85.96% of the companies are having their own planning departments/planning cells/strategic business units for strategic planning. This shows in-house strategic planning facilities which are developing in Indian companies. Eicher, Vam Organic, Ranbaxy, Escorts, Pepsi Foods and others have established their corporate planning cells for strategic planning. Some have set-up their strategic business units (SBUs). Godrej has SBUs in every business, consisting of a team of 10 people having a single day session once a quarter on strategy. 82.46% of the respondents report that strategic planning is a regular feature in their companies while in 31.58% companies it is need based. In some companies strategic planning is a regular feature as well as need based. In 71.93% of the sample companies strategic planning is based on planning techniques while a small number of companies (29.82%) use rough estimates for planning. 71.93% of the respondents reported that strategic planning started in their companies after the year 1991 when the liberalization process was initiated, whereas 28.07% of them mentioned that it had started in their companies before 1991. Before liberalization few managements bothered about

Table 2
Objectives Pursued Through Strategic Planning (SP)

Objectives	*Total score (No. of mentions)*	*Percentage of maximum possible score*	*Rank*
Profits	48	84.21	1
Stability	20	35.08	6
Growth	45	78.94	2
Gaining strategic advantages	31	54.38	4
Market leadership	39	68.42	3
Social responsibility	18	31.57	7
Diversification	21	36.84	5

strategic planning. Even Godrej admits that his group did little strategic planning before liberalization. 52.63% of the sample companies consult with their consultants for strategic planning and in 26.32% companies strategic planning is the exclusive responsibility of the consultants. The burst of corporate interest in strategic planning has fuelled a boom in the consultancy business in India.

Table 2 presents the objectives pursued through strategic planning shows that companies attach the primary importance to the profit objective followed by growth, market leadership and gaining strategic advantages. These objectives were ranked as 1st, 2nd, 3rd and 4th respectively on the basis of overall score. The results underscore the importance of profit objective. 84.21% of the sample companies are pursuing profit as their basic objectives. This is because profit is the only way by which an organization can protect its capital. In fact, to earn profit an enterprise has to set multiple objectives in key result areas. Growth objective has also been receiving high importance as 78.95% of the respondents mentioned it as their objective. It is interesting to observe that companies are showing keen interest in gaining market leadership and strategic advantages. They are attempting to improve product's quality, productivity and efficiency and want to be first to market with innovations. This is mainly because of emerging competition which Indian companies are facing today. Stability and diversification objectives have received low importance with only 35.08% to 36.84% of the respondents mentioning them as their objectives. They were ranked as 6th and 5th on the basis of overall score. This reveals that most of the companies are more interested to achieve growth by specializing in some selected fields of their interest. Social responsibility continues to receive considerably low importance as compared to other objectives. Only 31.58 % of the companies have been pursuing it as their objective and it has been ranked as 7th.

Executives responses to questions about need of strategic planning in Indian companies are summarized in Table 3. The results reflect that more than 80% of the respondents feel that strategic planning is needed for analyzing opportunities and threats in the external environment; for assessing business strengths and weaknesses; for formulating, evaluating and

Table 3
Need of Strategic Planning in Indian Companies

(N = 57)

Activity	*Percentage Response*			*Mean response*
	Agree	*Uncertain*	*Disagree*	
SP is needed for assessing and maintaining congruence among corporate and divisional objectives	80.70	5.26	14.04	2.04
SP is needed for analyzing opportunities and threats in the external environment	84.21	5.26	10.53	1.67
SP is needed for assessing business strengths and weaknesses	84.21	3.51	12.28	1.72
SP is needed for formulating, evaluating and selecting strategic alternatives	82.46	7.02	10.52	1.91
SP is needed for determining and modifying the organizational structure of business	78.95	8.77	12.28	2.23
SP is needed for ensuring the optimum availability and allocation of resources	73.68	12.28	14.04	2.00
SP is needed for developing and implementing contingency plans	80.70	3.51	15.79	1.96
SP is needed for managing human resources	71.93	8.77	19.30	2.21
SP is needed for tracking and regulating performance	70.18	10.52	19.30	2.25
SP is needed for market-orientation	61.40	14.04	24.56	2.44
SP is needed in response to competitive actions	63.16	15.79	21.05	2.28
SP is needed for managing strategic issues	68.42	17.54	14.04	2.09

Notes: 1. Agree represents the sum of percentage responses for the strongly agree and agree categories. 2. Disagree represent the sum of percentage responses for strongly disagree and disagree categories.

selecting strategic alternatives, for assessing and maintaining congruence among corporate and divisional objectives and for developing and implementing contingency plans. The resultant mean response in these activities was close to agree category.

Table 4

Potential Benefits of Strategic Planning (SP).

(N = 57)

Benefits	*Percentage Response*			*Mean response*
	Agree	*Uncertain*	*Disagree*	
SP improves long-term performance	80.70	8.77	10.53	1.81
SP improves the channelling of effort towards attainment of predetermined objectives	71.93	12.28	15.79	1.98
SP provides better balance between long-term and short-term goals	73.68	7.02	19.30	2.07
SP develops a closer linkage between strategy and operations	68.42	3.51	28.07	2.25
SP gives improved under-standing of changing environment and identifies greater opportunities	82.46	3.51	14.03	1.68
SP renders more effective the allocation of time and resources to identified opportunities	73.68	8.77	17.55	2.12
SP gives the firm an advantage over competitors	61.40	17.55	21.05	2.25
SP helps managers to become more genuinely interested in an organization	78.95	5.26	15.79	2.02
SP emphasize creativity among managers	70.18	10.53	19.29	1.91
SP helps marshal the behaviour of individual's in the organization into a total effort	63.16	14.04	22.80	2.21
SP reduces vulnerability to surprises	77.19	5.26	17.55	1.79
SP provides greater flexibility of response	64.91	10.53	24.56	2.16

Note : Same as in Table 3.

It ranged from 1.67 to 2.04. Over 70% of the executives agreed that the statements that strategic planning is needed, for determining and modifying the organizational structure of business; for ensuring the optimum availability and allocation of resources; for managing human resources and for tracking and regulating performance. The mean response which ranged from 2.00 to 2.25 in these statements was also closer to agree category. More than 60% of the respondents also agreed with the other statements. A small number of respondents ranging from 10.52% to 24.56% disagreed with the aforesaid statements. In all the statements the resultant mean was closer to agree category. Thus, strategic planning is needed by organizations for adaptation to environmental change and for facing external and internal challenges confronting organizations today.

In a similar way Table 4 reports the response of executives to 12 Likert type statements pertaining to the benefits of strategic planning. The results show that over 80% of the respondents feel that strategic planning improves long-term performance and gives improved understanding of changing business environment and identifies greater opportunities. Executives believed that this process allows more accurate anticipation of environmental changes and improved preparedness for reacting to unexpected internal or competitive demands. More than 70% respondents agreed that strategic planning improves the channeling of effort towards the attainment of predetermined objectives; provides better balance between long-term and short- term goals; renders more effective allocation of time and resources to identified opportunities; helps managers become more genuinely interested in an organization; emphasizes creativity among managers and reduces vulnerability to surprises. The resultant mean in all these benefits was between agree and strongly agree categories. It ranged from 1.68 to 2.12%. Majority of the respondents also agreed than disagreed with the other statements of benefits. Hence, in the collective view of the responding executives, strategic planning clearly is critical to their individual and organizational success, thus companies have high and diverse hopes from it. Therefore, it can be concluded that adopting strategic planning practices reduces the risk of catastrophic failures and increases the probability of an organization being able to face the changing environment successfully.

Table 5

Benefits Derived from Strategic Planning

(N = 57)

Benefits	*Total score (No. of mentions)*	*percent of maximum possible score*	*Rank*
Profitability	40	70.17	4
Growth	38	66.66	5
Improved decisions	48	84.21	1
Market leadership	33	57.89	8
Identification of greater opportunities	46	80.70	2.5
Clear objectives	36	63.15	6.5
Better coordination	46	80.70	2.5
Adaptability and flexibility	36	63.15	6.5
Cost control	26	45.61	11
Better employee motivation	28	49.12	10
Improved productivity	30	52.63	9

Table 5 summarizes the response to the benefits derived from strategic planning. The results reveal that improved decisions, better coordination and identification of greater opportunities are the major benefits that have accrued to the companies through strategic planning. These benefits have resulted into the achievement of two basic objectives—Profitability and growth. 66.66% to 84.21% of the companies surveyed have derived the abovementioned benefits from strategic planning while 63.15% of the respondents mentioned that their companies have also realized the benefits of clear objectives and general direction and adaptability and flexibility. A further examination of the Table 5 depicts that majority of the companies have realized the benefits of market leadership and improved productivity also. The percentage of respondents reporting realization of these benefits ranged from 52.63% to 57.89% whereas 45.61% to 49.12% of the executives revealed that their companies achieved the benefits of cost control and better employee motivation through strategic planning. This leads us to conclude that strategic planning provides various benefits to organizations and helps them to achieve desired objectives.

Conclusion

Today organizations need a planning system which is sensitive in detecting and responding to critical issues that surface sporadically and can cope with the increasingly volatile environment facing the companies currently. The research results of this study paint a striking picture of the importance of the strategic planning system for organizational performance. The process is generally seen as instrumental to high performance, evolutionary and perhaps revolutionary in its ever-increasing sophistication, increasingly pervasive throughout the organizations and action-oriented.

Strategic planning has been enjoying a high degree of corporate popularity in Indian companies, especially after the liberalization of the Indian economy. Companies pursue more ambitious objectives through strategic planning. They appear to seek profit with growth and market leadership. They expect a variety of benefits to flow by adopting strategic planning systems. Improved decision-making, better coordination, and identification of greater opportunities which result in growth and profitability appears to be the major benefits realized by organizations through strategic planning. Besides this, strategic planning changes management's thinking from short-term reactive stance to a long-term proactive stance. Managements' decision- making becomes offensive rather than defensive. Furthermore, the strategic planning gives the organizations an opportunity of taking a greater degree of control over the ever-changing environment. It gives a better understanding of the dynamics of change in the business environment and hopefully reduces vulnerability of being blindsided by surprise. The system develops a better balance between long-term and short-term goals, a closer linkage between strategy and operations and creates a willingness to change and greater flexibility among the staff.

The overall results of this study clearly reflects the value of strategic planning as gauged by a variety of benefits. The great majority of respondents indicated that strategic planning is highly useful to Indian companies. Despite some risks, the numerous benefits flowing from it justify the approach. However, it may be mentioned that strategic planning might not always produce the expected results. The reasons for this may be legion which may vary from company to company. But, research exposes at least one common denominator namely the rate and nature of environmental change as directly influencing results (Murphy: 1989). The environmental change has a direct linkage to the strategic planning process has been established (Hofer and Schendell: 1974). Perhaps strategic planning has failed in some cases not because of inherent weaknesses but because of inadequate scanning of environmental change (Murphy: 1989). Therefore, Indian organizations should develop their internal scanning and early warning groups so that the Board-rooms are provided with several scenarios and detailed information. Moreover the planning systems should not be allowed to fall victim to bureaucratic obstacles. Marx (1991) has identified numerous bureaucratic obstacles to effective planning, and suggested how these obstacles can most effectively be eliminated by attacking their root cause. Indian companies needs to be aware about all such obstacles and should not allow them to emerge in their companies, otherwise the strategic planning will fall from its pedestal and would be an exercise in futility.

References

1. Ansof, H.I., Avner, J., Brandenburg, R.B., Portner, F.E. and Radosevich, R. (1970), 'Does Planning Pay? The Effect of Planning on Success of Acquisitions in American Firms', *Long-Range Planning 3(2)*, pp. 2-7.
2. Armstrong, J.S. (1991), Strategic Planning Improves Manufacturing Performance, *Long-Range Planning* 24(5), pp. 127-29.
3. Camillus, J.C. and Dalta, D.K. (1991), 'Managing Strategic Issues in a Turbulent Environment', *Long-Range Planning* 24(2), pp. 67-74.

4. De Khuyver, C.A. and McNally, G.M. (1982), 'Developing a Corporate Planning Model for a Small Company,' *Long-Range Planning,* 15(1), pp. 97-106.

5. Fulmer, R.M. and Rue L.W. (1974) 'The Practice and Profitability of Long-Range Planning', *Managerial Planning, 22,* pp. 1-7.

6. Gibb, A. and Scot, M. (1985), 'Strategic Awareness, Personal Commitment and the Process of Planning in the Small Business', *Journal of Management Studies,* 22(6), pp. 597-627.

7. Hofer, C.W. and Schendell, D. (1974), *Strategy Formulation: Analytical Concepts*", West Publishing Company, St. Paul NM.

8. Kargar, D.W. and Malik, Z.A. (1975), Long-Range Planning and Organizational Performance, *Long-Range Planning,* December, pp. 60-64.

9. Lorenz, C., (1990), Too Much Informality can be Dangerous", *The Financial Times,* London, 14 May.

10. Marx, T.G. (1991), Removing the Obstacles to Effective Strategic Planning, Long-Range Planning 24(4), pp. 21-28.

11. Mintzberg, H. (1994), The Fall and Rise of Strategic Planning, *Harvard Business Review,* January-February, pp. 107-14.

12. Murphy, J.J. (1989), Identifying Strategic Issues, *Long-Range Planning* 22(2), pp. 101-105.

13. Paul, R.N., Donovan, N.B. and Taylor, J.W. (1978), *Harvard Business Review,* May-June.

14. Robinson, R.B. Jr. (1982), The importance of Outsiders in Small Firms Strategic Planning', *Academy of Management Journal,* March, pp. 80-93.

15. Steiner, G.A. (1967), Approaches to Long-Range Planning for Smaller Business, *California Management Review,* 10(1), pp. 3-16.

16. Steiner, G.A., Miner, J.R. and Gray, E.R. (1989), *Management Policy and Strategy,* McMillan Publishing Company, New York, p. 81.

17. Thune, S.S. and House, R.J. (1970), Where Long-Range Planning Pays Off, *Business Horizons,* August, pp. 81-87.

18. Wilson Ian, (1994), Strategic Planning Isn't Dead—It Changed, *Long-Range Planning,* 27(4), pp. 12-24.

3. [illegible] (1988). [illegible]

4. [illegible] (1977). [illegible]

5. [illegible] (1988). [illegible]

6. [illegible] (1979). [illegible]

7. [illegible] (1974). [illegible]

8. [illegible] (1978). [illegible]

9. [illegible] (1961). [illegible]

10. [illegible]

11. [illegible]

12. [illegible]

13. [illegible]

14. [illegible] (1982). [illegible]

15. [illegible]

16. [illegible]

17. [illegible]

15

Performance Differences among Various Industries in India

G.S. Shergill
and
Maninder S. Sarkaria

Following the pioneering work of Chandler (1962) in the field of strategic management, Rumelt (1974, 1977) examined the relationship among diversification strategy, organizational structure and economic performance. He developed nine categories of diversification and found that related diversification strategy outperformed the other strategies. But he could not show the causes of dispersion in performance among various diversification strategies. However, he asserted that related diversified firms enjoyed superior returns because of their common skills or resources into related areas. He commented that:

> Each of these industries is characterized by an extensible core skill and many opportunities for product differentiation and segmentation. They are excellent fields for using a difficult-to-replicate competence to create unique and defensible product—market position (1977, p. 16).

Thus, Rumelt indicated that each industry has different structural characteristics which have an impact on all firms in that industry.

Rumelt's (1974, 1977) works have been criticized because it did not control industry effects. Rumelt (1982) extended the analysis by controlling the industry effects on performance. Here again he obtained the similar results and identified that industry effect was primarily responsible for the high performance of related constrained firms.

Apart from Rumelt, many other researchers have also indicated that industry characteristics play an important role in the analysis of company performance. Firms operating in new and expanding industries are likely to perform better than those operating in traditional and declining industries (Kumar, 1985). Firms in some industries may earn comparatively higher profits on account of certain favourable structural characteristics. The structural variables such as industry's concentration ratio, growth rate, research and development expenditure, etc., have been persistently shown to have an impact on the performance of firms.

Pant (1991) indicated that some structural variables might allow firms to be in a better position to implement their strategies successfully and profitably. Besides this, certain other factors are also considered to affect firms in a particular industry. To quote, Jones and Cockrill (1985):

> Governments can influence industrial structure and market performance by implementing policies designed to affect the economic environment in which the enterprises operate (e.g. by encouraging consumer expenditure or by reducing interest rates to stimulate investment) and by the use of instruments that directly affect firm's costs, prices and organisation. (p. 59)

This phenomenon is omnipresent and India is no exception. The perusal of industrial policies, annual and five-year plans, fiscal policies, export-import policies, etc., reveals that the government does not give impartial treatment to all the industries. In other words different industries are subjected to varied policies. There is no denying the fact that inter-industry differences exist in respect of nature and rates of taxation, Exim policies etc. (see various issues of Reserve Bank of India Bulletin, Economic Survey, Report on Currency and Finance). The government sometimes favours an industry by providing incentives in terms of reduced tax rates, financial support, subsidies, and other such facilities. The development of industries is also influenced by government regulations. The sale of particular class of goods may be limited (e.g. alcoholic drink, petrol), similarly prices may be controlled, thus influencing profitability and growth of companies (Jones and Cockrill, 1985, p. 60). Sometimes the government intervene in the free operation of market forces to maintain the composition of industrial activities that is best suited to the needs of the country, for example, the erstwhile Monopolies and Restrictive Trade Practices Act, 1969 was a piece of economic legislation which sought to assure that the operation of economic system did not result in the concentration of economic power to the common detriment. Similarly, the benefits of industrial licensing procedure may go to few industries resulting in their disproportionate growth (Kapoor, 1989). Such things may contribute to varied performance of companies operating in different industries.

Many researchers have provided empirical support to the phenomenon of inter-industry performance differences. Porter (1985) reported that all industries did not offer equal opportunities for sustained profitability. Porter (1980) asserted that the overall firm performance was influenced by the characteristics of the industry to which a firm belonged. Carleton and Lakonishok (1986) and Hamilton and Shergill (1993) showed that industry effects explained a significant portion of the variation in profitability. Similarly, both Schmalensee (1985) and Kessides (1990) supported the industrial economists' focus on industry level analysis by finding the industry effects to be important. Kumar (1985) revealed that average growth rates were significantly different among various industries in India. The industrywise analysis of performance of companies, as is conducted by Reserve Bank of India, revealed the existence of varied growth rates in different industries (RBI Bulletin, Nov., 1991 March, 1992, and other issues). Hence, inter-industry research can help a great deal in formulating sound theory and policies for specific industries (Schmalensee, 1989).

The Objectives

In the light of the facts discussed above in section I, the objectives of this study are:

(i) To investigate inter-industry performance differentials among input based industry categories.

(ii) To carry out pairwise comparison of performance to explore the extent of dispersion among Agro, Metal and Chemical-based industry groups.

(iii) To relate performance differences to certain attributes of Indian economy.

Besides, this study also compares the findings with that of Ahluwalia (1985) who studied growth rates for a period of 20 years immediately preceeding this study. The objective of this study is also, from the strategic management point of view, in terms of its implications, to suggest firms that whenever they elect to diversify they should very carefully make the choice of the industry in which they want to enter as some such industries have the advantage of better performance due to inherent industry characteristics.

The Sample and Data

This study is based on the data of 115 largest manufacturing companies in India operating in the private corporate sector over a period of 11 years. The data were collected mainly from the various issues of Stock Exchange Official Directory (SEOD). The SEOD is primarily based on annual reports which include Balance Sheets and Profit and Loss Statements published by its member companies every year.

Industry-wise Classification of Companies

There exists a number of different classification systems of industries and there is as yet no one unanimously accepted industry classification suitable for all purposes. In this study companies have been grouped into three categories in accordance with Input-based industry classification. This classification system is basically extracted from the National Industrial Classification (NIC) and is widely used by policymakers and researchers (e.g. Ahluwalia 1985, Kahlon 1992).

The Scope of Study

The sample is extracted from amongst the largest manufacturing companies which were in operation over the period 1980-81 to 1990-91. The Stock Exchange Official Directory (SEOD) and Centre for Monitoring Indian Economy (CMIE)'s publications proved to be complementary to finalise the sample for this study. Unlike SEOD, CMIE provides information on ownership of every company. Moreover, CMIE's industry classification system is more specific. We assigned a company to a particular industry if it derived more than half of its sales from that company. We could get an exhaustive list of companies pertaining to different industries from SEOD and cross-checked every company with CMIE to sort out companies operating in the private sector in different industries. Eleven years sales data were compiled for each company and then companies were ranked in descending order in each industry according to the magnitude of 11 years total sales. The largest companies were picked up from each industry to form our sample. The final list of companies consisted of 115 spread over the three categories of Input-based classification. The make-up of sample is shown in Table 1.

Table 1

Input-based Classification of Industries: Make up of Sample

Industry Group	*No. of Companies*	*Sample Percentage*
Agro-based	56	49
Metal-based	23	20
Chemical-based	36	31
Total	115	100

This study has been confined to private sector only. The public sector enterprises are different from those operating in the private sector and it is very difficult and unfair to compare their performances (Millward, 1982; Lord Roll of Ipsat, 1982;

Bhatt, 1990; Khandwalla, 1990). The private sector has been playing an important and dominant role in Indian economy since independence. Table 2 shows that the share of the public sector has increased significantly in NDP. Nevertheless, the private sector occupies a dominant position in the economy.

Table 2

Percentage Share of Public and Private Sector in NDP (at current prices)

	1950-51	*1960-61*	*1970-71*	*1990-91*
Public Sector	7.5	10.6	14.5	23.8
Private Sector	92.5	89.4	85.5	76.2

Source: *Central Statistical Organisation, National Accounts Statistics, 1970-71, 1984-85 January, 1987, 1993*

Performance

Performance is a generic term and it can be interpreted and measured in a variety of different ways (Goodman and Penning, 1977; Devine et al, 1979; Millward, 1982). Performance simply reflects the degree of success achieved in terms of stated objectives and as the objectives differ widely, so does the concept of performance. This is why it cannot be put into the tight framework of definition.

Berle and Means (1932) observed that there is a separation between ownership and management in large companies and in such companies, different interested parties view company performance from different viewpoints. Penrose (1959) has rightly remarked that owners are interested in profitability, while managers are interested in growth of the firm. This study measures company performance by incorporating profitability and growth dimensions. Return on Assets (ROA) has been employed as profitability indicator while Growth in Sales (GSALES) represents growth performance of the company. ROA is the most widely used return measure and it serves as the measure of management's efficiency and effectiveness in utilising all the assets under its control. GSALES represents the firm's success in its markets.

Methodology

Analysis has been carried out for ROA and GSALES separately. The ROA has been computed by employing the following formula:

$$ROA = \frac{EBIT}{Total\ Assets} \times 100$$

The compound growth rate of sales over the period 1980-81 to 1990-91 have been computed with the help of following model:

$$Y = a + bt + e$$

where Y=Value of variable

a=Intercept

b=Slope

t=Time variable

e=Error term

The formula to compute the compound growth rate 'r' is:

$$r = (\text{antilog } b\hat{} - 1) \times 100$$

where b^ is the Ordinary Least Square estimator of b in the regression model given above.

This is a commonly used formula of computing growth rate (Ahluwalia, 1985, Kumar, 1985).

ANOVA has been employed to study the performance dispersions among the three categories of Input-based industry classification and their significance level. Pairwise comparison has been done by using Tukey's test of multiple comparisons.

Results and Discussion

Empirical Result

Table 3 shows the results of analysis of industry category and performance. Estimation is based on 11 years data on ROA and GSALES for 115 companies over the period 1980-81 to 1990-91. The F-ratios depicted in the Table provide a test of the level of significance of inter-industry differentials within input-based industry classification.

Table 3

One Way Analysis of Variance at Industry and Performance

Performance		*Industry*				
		Agro-based	*Metal-based*	*Chemical-based*	*Overall*	*F-Ratio*
ROA	MEAN	11.20	12.06	11.23	11.38	
	SD	7.65	5.14	3.59	6.11	0.18
	NO.	56	23	36	115	
GSALES	MEAN	11.52	19.89	14.31	14.07	
	SD	6.15	24.68	6.54	12.61	3.78*
	NO.	56	23	36	115	

Note: * Significant at 5% level.

Of the three categories, the Metal-based industry scores the highest while the Chemical-based group ranks second on both the indicators of performance. The Agro-based group is the poorest on both the measures and its mean values are consistently below the corresponding overall mean values. The F-ratios indicate that the null hypothesis of inter-industry performance differences is rejected on only GSALES at 5% level of significance. Figures 1 and 2 depict the comparative performance of different segments of Input-based industry classification for ROA and GSALES respectively.

The finding of lowest growth performance of Agro-based group is exactly similar to that of Ahluwalia, (1985) who conducted a study on growth rates for the period immediately preceeding this study. Table 4 shows her results.

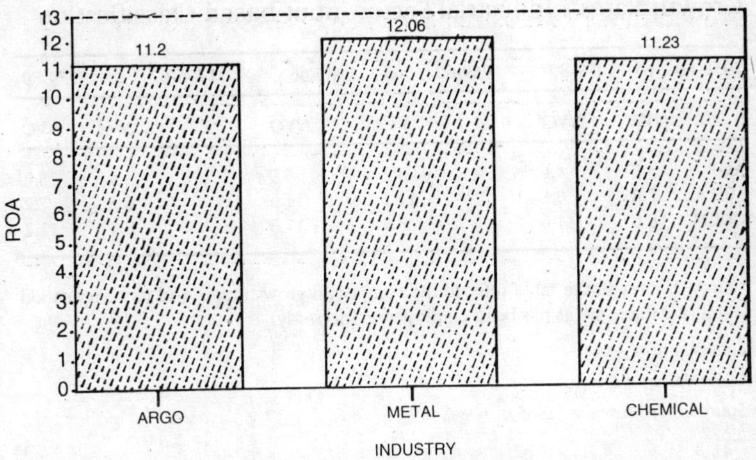

COMPARATIVE PERFORMANCE OF INDUSTRIES : ROA

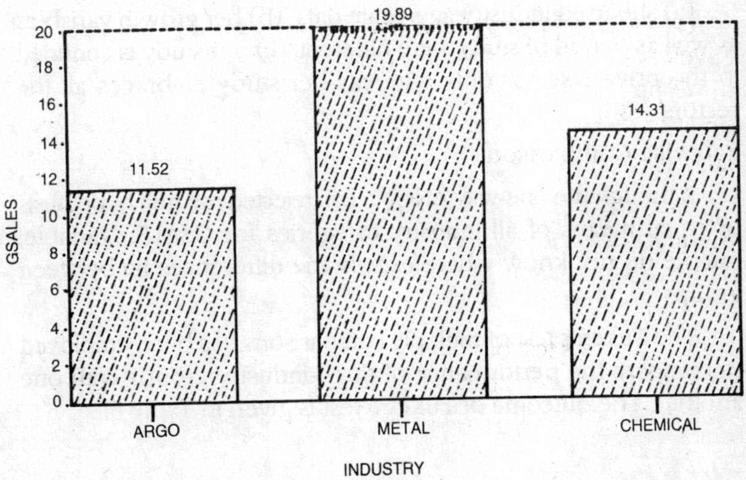

COMPARATIVE PERFORMANCE OF INDUSTRIES : GSALES

Table 4

Growth Rates*: Industrial Sector Input-based Classification

	1959-60 to 1979-80		1959-60 to 1965-66		1966-67 to 1979-80	
	NVA#	NVO$	NVA	NVO	NVA	NVO
AGRO	3.2	4.6	3.7	5.9	4.4	5.0
METAL	7.8	8.8	14.1	14.6	6.5	7.2
CHEM.	8.6	11.6	8.2	11.3	8.1	11.2

* Growth rates in the table refer to the compound growth rates and its computation formula is the same as has been employed in this study.

Net Value Added

$ Net Value of Output

Source: Ahluwalia (1985).

However, her findings for other two groups are not congruous with ours for all the periods. The differences in findings may be attributed to the following reasons:

(a) she used industry aggregate data, (b) her growth variables as well as period of study were different, (c) our study is confined to the private sector only whereas her study embraces all the sectors.

Pairwise Comparison

Although the one-way ANOVA has rejected the null hypothesis of equal means of all industry categories for GSALES variable, but we do not know where exactly the differences lie between groups.

The Tukey's test of multiple comparisons has been employed to compare the performance of three-industry groups with one another. The outcome of Tukey's test is given in Table 5.

Table 5

Tukey's Test of Multiple Comparison on Industry and Performance (elements are different between means)

Performance	*Pairs of Industry Groups* Being Compared*			*HSD*
	A-M	*A-C*	*M-C*	
ROA	–0.86	–0.03	0.84	3.37
GSALES	–8.37$	–2.79	5.58	7.59

*A, M and C stand for respectively Agro-based, Metal-based and Chemical-based industry groups.

$ Significant at 5% level.

Evidently there is significant difference between groups A and M in respect of GSALES. In other words, significant difference exists between the growth performance of Agro-based group and Metal-based group. To be more specific, the growth rate of Agro-based group is significantly less than that of Metal-based group of companies. No other pair shows statistically significant differences.

Discussion of Results

The causes of poor performance of Agro-based segment can be attributed to various factors. Many researchers have examined the link between agriculture and industry in India (Ahluwalia, 1985 has provided a long list of references). Our sample of Agro-based group includes companies from Tea (10), Tobacco (4), Cotton (10), Jute (8), Vanaspati (4), Sugar (10), and Tyre and Tube (10) industries. (Figures in brackets show the number of companies in each industry). The availability of agriculture raw materials significantly affects the performance of Agro-based industries. Sastry (1984) provided empirical evidences in his study on cotton mills in India for 1950-73. Cotton textile and jute industries are dependent on raw cotton and raw Jute respectively. During the Sixth Plan (1980-85) textile industry suffered from prolonged labour unrest, and insufficient demand and later suffered due to capture of its big market share by man-made fibre industry. The share of man-made fibre has been consistently increasing in the consumption pattern of textiles. It is the distinctive qualities of this fibre by virtue of which its consumption increased tremendously over the years. The cotton textile mills have also been facing the problems of replacement of old and obsolete machinery.

The condition of sugar industry has been rather comfortable mainly because of the measures initiated by the government. The ratio of free sale quota has been reduced continuously over the period under our study for the betterment of the industry. The prices of Molasses have been on the rise during the Sixth and Seventh Five-Year Plans. Tea industry is a foreign exchange earning industry and the government has made efforts to boost the production of this industry consistently (*Economic Survey*—various issues).

The Metal-based group is ranking top on both the indicators of performance. This group is fluctuating between first and second place for growth performance in the study of Ahluwalia (1985). The constituents of this industry rather did well during the Sixth Plan. The production of machinetools, passenger cars, and motorcycles exceeded targets during the Sixth Plan. The government has helped this industry group from time to time by solving its problems, strengthening its competitive position and reducing its cost disadvantages. For example, the budget for 1987-88 revised the tariff rates upward on selected imports from 55% to 85% in order to provide protection to indigenous manufacturers (*Economic Survey*, 1987-88, p. 36.) The Chemical-based group stands second on both the performance dimensions. Ahluwalia (1985) found it fluctuating between first and second position on growth performance. The contents of this group in our study are fertilizer (6), man-made fibre (14), paint (6) and pharmaceutical (10) industries. The fertilizer and pharmaceutical industries have been subjected to price controls by the government which is supposed to affect the growth of industries adversely (for details see Ahluwalia, 1985, pp. 153-54). Fertilizer industry has suffered from time to time because of power cuts, water shortages, equipment breakdown and non-availability of input materials (*Economic Survey*, 1987-88, 1988-89, and other relevant issues). Pharmaceutical industry has achieved a good performance due to certain government favours, e.g., government has extended the system of delicensing many a times for this industry (*Economic Survey*—various issues). The man-made fibre industry has had a high time and would continue to retain exceeding position. It has captured a big market share from the cotton textile by virtue of its distinctive qualities (discussed above). Paint industry is an intermediate industry and has been performing well because the industries on which its demand is dependent (e.g. automobile) have been doing well in production.

Summary and Implications

This study considers the performance differences across industries in India. The results are based on the analysis of 115 large (in terms of sales) Indian companies operating in the private sector. Companies have been grouped into three categories in accordance with Input-based industry classification. The three categories of this classification are: Agro-based, Metal-based and Chemical-based. The data pertains to a period of 11 years from 1980-81 to 1990-91. The performance has been operationalized in terms of profitability and growth. ROA represents profitability while GSALES has been employed as an indicator of growth. ANOVA has been used to study the performance dispersions among different categories and their significance level. The industry-wise analysis points to the existence of performance differences among the three categories although the statistical significance is only for the growth measure. The Metal-based group performs the best while the Agro-based group ranks the lowest on profitability as well as growth dimensions. The findings have also been compared with that of Ahluwalia (1985) who studied growth rates for a period immediately preceding this study. Pairwise comparison has also been made by using Tukey's test of multiple comparisons. This test reveals that only the growth performance of Agro-based group is significantly lower than that of Metal-based group. This study concludes by relating the inter-industry differences to certain attributes of Indian economy.

Studies such as this could help us find the factors responsible for poor performance of certain industries and guide the formulation of strategies to remove the disparities among industries. The government should not make uniform policies for all the industries. The Agro-based industries are the most vulnerable to monsoons (excess or dearth), droughts, etc. The policies should contain special provisions to provide such industries protection and incentives in the form of tax holidays, subsidies and/or the like.

From the investors' and entrepreneurs' viewpoints, the investment in the Metal-based industry and also the Chemical-based may be stated to be the most profitable. The existing companies may reduce their risk by expanding or diversifying their operations in the industries which are Metal-based or Chemical-based (the second best in our analysis). Creditors and lenders can also visualize this industry group as the most potential area to invest in as they always want to get the interest regularly and return of their principal at maturity. Also, the higher profitability and growth can certainly contribute to make the solvency position of the firm stronger. Finally, the managements of the firms functioning in these industry groups may feel at ease as they have to protect the interests of shareholders (who concentrate on profitability), and at the same time see that the companies grow profitably.

References

1. Ahluwalia, I.J. (1985), Industrial Growth in India, Oxford University Press, Delhi.
2. Berle, A.A. and Means, G.C. (1932), *The Modern Corporation and Private Property*, New York, Macmillan.
3. Bhatt, V.V. (1990), Foreword in P.N. Khandwalla's book (1992)', *Excellent Management in the Public Sector*, Vision Books, New Delhi.
4. Carleton, W.T. and Lakonishok, J. (1986), The Size Anomaly: Does Industry Group Matter? *The Journal of Portfolio Management*, (spring), pp. 36-40.
5. The Centre for *Monitoring Indian Economy*, (Jan. 1993 and earlier issues), Bombay, Key Financial Data on Larger Business Units.
6. Chandler, A.D. (1962), Strategy and Structure—Chapters in the History of American Industrial Enterprise, Cambridge, Mars, the MIT Press.
7. Devine, P.J., Lee, N., Jones, R.M., and Tyson, W.T. (1979), An Introduction to Industrial Economics, Third edition, George Allen & Unwin Ltd. London.
8. *Economic Survey*, (Issues of the relevant years), Ministry of Finance, Government of India.

9. Goodman, P.S. and Pennings, J.M. (eds.) (1977), *New Perspectives on Organisational Effectiveness* San Francisco, Jossy Bass.

10. Hamilton, R.T. and Shergill, G.S., (1993), The Logic of New Zealand Business, Oxford University Press, Auckland.

11. Jones, T.T. and Cockrill, T.A.J. (1985), *Structure and Performance of Industries*, Heritage Publishers, New Delhi-6.

12. Kahlon, P.K. (1992), *Capacity Utilisation in Indian Industry: An Empirical Analysis*, unpublished Ph.D. thesis submitted to Guru Nanak Dev University, Amritsar.

13. Kapoor, N.D. (1989), *The Monopolies and Restrictive Trade Practices Act, 1969—A Compendium*, Sultan Chand & Sons, New Delhi.

14. Kessides, I.N. (1990), Internal versus External Market—Conditions and Firm Profitability: An Exploratory Model, *The Economic Journal*, Vol. 100, pp. 773-92.

15. Khandwalla, P.N. (1990), *Excellent Management in the Public Sector*, Vision Books, New Delhi.

16. Kumar, P. (1985), Growth of Industrial Corporations in India, Deep and Deep Publications, New Delhi.

17. Lord Roll of Ispat (1982), *The Mixed Economy*, Macmillan Press.

18. Millward, R. (1982), The Comparative Performance of Public and Private Ownership, in the book *The Mixed Economy*, edited by Lord Roll of Ispat (1982), Macmillan Press, pp. 58-93.

19. Pant, L.W. (1991), An Investigation of Industry and Firm Structural Characteristics in Corporate Turnarounds, *Journal of Management Studies*, Vol. 28, No. 6, Nov., pp. 623-43.

20. Penrose, E.T. (1959), *The Theory of Growth of Firm*, London Basil Black.

21. Porter, M.E. (1980), *Competitive Strategy*, The Free Press, New York.

22. Porter, M.E. (1985), Competitive Advantage, The Free Press, New York.

23. Report on Currency and Finance, (relevant issues), Issued by the Department of Economic Analysis and Policy, Reserve Bank of India, Bombay.

24. *Reserve Bank of India Bulletin*, (March 1992, Nov. 1991 and other relevant issues), Issued by the Department of Economic Analysis and Policy, Reserve Bank of India, Bombay.

25. Rumelt, R.P. (1974), *Strategy, Structure and Economic Performance*. Cambridge Mass, Harvard University Press.

26. Rumelt, R.P. (1977), *Diversity and Profitability*, Working Paper MGL-51, Managerial Study Center, Graduate School of Management, University of California, Los Angeles.

27. Rumelt, R.P. (1982), How Important is Industry in Explaining Firm Profitability? Unpublished Working Paper, UCLA.

28. Sastry, D.U. (1984), *The Cotton Mill Industry in India*, Institute of Economic Growth Studies, Oxford University Press.

29. Schmalensee, R. (1989), Inter-Industry Studies of Structure and Performance, in

Handbook of Industrial Organisation (ed. R. Schmalensee and R. Willig), Amsterdam: North Holland.

30. Schmalensee, R. (1985), Do Markets Differ Much?, *The American Economic Review*, Vol. 75, No. 1, March, pp. 341-51.

31. *The Stock Exchange Official Directory*, Bombay, (Relevant issues), Bombay.

16

Strategic Management of Small Scale Industries in India (Impact of Policy Changes)

G.S. Batra

In the developing countries, Small Scale Enterprises (SSE) play a significant role in the overall economic development of the country. These industries, by and large represent a stage in economic transition from traditional to modern technology. The variation in transitional nature of this process is reflected in the diversity of these industries. Most of these enterprises use simple skills and machinery. Besides playing economic role for the country, small enterprises because of its unique economic and organizational characteristics also play social and political role in creating local employment, balanced resource utilization, income generation and in helping to promote change in a gradual and peaceful manner. Socio-economic factors effecting SSE came to being during industrial revolution with nations of entrepreneurial importance gaining favour by the mid-twentieth century. During the 1960s, the behaviour of the individual came to be highlighted as a major factor contributing to SSE development as entrepreneurship and therefore supply of entrepreneurs came to be recognised as critical to development.

The Role of Small Industries

The Industrial Policy Statement of 1980 emphasized the balanced and harmonious development of all sectors of industries. It stated that while making all efforts towards integrated industrial development, it is proposed to promote the concept of economic federalism with the setting up of a few nucleus plants in each district, identified as industrially backward, to generate as many ancillaries and small and cottage units as possible. Small industries have now been redefined to include those manufacturing and repairing units having investment in plant and machinery upto Rs. 35 lakhs (in the case of ancillary units upto Rs. 45 lakhs). To facilitate modernization and achieve rapid growth, the upper limit on investment (Plant and Machinery) has been raised in respect of small scale units from Rs. 20 lakhs to Rs. 35 lakhs and in the case of ancillary units from Rs. 25 lakhs to Rs. 45 lakhs. With this as the upper limit, the village and small industries sector consists of (i) traditional industries, namely, handlooms, cottage and village industries, handicrafts, etc.; and (ii) modern small scale industries including tiny units and powerlooms. The traditional industries are generally artisan-based, located mostly in rural and semi-urban areas, involving lower levels of investment in machinery and provide largely part-time employment. Modern small scale industries use mostly power-operated appliances and machinery, having some technological sophistication and are generally located close to or in the urban areas, including the large industrial sectors.

Along with the growth in the volume of production, employment and exports, there has been progressive diversification in this sector. Beginning with simple consumer goods like soap, detergents, leather goods, this sector has now entered into many sophisticated fields like micro-processors, minicomputers, electronic appliances and watches, colour TV and electronic devices. In recent years, significant efforts have been made towards a progressive diversification and updating of technology. This has been possible because of the continuing incentives combined with positive response from small entrepreneurs. The incentives include reservation of items for exclusive development in the small scale sector, marketing assistance, preferential prices and purchase from DGS & D, provision of credit facilities on soft terms, supply of critical raw materials on priority basis, etc.

Government, for the first time, announced a separate policy for small and tiny industry sector (NSIP) on August 6, 1991. Debate on the impact of New Economic Policy on large-scale sector has generated lot of interest among academicians, entrepreneurs, planners, and policymakers. However, the implications of this policy thrust for small scale sector have not been adequately debated despite its vital role in the economic development of the country.

Policy reforms across the world economies have succeeded only when the directly affected agents have perceived them as contributory to development.

Objectives and Methodology

The present study is an attempt to understand the perceptions of the entrepreneurs on various policy measures launched since 1991. The main object of this study is to highlight the role of small scale sector in the changing global business scenario. Within the small scale sector, all the product groups will not be affected in a uniform pattern by a given policy measure.

Through simple random techniques 100 entrepreneurs were selected for study. Besides entrepreneurs, staff of industry associations, officials from Industries Departments, State Financial Corporations and Commercial Banks were also interviewed to understand their viewpoint.

Performance of Small Business Enterprises

A number of small scale units are provisionally estimated to have gone up from 19.48 lakhs in 1990-91 to 20.80 lakhs in 1991-92—14.96 lakhs registered units on the rolls of the State Industries Departments and 5.84 lakhs unregistered units—registering an increase of about 6.8%. However, if the results of the census of SSI units 1987-88 are any guide, about 30 to 40% of these registered units might be non-functional. The value of output of the SSI sector in 1991-92 at current prices, is estimated at Rs. 178700 crores, about 15% higher than the output of Rs.

155340 crores in 1990-91. Adjusted for inflation, the real growth of output of the sector in 1991-92 might be less than 2%. Estimated employment in the sector has also increased from 125.3 lakhs in 1990-91 to 128.8 lakhs in 1991-92, an increase of about 3%. The growth of this sector in 1991-92 was in spite of a number of constraints like import restrictions affecting the availability of requisite raw materials and credit squeeze and a rise in the interest rates leading to severe erosion of the liquidity position of the SSI units.

Table I

Indicators of Performance of Small Scale Industries

S. No.	*Ratio/Co-efficient*	*SSI Census* 1972	1990-91
1.	Fixed Investment per unit (Rs. lakh)	0.76	1.60
2.	Investment in Plant and Machinery per unit (Original value) (Rs. lakh)	0.38	0.95
3.	Employment per unit (Number)	12.00	6.29
4.	Value of output per unit (Rs. lakh)	1.86	7.38
5.	Fixed investment per employee Rs. 8,000	6.38	25.36
6.	Value of output per employee Rs. 8,000	15.74	117.22
7.	Net value added per employee Rs. 8,000	5.10	27.99
8.	Wages and employee Rs. 8,000	1.56	6.27
9.	Value of output/investment in fixed assets	2.47	4.62
10.	Net value added/investment in fixed assets	0.32	1.10

Source : *Economic Survey*, Government of India, 1992-93.

The second all-India census of registered small scale industrial units, was conducted by the Small Industries Development Organisation (SIDO) in 1987-88, and its published results show that out of 9.87 lakh registered SSI units as on 31.3.1988 included in the frame, 3.05 lakh units, which constituted about 31% of total registered units, were closed and another 57,000 units were not traceable. Out of 5.82 lakh working units for which data were tabulated, 96.2% were SSI units, 3.2% small service establishments and 0.5% ancillary units. Some of the important structural ratios and coefficients derived from the results of the two SSI censuses of 1972 and 1987-88 are contrasted with the corresponding ratios and coefficients derived from the summary results of the Annual Survey of Industries (ASI) 1987-88, in Table 1. The ASI covers factory sector SSI units also and is therefore not strictly comparable.

The census results provide the much-needed data base for the SSI sector. Findings of the census also give added empirical support to the generally accepted hypotheses about the distinct characteristics of the SSI sector compared with those of the large and medium sector, namely lower capital base, lower capital/ labour ratio, lower productivity of labour and higher productivity of capital and lower wage rates.

Recent Restructuring Measures

Government has taken a number of steps for the promotion of small scale industries in accordance with the measures announced on 6 August, 1991.

1. There were restrictions on registering new SSI units for the manufacture of certain products although the products are reserved for the small scale sector. The list of such restricted products was disbanded.
2. Industry-related service and business enterprises with investment upto Rs. 5 lakhs in fixed assets (excluding land and building) irrespective of their location are now treated on par with small scale industries.
3. Steps have been taken to alleviate the credit bottlenecks of this sector. The eligibility limit of projects under the National Equity Fund Scheme has been doubled from Rs. 5 lakhs to Rs. 10 lakhs.
4. The Single Window Scheme was extended to be operated by Scheduled Banks also in addition to State Financial Institutions.
5. An Ordinance was promulgated on 23 September, 1992 making payment of interest obligatory on delayed payments to small scale and ancillary industrial undertakings. It has been re-promulgated in January 1993.

Khadi and Village Industries

The Khadi and Village Industries Commission (KVIC) covers about 2.1 lakh villages throughout the country through 30 state KVI Boards, 2320 registered institutions, 29,813 cooperatives and over 5 lakh individuals. Over the years, the main thrust of KVIC activities has been to provide a larger share of employment to SC/STs and women. At present SC/ST comprise nearly 30 per cent of workers and nearly 46% women.

It is provisionally estimated that during 1991-92 the KVI sector produced goods worth Rs. 2458 crores and provided employment to 49.7 lakh persons. During 1992-93, the production level went up to Rs. 2670 crores and employment to 51.05 lakh persons.

Industrial Sickness in Small Business

As at the end of March 1991, there were 2.24 lakh sick or weak industrial units on the rolls of commercial banks. A little over 2.21 lakhs (99%) of them were in the small scale sector. Outstanding bank credit of Rs. 10,768 crores, which constituted about 17.5% of total industrial credit, was locked in these 2.24 lakhs sick or weak industrial units (excluding 127575 non-existent and non-traceable SSI units with an outstanding bank credit of Rs. 284 crores) (Table 2). A slight abatement in the increasing incidence of sickness due to early detection and preventive measures taken by the banking system is in evidence. Total outstanding bank credit locked in sick or weak industrial units which had increased by 23.2% between December 1987 and December 1988 and by 21.4% between December 1988 and March 1990 (17.1% on an annualised basis) showed a much lower increase of 15.1% during the year ended March 1991. Although small scale industries accounted for 99% of the total sick or weak units at the end of March 1991, their share in the aggregate locked in bank credit was only 25.9%, same as at the end of March 1990. The bank credit outstanding in respect of sick SSI units at the end of March 1991, accounted for about 16.2% of total credit to small scale industries. For sick or weak, large and medium scale industrial units, the ratio was 17.9%. Out of the 2337 non-SSI sick or weak units, 1896 (81.1%) were in the private-sector which accounted for 72.7% of the total outstanding bank credit to the non-SSI sick or weak units. Industry-group-wise, the incidence of sickness and weakness in the non-SSI sector in terms of credit outstanding was the highest in textiles (25.0%) followed by engineering (18.3%), chemicals (7.0%), iron and steel (6.2%), electricals (5.5%) and paper (4.5%).

Table 3 gives the viability status of the identified sick and weak industrial units as at the end of March 1991. The viability of sick units was lower in the SSI sector (7.3%) than in the non-SSI sector (40.3%). However, the coverage of the nursing programme at about 82% in the SSI sector was significantly higher than 61.4% in the non-SSI sector.

The entrepreneurs viewpoint was elicited on the following policy measures :

1. In India, small scale sector has been defined in terms of investment in plant and machinery. The NSIP, now, expands the ceiling limit on investment in P&M from Rs. 2 lakhs to Rs. 5 lakhs in case of tiny enterprises, from Rs. 35 lakhs to Rs. 60 lakhs in case of small enterprises and Rs. 45 lakhs in case of ancillary enterprises.
2. Emphasis of government intervention would henceforth shift from subsidised, cheap credit, except for special target groups, to free flow of credit. This amounts to the withdrawal of both preferential lending and concessional credit which small scale sector use to enjoy hitherto.
3. The new policy has allowed equity participation by large as well as foreign undertakings in small scale units not exceeding 24 per cent of the total share holding.
4. The new policy has introduced a new legal form of business organization known as limited partnership. It stipulates that the liability of at least one partner will be unlimited and that of the other partners will be limited to their equity participation.
5. The Government of India passed an Ordinance on 23rd September, 1992 providing for payment of interest on delayed payments to the SSI firms.

6. In India, 836 products are reserved for exclusive production in small scale sector. Despite representations from various industry associations to de-reserve, the new policy has pronounced continuation of the reservation policy.
7. There has been a major shift in the trade policy towards liberalization. Four policy measures introduced recently are of special significance to small scale sector. One, liberalization of export promotion capital goods scheme; two, slashing of the customs duties across the board from 150% to 85% (even 35% in few cases); three, a large number of products are put under Open General Licence; and four, devaluation and 100% contribution of rupee on trade account.

Analysis and Discussion

About 49% respondents felt that relaxation in investment ceiling limit would contribute to the growth of their enterprises in terms of technology upgradation. Across the centres, the entrepreneurs' perception on this policy measures shows a uniform pattern. By the investment size, which is a more relevant criterion in this context, the percentage of entrepreneurs with positive perception increases as one moves from smaller to larger. However, more than 50% of the entrepreneurs felt it quite dampening inasmuch as it brings relatively larger competeing units into the protection umbrella.

Only about 35% entrepreneurs felt that de-reservation of products is not harmful for their enterprises. This proportion is extremely low in Patiala. However, along with investment classes and turnover classes it increases. Entrepreneurs with higher investment base as well as those with higher turnover opine that entry of large units in the manufacture of their products is prevented in any case by the diseconomies of scale. About 55% of entrepreneurs felt limited partnership form of organization as useful in raising funds.

However, as high as 68% entrepreneurs in Ludhiana are quite hopeful about this policy initiative to the extent that it would save the women as well as sleeping partners from being pulled into public. Neither investment level nor type of the product

Table II
Industrial Sickness

		Number of Units			Amount outstanding		
		End-December 1988	End-March 1990	End-March 1992	End-December 1988	End-March 1990 Rs. Crore	End-March 1992
1.	Non-sick Units	240573	218828	221472	2141.00	2426.94	2792.04
2.	Non-SSI Sick Units	1241	1455	1461	3387.30	4538.82	5105.57
3.	Non-SSI Weak Units	770	814	876	2177.00	2386.77	2870.21
	Total	242534	221097	223809	7705.30	9352.53	10767.82
		Change over previous year—per cent					
1.	SSI Sick Units	17.80	-9.04	1.21	19.10	13.36	15.04
2.	Non-SSI Sick Units	20.90	17.24	0.41	20.90	34.00	12.49
3.	Non-SSI Weak Units	3.90	5.71	7.62	31.40	9.64	20.25
	Total	17.70	-8.84	1.23	23.20	21.38	15.13

Source : *Economic Survey*, Government of India, 1992-93.

Table III
Viability Status of Sick or Weak Units

		SSI		Non-SSI		Total	
		Number	Outstanding Bank Credit (Rs. Crore)	Number	Outstanding Bank Credit (Rs. Crore)	Number	Outstanding Bank Credit (Rs. Crore)
1	2	3	4	5	6	7	8
1.	Viable Units	16140	693.10	941	3699.63	17081	4392.73
2.	Non-viable Units	202998	1997.13	974	2206.97	203972	4204.10
3.	Viability not assessed	2334	101.81	422	2069.18	2756	2170.99
4.	Total	221472	2792.04	2337	7975.78	223809	10767.82
5.	(a) Units under nursing Programme	13224	550.08	578	2336.07	13802	2886.15
	Per Cent						
	(b) As per cent of viable units	81.93	79.37	61.42	63.14	80.80	65.70
	Composition						
1.	Viable Units	7.29	24.82	40.27	46.39	7.60	40.79
2.	Non-viable units	91.66	71.53	41.68	27.67	91.20	39.04
3.	Viability not assessed	1.00	3.70	18.00	25.94	1.20	20.16
4.	Total	100.00	100.00	100.00	100.00	100.00	100.00

Source : *Economic Survey*, Government of India, 1992-93.

has significant influence on this perception. It seems the centres with high incidence of private limited companies are more in favour of immediate implementation of this policy option.

As regards 24% equity participation most (60%) of the respondents viewed it favourably in terms of its contribution to technology, finance and marketing. In Ludhiana and Jalandhar the response is overwhelming (65% and 75% respectively). More than 60% respondents felt that the Delayed Payments Ordinance would not serve the purpose. Majority (69%) of the respondents felt that liberalization of trade will be helpful in technology upgradation.

Implications of Policy Changes on the Small Sector

The growth and development of small sector units has been constrained by several factors including technological obsolescence, inadequate and irregular supply of raw materials, lack of organized marketing channels, imperfect knowledge of market conditions, unorganized nature of operations, inadequate availability of credit, constraints of infrastructural facilities including power and deficient managerial and technical skills. There has been lack of effective cooperation among the various support organizations set up over the period for the promotion and development of these small industries. Quality consciousness has not been generated to the desired level. Some of the fiscal policies pursued have resulted in unintended splitting-up of the capacities into uneconomic operations and have inhibited their smooth transfer to the medium and large sectors. All these constraints have resulted in a skewed cost structure placing the sector at a disadvantage in relation to large industries both in the domestic and export markets.

Investment

Finance is the life-blood of an industry. It is one of the constant problems faced by SSE. In the process of development, the non-availability of timely and adequate finance generally acts as a severe restraining factor. The small enterprises find problem of finance and investment at all stages. Even in beginning they have to run from pillar to post for getting initial investment. They have to depend more on their own funds, borrowed funds mainly from relatives, friends and professional lenders. This is because of the fact that established financial institutions like banks and financial corporations are generally reluctant to advance money to these small units since they have not established themselves.

Poor Technology

Technology is the base of the industry. In modern times a lot of attention is being devoted towards the improvement of the technology. Fortunately the technology is developing rapidly and we can find a very sophisticated technology in the market. But the small enterprises cannot think of using the sophistication of the latest technologies because of their poor financial structure. The small enterprises need to keep pace with development of the technology so as to remain in the market;

(i) improve the quality of the product;

(ii) lower the cost of the production; and

(iii) pass on the benefits of the customers.

But they have to depend upon the traditional technologies and find themselves squeezed out of the business. So the absence of the latest technology which can ensure quality and a high rate of productivity makes the small enterprises handicapped.

Marketing

Marketing is a key factor in determining the success of an industrial concern. The marketing view looks at the business as directed towards the satisfaction of a customer and as a purveyor of a customer utility. Market of the product is a crucial area, which is one of the major stumbling blocks, for small scale industries. A SSI may be able to establish a good unit and to bring out a quality product but if that entrepreneur is not able to market the product, he cannot be called a successful entrepreneur.

International Competition

The modern world of business is full of complexities and needs a constant attention and efforts to face the problems particularly when a tough competition is creating a lot of problems, then it is necessary for every entrepreneur to understand the competitive situation. In fact, it may be a matter of life and death for business. A typical small entrepreneur may face competition from other small firms and from large companies having established and well-known brand names. However, the true nature and extent of competition can hardly be judged from the market share being enjoyed by each competitor. In a vast country like India, the nature of competition may vary drastically from market to market. which one highly price-sensitive as well as price insensitive, quality sensitive markets.

It is, therefore, important for the entrepreneur to study the competitive situation with reference to chosen market segments. In case of many products, the household and institutional markets may have altogether different types of competitions.

Recent Strategies

The strategies for the development of small scale industries in the Seventh Plan can be summarised as follows:

(i) Improve productivity, enhance quality, reduce costs and re-structure product-mix through upgradation of technology and modernization.

(ii) Optimise utilization of existing capacities through supply of adequate inputs including credit, power, and raw materials, etc.

(iii) Expand share of small industry products in the domestic markets through publicity, standardization, market support and increased participation in the government purchase programme.

(iv) Strengthen the programmes of ancillarization to establish and improve linkage between large and small industries leading to harmonious growth of the total industrial sector.

(v) Promote specialization in production and export-oriented industries.

(vi) Strengthen and enlarge skill profile and entrepreneurial base and management practices to increase opportunities for self-employment.

(vii) Improve general levels of welfare of workers and artisans through better working conditions, welfare measures and security of employment.

Conclusion

The policies to be pursued during the Eighth Plan aim at rationalization of fiscal measures to ensure the rapid growth of small industries. Infrastructural facilities would be strengthened at various levels. Adoption of modern management techniques will be encouraged. Development and dissemination of an appropriate technology to improve productivity and quality and lessen the dependence on subsidies would receive due emphasis. Skills would be further upgraded in line with the degree of sophistication of the products and processes. Measures would be taken to adopt coherent marketing strategies both for internal and export markets and research and development efforts would be enhanced. New incentives required for increasing production of an ancillary items through the sub-contracting system would be taken up both in the public and private sectors. Adequate infrastructure would be created in the less developed areas to attract small industries. There has been increase in the number of cooperatives, but a large number of them are either sick or dormant mainly due to weak quality of leadership, management, and marketing infrastructure. Attention would be focused on education of members and officebearers of the cooperatives.

The government has liberalized its policy towards small industries to bring about better coordination between a small sector and the medium and large sectors. They have to rise to the challenge of ancillarisation process now evolving in the country and should think big and grow bigger. It has been noted that the vested interest in small industries want to remain small because of the protective shelter. But protection cannot be for ever. It creates a permanent interest in remaining an inefficient and incompetent industry in order to enjoy the benefits that go to the weak.

Entrepreneurs have become more quality conscious and have started looking-up for technological upgradation by investing in HRD, in whatsoever small way it could be. All these indicate that the small scale sector has come of age and is gearing up to face the competition with full vigour.

In the past, the policy of promoting and protecting small scale sector was based on its low capital requirement, high employment potential, locational flexibility, optimal use of resources both human and physical, balanced regional growth and decentralization of economic power.

Problems of small enterprises are multi-dimensional, and these can be solved by the coordinated efforts of entrepreneur, and functioning of promotional agencies and government assistance without red-tape or bureaucratic delays. A proper environment must be created where an entrepreneur is educated and trained in acquiring the necessary skill in running the small business enterprises.

References

1. Pathy, Jagannath, *Anthropology of Development : Demystifications and Relevance*, Gyan Publishing House, Delhi, 1987.
2. Malenbaum, W. Prospects for Indian Development : The Free Press, Glencoe III, 1962, Also cited in Hoselitz, B.F. (ed.) *The Role of Small Industry in the Process of Economic Growth*, The Hague, Mouton, Paris, 1968.
3. UNESCO, *Social Research of Small Industries in India*, 1963, pp. 7-39.
4. Hoselitz, B.F. (ed.), *The Role of Small Industry in the Process of Economic Growth*, The Hague, Mouton, Paris, 1968, pp. 140-44.
5. UNESCO, *Social Aspects of Small Industries in India*, Studies in Howrah, Bombay, 1962.
6. UNESCO, *Small Industries and Social Change : Four Studies in India*, 1968.
7. Sharma, R.K., *Industrial Entrepreneurship in a Developing Economies*, Kalyani Publishers, 1989.
8. Cohen, William A., *The Entrepreneur and Small Business Problem Solver*, John Wiley and Sons, New York, 1990.
9. Jain, Gautam Raj and Ansari Akbar, M., *Self-made Impact Making Entrepreneurs*, Entrepreneurship Development Institute of India, Ahmedabad, 1988.
10. Bhattacharya, S.N., Development of Small Scale and Cottage Industries, Metropolitan Book Co., New Delhi, 1986, p. 44.
11. Batra, G.S. Industrial Entrepreneurship, Babson World Conference on Entrepreneurship, Babson., 1972.
12. Government of India, *Economic Survey*, 1995.

[illegible] product and [illegible] small [illegible] low capital requirement [illegible] optimal use of [illegible] regional [illegible]

[illegible] small enterprises are [illegible] and these can be solved by the [illegible] efforts of [illegible] and [illegible] promotional agencies and government [illegible] business enterprises.

References

[illegible]

17

Peerless Group: A Look at the Past and Future

Sukti Ghosh

According to Glueck (1980), "Past strategies are the beginning point of strategic choice and may eliminate some strategic choices as a result". This implies that Strategic Management process is a continuous one. Therefore a look at the past strategies is a must for formulating the strategies for the future. And to know the past strategies we need to know the past developments of the Peerless Group.

Background

From 1930-32, the country was in the midst of Nationalist Movement which witnessed the boycott of everything foreign in order to liberate the country from the bondage of the British Raj. Late Shri Radhashyam Roy too could not remain untouched for he was a patriot from the core of his heart. Being a great visionary and idealist he rightly perceived that the foreign companies dominated the arena of insurance business and there by syphon off a big chunk of Indian money regularly to foreign lands. To check, to some extent, this unwarranted flow of Indian money to foreign lands, he visualized the idea of floating a *Swadeshi*, company at Narayanganj.

25th October, 1932 was a glorious day in the history of Peerless. On this day Shri Radhashyam Roy founded 'The Peerless Insurance Company Limited' with a meagre initial capital of Rs. 300. In this venture he was joined by Shri K.K. Chatterjee, an idealist and a life-time friend and soon after started Provident Insurance, the authorized capital of which stood at Rs. 20,000.

Though The Peerless Insurance Company Limited, faced strong challenge from the well-established foreign companies, it was destined to become a pioneer non-banking financial company under the administrative acumen and farsightedness of late Shri Radhashyam Roy. Soon this company achieved the distinction of becoming one of the leading Provident Insurance Companies in India.

Shifting of Office to Calcutta

In 1935, the management of Peerless took a very significant decision of shifting its office to Calcutta, which was the seat of political and economic power, and could have far reaching consequences. Here, the company witnessed a rapid growth as years rolled on. The Board of Directors of the company too was enlarged to include among others, Hon'ble Mr. Kumar Shankar Roy, Bar-at-law and member, council of state, Khan Sahib Abdul Jabbar Biswas, Hon'y Magistrate.

Introduction of Insurance Act 1938

In 1938, the wellknown Insurance Act of 1938 was passed and the company paid the requisite amount to the RBI as stipulated by the act. Authorised capital was increased to Rs. 3,00,000/ and a sum of Rs. 50,000 was disbursed as claimed by the company under its Provident Insurance schemes.

Commencement of Life Insurance Business

By 1942-43, there were too many players in the Provident Insurance business as it was a profitable venture. At this juncture, the company took a historical decision to switch over to life insurance business resulting in "Peerless Life Assurance Co. Ltd." in 1943. The life insurance business flourished by leaps and bounds and was later renamed "The Peerless General Insurance and Investment Company Ltd." in 1947.

Executives

As the guiding force, Shri B. K. Roy ushered in a new era in the corporate history of Peerless. With the success of the saving schemes, Peerless witnessed the assimilation of many brilliant executives with proven track records and expertise, into its fold. In 1960, Shri M.R. Mukherjee joined the Board of Directors with Shri K.K. Chatterjee, becoming the chairman of the company. And despite facing some adversities, Peerless reached a respectable height, to be renowned as a highly reputed non-banking savings company. In 1967, the company shifted its office from 8/2 Hastings Street to 5/2, Fakir De Lane in order to cope up with the increase in its activities.

Field Force: The Harbinger of the Peerless Message

The field force undisputably has been the kernel of all activities in the Peerless. The wonderful achievement of Peerless has been possible, largely due to their painstaking and concerted effort of their dedicated field force. They have strived to spread the Peerless message of savings across the country, which has gone a long way in shaping the nation's destiny. Partition of the country, the turmoil and the communal riots have left a scar in the history of India with thousands of people displaced. There remained an immediate task of nation-building and rehabilitation in which Peerless had to play a decisive role.

A Midstream Threat

In 1956, Life Insurance business was nationalised. Along with other Life Insurance Companies, Peerless Life Assurance Co. Ltd. too came in its purview. Notwithstanding this big jolt, the parent company kept on its onward voyage on the troubled high sea by devising new schemes to encourage savings and ensure secured investments.

Managing the Threat

In spite of some adversity, 1956, this year was indeed an epoch-making year for Peerless, when it introduced the 'Social Welfare Schemes' based on scientific acturial principles on the recommendations of some eminent actuaries. This scheme became an instant success as it served the needs of the common man with small means who was still not being served by the banks or post offices.

The year 1972 marked the beginning of a new era in the history of Peerless with the introduction of Automatic Promotion System which envisaged a unique plan for promotion by which any member of the field force could get automatic promotion with the fulfilment of preset performance targets.

In 1974, the Registered Office of the company was again shifted to 3, Esplanade East, Calcutta, because enlarging operations called for a larger office accommodation. In the same year "The Peerless General Insurance and Investment Company Limited" was renamed "The Peerless General Finance and Investment Company Limited".

Golden Jubilee: A Landmark

In 1982, Peerless completed the first fifty years of its glorious existence. By this year, Peerless had become a symbol of the 'small savings movement' by mobilising small savings on an unprecedented scale with over 12 million certificate holders. About 3000 members of its office staff manned 75 offices in every corner of the country.

Particulars	*1962*	*1972*	*1984*	*1986*
No. of Agents and Field Officer	1,450	14,600	Over 4,00,000	4,50,000
No. of Certificate Holders	4,600	1,50,000	Nearly 167,00,000	187,00,000
Investment in Govt. Securities/Bank Deposits (in Rs.)	1,10,000	105,37,645	582.88 crores	707.82 crores

Peerless comfortably crossed Rs. 2100 crores mark for the new business secured in one year period. The value of total assets exceeded Rs. 325 crores and profit after tax for the Golden Jubilee year was Rs. 4.29 crores and the paid-up Capital and Reserve stood at Rs. 3.7 crores. As usual, Peerless offered utmost security to the certificate holders by having invested in the government custody an amount exceeding Rs. 275 crores against contractual liability of Rs. 229 crores.

The year 1984 marked a turning-point in the history of Peerless with the induction of professionals in the management cadre to facilitate scientific administration and prompt functioning through decentralization of operations. In this very year it also resolved to explore untrodden avenues for greater utilization of infrastructural strength and achieve its corporate goals.

Spreading out for Brighter Days Ahead

The transition period from Golden Jubilee to the Diamond Jubilee has witnessed Peerless to vacillate between expectations and disappointments.

Notwithstanding the various problems, the company continued its rapid strides towards the lofty heights of success, first under the versatile business acumen of Shri B. K. Roy and thereafter under the wise counsel and administrative abilities of Shri S. K. Roy and then the intrepid and dynamic leadership of Shri P. C. Sen.

In 1985, however, the total assets of the company reached an all time high figure of Rs. 750 crores but at the same time the status of the company was challenged in the court of law. The company at that time was not sailing smoothly as the sad demise of Shri B. K. Roy had caused an irrepairable loss to the company. In 1987, however, the long-drawn legal battle came to an end with the Supreme Court declaring the saving schemes of Peerless to be legal. This favourable verdict of the Supreme Court nullified all the charges regarding viability and status of the company. Flushed with success, the management set about to rejuvenate the workforce, once again the certificate holders reposed their faith with renewed vigour and greater confidence.

Peerless today has the distinction of being a pioneer non-banking financial institution with a remarkable track-record commanding admiration and as a corollary some envy it too. But the journey has not yet ended, with many a milestones to be still reached and thus Peerless' march towards the Platinum Jubilee continues unabated.

...t in Recent Past

A resplendent star in the economic firmament, Peerless has secured a niche for itself in the corporate world. Though it is gearing up its activities to keep pace with the fast changing business environment, it has still not severed its activities from the ideals and basic principles of late Shri B.K. Roy. This includes opening up of more and more branches to provide service at the doorstep; computerization in a phased manner; decentralization of operations; installation of modern management tools and gadgets with a mission to provide better and expeditious service to the certificate holders.

At Peerless, the certificate holder's interests get the highest priority and it has been the unwavering philosophy of Peerless to ensure that this basic objective is realised through the various schemes it has undertaken in the recent past; launching attractive saving schemes with greater returns; offering Free Accidental Death Benefits; providing Mediclaim facilities. Each of the 100 odd Peerless branch offices now has authority to settle claims. And with state-of-the-art modern communication networks, delay and discomfort for the customer has been reduced.

Secured Investments

Peerless has been resolute in its policy of providing iron-clad security to the investors. It is still pursuing the time-honoured policy of lodging a major portion of its resources with the government. In 1976, even prior to the regulatory provision in respect of investment of mobilised funds, Peerless had on its own, fortified the security in a manner that was unparalleled in the history of non-banking saving's companies in India. The services of a competent actuary is secured in order to value the accumulated funds so as to make sure that there is enough funds set aside against contractual liabilities.

Swift Settlement of Claims: An Unequalled Peerless Tradition

Prompt and hassle-free settlement of claims has been one of major objectives of the company management believes that payment of maturity and other claims ought to be not only speedy but also easy and comfortable as it adds to consumer satisfaction. Peerless has been striving with unflinching determination to settle certificate holders' claims as fast as possible.

Spectacular Peerless Growth (4 years at a glance)

Particulars	*1987-88*	*1988-89*	*1989-90*	*1990-91*
Total No. of Officers	99	103	116	121
Total No. of Certificate Holders	194,00,000	2,09,000	233,00,000	266,00,000
Maturity and other Claims Paid	Rs. 135.46 Cr. as on 31/10/87	Rs. 260.30 Cr. as on 31/10/89	Rs. 334.99 Cr. as on 31/03/90	Rs. 409.83 Cr. as on 31/03/91
Total Asset	Rs. 899.71 Cr. as on 31/03/88	Rs. 1002.74 Cr. as on 31/03/89	Rs. 1172.53 Cr. as on 31/03/90	Rs. 1386.16 Cr. as on 31/03/91

Exploring New Markets: Reaching New Horizons

Over the years, it has been the members of the Peerless field force who have been working tirelessly and with sincerity to assist common man to save for a better tomorrow. They have braved every hazard to offer service at the customer's doorsteps. In their ceaseless endeavour, they have been able to tap the resources in the remote segments which has hitherto remained untapped. Admittedly, this has been one of the major contributions of Peerless to the country and its people.

New Endeavours : New Prospects

The achievement Peerless have been a phenomenal success story with the help of the trust and confidence of the certificate holders. But this success only added fuel to the fire as Peerless aspired for greater success with the expansion of its activities. And to fulfil this mission, Shri P.C. Sen embarked on a well-chalked-out and need-based plan for diversifications. Admittedly, it was Sen's dynamism, business acumen, entrepreneurial flair and far-sightedness which has been instrumental in paving the path for these new ventures.

The corporate aims and objectives behind the new endeavours of Peerless were based on a sharply analytical, tactical and realistic approach, taking account the enormous latent potentiality of its infrastructural strength in order to widen the scope of its activities, to realise overall corporate growth and to ensure all round benefit to the country and its people. The new endeavours of Peerless are in tune with the national priorities contributing immensely to enrich the quality of life.

Peerless Abasan Finance Limited

A wholly owned subsidiary of Peerless, Peerless Abasan Finance Limited, has undertaken a herculean task of aiding the national endeavour to provide a solution to the ever-increasing problem of ensuring a roof for every citizen. Its function pertains mainly to making available finance to people in order to make their dreams of owning a house come true. The company has envisaged a special loan scheme termed Peerless Griha Mitra Yojana which has gained immense popularity. Apart from these, it also offers special facilities to the certificate holders of Peerless. The company has also entered into the field of financing the housing schemes of government/semi-government and corporate sectors.

Peerless Developers Limited

With a humble beginning in 1990 set up to cater to the increasing domestic needs in the consumer market, Peerless Developers Limited, is all set to storm the country's consumer market. Peerless Bazaar : a sophisticated showroom of electronic and other home appliances in Calcutta has been the talk of the town for quite some time now. Plans are on the anvil to have similar projects in other cities where it has not been able to reach yet.

Peerless Shipping and Oilfields Ltd.

The company is a Indo-Norwegian joint-venture engaged in hi-tech sub-sea engineering support service in the offshore oil-fields and onshore land drilling for oil exploration.

'Drive Ocean', the highly sophisticated multipurpose diving support vessel, equipped with fire fighting in the offshore oil-fields, pollution control and rescue operations and also a dynamic positioning system making it capable of stationing in one place withstanding high velocity winds and waves, was selected by the ONGC against a global tender for a fire fighting and rescue vessel with dive support. 'Drive Ocean' however helped the country to earn substantial foreign exchange when it was deployed by the company to foreign charters.

The cooperation with ONGC has been fruitful for Peerless as it has been awarded the contract for management and operation of the state-of-the-art "MSV Samudraprabha"

Peerless Hotels and Travels Limited

Promoting tourism constitutes the basic objective of this subsidiary. By opening a chain of hotels and resorts in both rural and urban sectors and operating a travel division, this subsidiary intends to contribute substantially to the socio-economic development of the country. Its maiden venture, Soma, the lake-side hotel and village resort in Mukutmanipur, Bankura, West Bengal is providing a recluse from the hustle and bustle of towns and cities. 'Peerless Inns' have also been set up in many cities across India with much success.

Peerless Financial Services Limited

An offshoot of the mother business, it is functioning in the country's capital market. With the aid of the infrastructural facilities of the mother company it has made deep inroads into the capital investment market of the country.

Peerless Hospital and B.K. Roy Research Centre Limited

It has been the fulfilment of a dream of late Shri B. K. Roy, who made a commitment wayback in 1982 to establish a modern hospital. After a decade the dream has come true in the form of a 300-bed modern hospital equipped with state-of-the-art diagnostic services. The hospital is run by experts in the field of medical science and offers specialized services in ophthalmology, neonatalogy, cardiology, medicine, pediatrics and general surgery.

Social Commitment

Backed by six decades of heritage and reputation, Peerless today occupies a secured position in the country's corporate world. And while fulfilling its corporate objective it has not turned its eyes from its social responsibilities, as serving the country and its people have been part of Peerless' unswerving philosophy. Peerless has contributed substantially to the humanitarian causes. The company has donated generously to Ramkrishna Mission, Bharat Sevashram Sangha, Ramkrishna Mission Seva Pratisthan, Balananda Brahmachari Hospital, Behala Cancer Centre and Welfare Home, Thakurpukur.

Brachy Therapy Unit at Cancer Centre and Welfare Home, Thakurpukur and Soil Testing Laboratory at Kamarpukur are still standing as tangible examples of outstanding social commitment of Peerlees. In this, it has taken up some unique ventures like Yatri Nivas at Kamarpukur and the Peerless Overbridge at V.I.P. Road, Ultadanga Crossing.

The company had diversified its activities into different areas of business alongwith its original business as stated in the preceeding section.

Here all the subsidiaries are to be taken as SBUs and this study attempts to determine the strategic position of each subsidiary on the basis of two variables, viz., 'business sector prospects' and 'company's competitive capability' through DPM model developed by Royal Dutch Shell (Ghosh, 1986).

Use of this strategic tool is for comparison and evaluation of strategic alternatives constituting a major aspect of the optimum allocation of resources amongst the SBU's for the attainment of the overall organization goals.

Business Sector Prospects

Company's Competitive capabilities	*Unattractive*	*Average*	*Attractive*
Weak	*Disinvest*	*Phased Withdrawl*	*Double or Quit*
Average	Phased Withdrawl	*Custodial* Peerless Hotels & Travels Ltd. Peerless Financial Services Ltd.	*Try Harder* Peerless Developers Peerless Hospital and B.K. Roy Research Centre Ltd.
Strong	*Cash Generation* The Peerless General Finance & Investment Co. Ltd.	*Growth* Peerless Abasan Peerless Shipping & Oilfields Ltd.	*Leader*

(1) Peerless Abasan Finance Limited

Though government and private developers are the main competitors of this subsidiary, government constitutes a major threat as it offers accommodation at a much lower price. But one advantageous factor seems to be the fact that its participation is not significant. The Peerless Abasan is also facing competition from the private developers, but owing to some unwanted incidents customers are losing faith on them. On the other hand, Peerless Abasan is giving better facilities to the certificate holders regarding the repayment of loans. It also has a goodwill along with strong financial position which gives it an edge over the others. Therefore, it may be concluded that competitive capability of Peerless Abasan is strong although the business prospect is average.

Therefore, the strategic position of Peerless Abasan is growth in the DPM model. This is suited for growth strategy supported by adequate investment to the business.

(2) Peerless Developers Ltd.

The business sector prospect of this S.B.U. is said to be "Attractive". As the Peerless Bazaar offers sophisticated electronic goods and home appliances which have an expanding market, and is located at the nerve centre of Calcutta, the business sector prospect is indeed attractive.

On the other hand, the company's competitive capabilities may be called average as there are many players in the field offering the same services. Therefore, the strategic position of the S.B.U. is "Try Harder" in the DPM model. This business should be provided with necessary resources so as to move it to the position of grwoth.

(3) Peerless Hotel and Travels Ltd.

Here both business sector prospect and the company's competitive capabilities are concluded as average.

If the instance of hotel Ritz Continental (Calcutta) is taken, though it is a five-star hotel, there are other five-star hotels in the vicinity (Grand Hotel, Park Hotel, Hotel Taj Bengal etc.) which offers stiff competition.

Again, the company has taken over hotel Maharaja International in Durgapur which is not a popular tourist spot and has introduced a resort 'Soma' in Mukutmanipur which has not yet caught the fancy of tourists. The business sector prospect may be concluded as average in this stage.

So the subsidiary is placed into the position "custodial" in the DPM model. Liberalization measures by the government is likely to encourage a large influx of tourists and business class tourists and thus resources should be pumped into it to take advantage of the same.

(4) Peerless Shipping and Oilfields Ltd.

The subsidiary is exploring untrodden paths and as such the 'business factor prospect' is assumed to be average. However, the only competitors, the foreign contractors, have been driven out by Peerless making the competitive capability 'strong'.

Therefore, this S.B.U. is in the position of growth leader in the DPM model. The company as it has the competitive capability should opt for growth strategy supported by R & D and production capacity.

(5) Peerless Financial Services Limited

Owing to the unstable economic condition and the ups and downs in the capital market, the business sector prospect is assumed to be average.

Again, although the mother company is sound in its financial resources, but there is little information regarding the choice of the area of investment. So again, it is concluded as average.

Therefore, strategic position of the S.B.U. is 'custodial'. Liberalization Measures is likely to infuse money into the stock though the goreign investment, which is likely to be advantageous for the company.

ETOP

Competitor / Market	Introduction of various housing loan schemes by HUDCO, HDFC, and other financial schemes by UTI, SBI, etc.
Government	(-) Government participation in

developing lands for lower/middle income groups and government interference in building MIG & LIG apartments around Calcutta. Tax concession by government on various schemes by government controlled F.I.

SAP

Marketing	(+) Large number of agents and a wide spread network.
	(-) Apathy in the use of print and electronic media.
Finance	(+) Ability to generate fund through the non-banking deposit schemes as well as through participation in the stock market.
Corporate Resources	(+) Efficient and experienced management team.

Matching of Internal Strengths with Environmental Factors

Internal Strengths	*Environmental Factors*
A large and widespread fieldforce	Awareness of people regarding the needs of insurance schemes and other long term deposits schemes as part of their future planning.
Ability to generate capital to diversify the activities	Unstable economic condition in the manufacturing sector for various reasons in the eastern region.
Efficient management team capable of coping with the change	Need for identifying the change in lifestyle and values of the middle and lower income groups.

SWOT

Strengths: A large and widespread fieldforce, efficient and experienced management team ability to generate funds to diversify into other activities.

Weaknesses: Apathy to use print and electronic media, over zealous diversification.

Opportunity: Awareness of the people regarding the needs of insurance schemes and other long term deposit schemes as part of their future planning. Liberalization measures by the government likely to infuse money into the hands of some sections of the society which is likely to create opportunity for Peerless Developers. Need for medical services in the society to be met by Peerless Hospital and B.K. Roy Research Centre.

Threat: Government participation in developing lands for lower/middle income groups and government interference in building MIG & LIG apartments around Calcutta. Tax concessions by government on various schemes by government controlled FI.

Conclusions

(i) Though Peerless has placed its major business in the cash generation cell of the directional policy matrix but it should have been placed in the leader zone.

In the context of the various liberalization measures taken by the government of India, it is foreseeable that insurance business market may expand in due time with probable threat from foreign companies.

Though in the recent past it has diversified from its mother business, it is likely to get neutralised if the "cash generation" business, driven by environmental threats is not able to keep its promise.

(ii) In the span of a short period, its overzealous diversification could cause the company some trouble and the company is likely to face tough competition from others. The corporate planners of Peerless should, in the years to come, lay more emphasis on stable growth as a pause strategy rather than going for overzealous diversification and aim for competitive advantage through core competency of the Group.

References

1. William F. Glueck (1980) : *Business Policy and Strategic Management* (Third Ed.) McGraw Hill.
2. P.K. Ghosh (1986) : *Business Policy—Strategic Planning and Management* (First Ed.) Sultan Chand & Sons.

18

An Innovator Archetype (Dr. Reddy's Laboratories)

Harendra Dey
and
Saikat Banerjee

In an era when the majority of the pharmaceutical industry is tending to its injured bottomlines, Dr. Reddy's Group is one of the success stories, which is all set to strengthen its position and expand its activities. The most significant fact that excites one's interest in this case-study is the company's tactful handling of the threats and the use of these very threats as opportunities for further growth.

The guiding force behind this company is its founder Dr. Anji Reddy, who was a senior scientist at the Hyderabad-based public sector pharma giant, Indian Drugs and Pharmaceuticals Ltd. (I.D.P.L). IDPL, set up with the resolve to improve the health of the nation, itself became sick with accumulated losses totalling Rs. 434 crores at the year ending 1988-89.

Dr. Reddy's stride towards a dream success began in 1979, when bitten by the entrepreneurial bug he quit his job at the

IDPL and started the Standard Organics Limited, a bulk drugs company. Bulk drugs are intermediate compounds used in the manufacture of capsules, tablets, solutions, etc. A huge market for these bulk drugs existed during that time without any accompanying danger in marketing them. In 1980, Dr. Anji Reddy was joined by C. Chandrashekhar Reddy, a NRI and an old friend who had made a fortune in textiles in Nigeria. Together they built up another bulk drug manufacturing company namely SOL Pharmaceuticals Ltd. Production rose from 23 tonnes in 1980 to 198 tonnes in 1983 while sales rose from 1.39 crores to 8.8 crores. Flushed with success, the Reddys launched other new companies, the most significant of which turned out to be Dr. Reddy's Laboratories Pvt. Ltd. and Standard Medical Leasing. (both set up in 1983).

But soon, they were to part their ways with Dr. Anji Reddy retaining Dr. Reddy's Laboratories and C. Reddy getting hold of Standard Medical Leasing Ltd. But this split was not total for both of them still held 50% controlling interest in SOL and Standard Organics and were the dual managing directors till 1986. In 1986, Dr. Anji Reddy sold his share in both these companies to C.C. Reddy thus becoming financially quite strong. Now Dr. Anji Reddy had only Dr. Reddy's Laboratories in his control (See Exhibit-1).

Duplicating Drugs at Much Cheaper Price

Indian drugs and pharmaceuticals industry has flourished under the regime of process patents as against the internationally accepted product patent. The Indian Patent Act of 1970 gives patent protection for the products themselves, that is, any Indian manufacturer can produce and market a patented drug as long as there is a change in the manufacturing process. The cost of developing a new product can be anything around Rs. 250 crores and an estimated time of about twelve years on an average is required for a new drug to reach the manufacturing stage. Therefore, it is a very costly and time-consuming process.

Exhibit-1

Reddy's Group

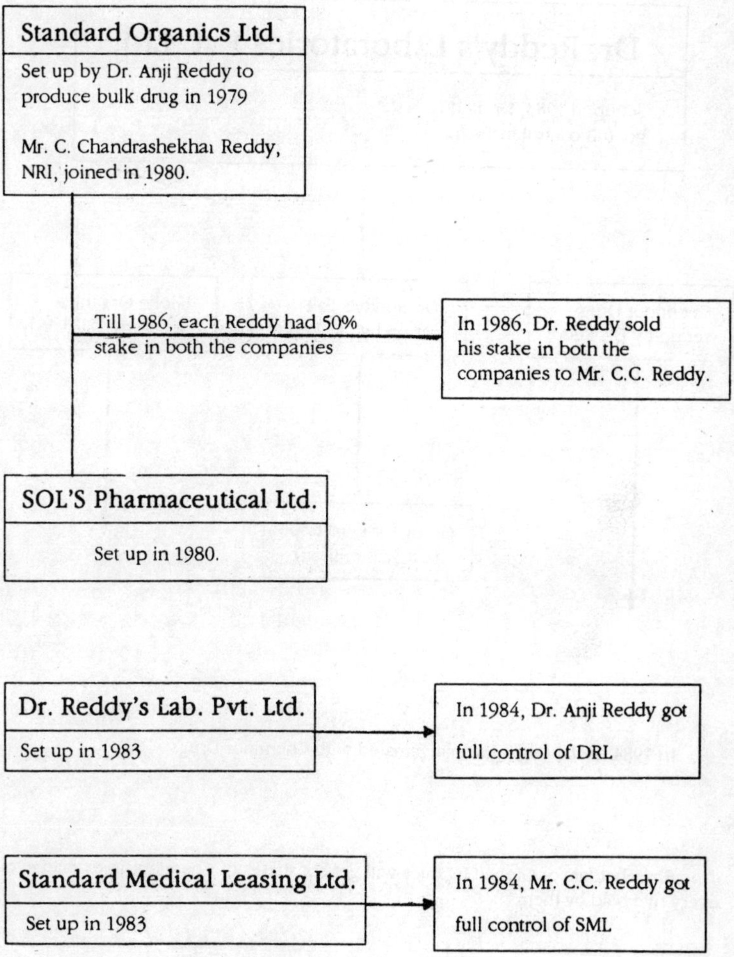

Exhibit-1

DR. ANJI REDDY

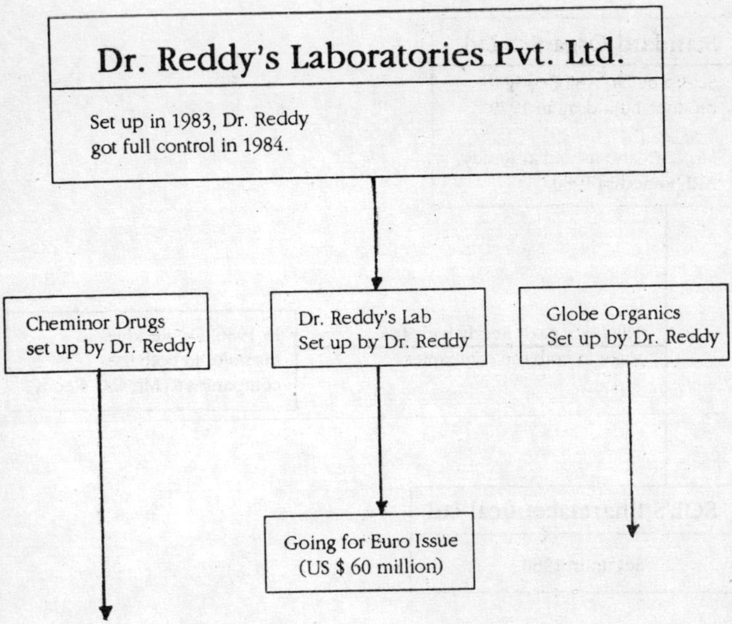

In 1984 Globe Organics amalgamated with Cheminor Drugs

Shareholders of Globe Organics will get six shares of Cheminor in exchange of every five held by them.

As such, when in 1984, the drug 1-methyl dopa (an anti-depressant) was in short supply, Dr. Anji Reddy took it as his personal challenge to duplicate the drug. Within a short period, Dr. Reddy succeded in his mission i.e. duplicated 1-methyl dopa, at a cheaper price, which foreign multinationals had often spent years and millions researching. With this began his giant stride towards success. He replicated a large number of patented drugs and by marketing them made huge profits, despite setting these drugs at a fraction of the price charged by the multinationals.

All these successes he could achieve mainly due to the fact that Dr. Reddy's Lab had developed some of the world's cheapest processes for the manufacture of drugs. In 1986, Dr. Reddy's Lab duplicated Ibuprofen (an analgesic) and manufactured it at a much lower price as compared to Glaxo, Pfizer and others. For three years it was the sole supplier of Ibuprofen in the Indian market. But as soon as Ibuprofen got off patented, Dr. Reddy flooded the U.S. markets with Ibuprofen at an abnormally low price which created a great problem for the US companies producing Ibuprofen as they were not in a position to sell their product at such a low price.

In 1989, the US-based Ethyl Corporation filed an anti-dumping case against Dr. Reddy's Laboratories. They were of the opinion that Dr. Reddy's. Lab was dumping Ibuprofen in the U.S.A. at a lower price, taking advantage of the cash compensatory support that the Indian government was providing at that time to such drug exporters. Ethyl Corporation also claimed that the methods used by DRL were also unfair.

But Dr. Reddy's Laboratories won the case and continued to export Ibuprofen in large quantities to the U.S. for he was able to prove that the cost of manufacturing Ibuprofen by his process was only a third to that of U.S. manufacturers. Moreover, he had the approval of the U.S. Food and Drug Administration and in turn claimed that the price charged by Ethyl Corporation is much higher and unfair.

One of the major strengths of DRL is adapting to the changing environment, which of course is necessary for the survival of any organization. For instance, Syntex Corporation of U.S.A.

discovered a pain-killer named Ketorolac, but before Syntex Corporation could introduce it in the South American market, Dr. Reddy's Laboratories duplicated the drug and flooded the South American market.

DRL's success is principally due to the fact that it has been able to manufacture drugs at an abnormally low price which is evident in the case of Ranitidine (an anti-ulcer drug) which was produced at such an absurdly low cost that even Glaxo, the original manufacturer began to buy from it. Though this made the multinationals, who were the hardest hit by these methods, unhappy with its modus operandi.

Export

Dr. Reddy's Laboratories has opted for exports as an integral part of its growth strategy, as it has always been lucrative. To promote exports DRL set up a marketing office, Reddy Cheminor in Los Angeles. For the Indian Drug Industry as a whole, export touches about 30% of production, i.e., approximately 722 crores as in 1992-93. Margins at 7% to 8% are much higher in export than in domestic markets, where prices are controlled by the government through Drug Price Control Order. Apart from this, 80% of the world's total pharmaceutical market one in the U.S., Europe and Japan selling only 5% patented products. Banking on these statistics, Dr. Reddy's strategy has been, as expected, to work on drugs that fall off the patents list, and also to export intermediate drugs which are off the patent list and does not require FDA approval. As for the Reddy's group, exports have risen from 39 crores in 1991-92 to 62 crores in 1992-93 and to 109 crores in 1993-94.

Exhibit-2

Strength: Adapting Quickly to a Changing Environment

Company's Strategies

(1) Duplicate patented drugs, e.g., 1-methyl dopa, Ranitidine, Ibuprofen, Katarolec, Terfinidine, Captopril, Astemazole, Famotidine, Enalarpil Omeprazole, etc.

(2) Produce drugs which do not fall under government's price control.

(3) Quality:- Purity of drugs produced are higher than other multinationals.

(4) Cost of manufacturing and overhead costs are very low as it developed some of the world's cheapest processes of manufacture of drugs. This will give much advantage to the company to fight with multinationals.

(5) Since margin in export is much higher than domestic trade, the company has made export an integral part of its growth strategy.

(6) To face competition in the post GATT era, the company has set up a research foundation which is the biggest R&D centre in the private sector in India, spending 15% of net sales in R&D whereas industrial average in india is 2% of net sales. To have the required resources, the company has gone for collaborative effort with a French company; patented a series of anti-cancer compounds in the US and also has patented other two drugs.

Government's Price Control on Drugs

One of the greatest hurdles in the way of profit-making for the pharmaceutical industry in India has been the Drug Price Control Order (DPCO). If we consider the whole of the pharmaceutical industry in India, we are likely to find about 3/4th of the turnover of the organized sector to be covered under price control. Notwithstanding the obstacle posed by DPCO, Dr. Reddy has been successful in his endeavour, chiefly due to his innovation, for most of the drugs produced by DRL lie outside the purview of DPCO.

Quality

With the liberalization of the Indian economy and globalization, quality is likely to acquire paramount importance. But it is one factor which has always been given the due consideration it deserved by Dr. Reddy's Lab. The purity of his Ibuprofen as tested by the concerned authority turned out to be 99.9% as against the multinationals whose purity stands at 98%.

Product Patent Regime will be in Force From 2005 AD

Now with the signing of the Dunkel Agreement on Intellectual Property Rights, companies like that of Dr. Reddy's will have to reconsider their strategies. But Dr. Reddy's group is unperturbed and subscribed to the idea of Intellectual Property Rights. The rationale behind is simple: by researching new drug molecules, rather than duplicating them, the company can patent the new drugs and make phenomenal profits.

A Dr. Reddy Research Foundation has thus been set up with an initial investment of Rs. 8 crore (which will be the biggest R&D centre in the private sector). The complex has twenty-eight modern labs, state-of-the-art equipment and 200 researchers.

But the question that comes to the mind is, whether independent research can be done in India with such nominal resources given the MNCs, which pump millions of dollars into it. However, Dr. Reddy's Group is of the view that in R & D the main cost is that of manpower. A researcher in the U.S.A. would entail a sum of $ 1,00,000. In India, however, one can get the services of eight scientists at this cost. Another solution to this problem can be a collaborative effort with foreign companies. With this in mind, it is also undertaking research in quinoles, antidiabetic and anti-cancer treatment. Dr. Reddy's Lab, in 1993, has patented two drugs in the U.S. and in 1994 the group's research arm has successfully discovered a series of novel anti-cancer compounds which are currently being patented. Thereafter the company expects to file six or seven patents a year in the U.S. and in Europe.

Exhibit 3
Strategic Advantage Profile (SAP)

Factors	*Impact*	*Diagnosis*
Financial/ Accounting	+30	Going for Euro issue to reduce cost of capital: Production, R&D and Marketing has never suffered due to shortage of working capital: Paying 30% dividend to shareholders and capitalized reserves twice by issuing bonus

		shares; debtequity ratio is 1.5:1 which is highly satisfactory.
Marketing/	+35	The Company is the market leader in many products in India. It can easily flood foreign countries with off the patent drugs very rapidly. Flooded South American market with Ketorolac, a bulk drug even before Syntex Corp. of U.S.A., the original manufacturer could introduce that product in South American market. Set up a marketing office in Los Angeles.
Production/ Operations and R&D	+38	Developed some of the world's cheapest process of manufacture of drugs. Very efficient in duplicating patented drugs. Discovered some new drugs and got them patented. Can manufacture huge volume of any drug at a short time.
Personnel/ Labour	+35	Highly experienced and efficient personnel are working miracles in the company. Labour relation is cordial and there is no strike or labour disturbances.
Corporate Resources	+45	Tactfully handled all the threats and used some of these very threats as opportunities for further growth and expansion. All the strategies were very successful that led to rapid growth and profitability of the company.

Financial Performance

DRL has had an enviable record in the past both in terms of performance and giving a share of the profit to the shareholders. Financial report has been shown in Exhibit 4.

Exhibit-4

Financial Results (Excellent Performance)

(Rs. in Crores)

Year Ending	*Equity*	*Sales*	*Export*	*Gross Profit*	*Net Profit (PAT)*	*Gross Profit Margin (%)*	*Bonus*	*Dividend*
8612	2.92	6.35		0.75				
9023	2.92	26			0.64	6.50		

9003	6.56	106.05	39	10.28	14.01	1:1	
9303	6.56	113.34	62	20.53	20.34		
9403	21.91	174.72	109	25.21	19.1	2:1	30%

Net profit has jumped from 0.64 crores in 1989-90 to 25.21 crores in 1993-94. Sales have increased from 6.35 crores in the year ending December 1986 to 174.72 crores in the year ending March 1994. Exports have jumped from 39 crores in 1991-92 to 109 crores in 1993-94. Gross profit margins increased from 6.5% in 1989-90 to 19.1% in 1994.

The company issued bonus shares to its shareholders in the year 1992 in the ratio 1:1 and again declared bonus share in 1994 in the ratio 2:1, i.e., the shareholders will get two free shares for every share held. Market price on ex-bonus basis is nearly Rs. 510 as in July 1994. The company have also declared 30% dividend to the shareholders.

Exhibit-5
How Shareholders are Rewarded

Year/ Month	*Market Price (Rs.)*	*Year*	*No. of Shares*	*Investments*
1986	10	1986	100	Rs. 1000/-
1990 Apr.	50	1992	(1:1 Bonus) 200	
1990 Nov.	90	1994	(2:1 Bonus) 600	
1992 Nov.	380	Total investment upto the year 1994 is Rs. 1000/-. Total no. of shares in possession is 600, market price as on July'94 is Rs. 510 Capital Appreciation as in July' 94 (Market price x No. of shares) = 510 x 600 = 3,06,000/- Less investment of Rs. 1000 gives 3,06,000 - 1000 = 3,05,000/- Duration from 1986-94, i.e., 8 years.		
1993 Jan.	525 (XB) (1:1)			
1994 Jan.	680			
1994 Feb.	1550 (CB)			
1994 Jul.	510 (XB) (2:1)			

Therefore, within 8 years invested money multiplied by 305 times. The company is at present giving a dividend of 30% to its shareholders.

19

SWOT Analysis for Babhanan Sugar Mills Ltd.

Samata Bhattacharjee

Babhanan Sugar Mills Ltd., a renowned name was established in Gonda, U.P. but all was not well with the company until a few years back. The company failed to achieve profitability due to irregular and uncertain availability of sugarcane and an inefficient management to cope with the situation. The company became a sick unit and continued to do so till the present management decided to take it over in 1989. Many experts at that time, felt the decision to be impulsive but opined that there was no scope of revival.

In 1990, Chairman-cum-Managing Director of Balarampur Chini Mills Ltd., Mr. K.N. Saraogi took over as the Chairman of Babhanan Sugar Mills Ltd. The new management aimed at better quality product, a dynamic work ethos and greater profitability. They achieved it by skilful management of manpower, raw materials and assets. So, in 1992, Babhanan Sugar Mills Ltd., earned profit for the first time and that is why the course they undertook may be a study of interest.

Sugarcane has been the common raw material for sugar, gur

and khandsari. Unlike sugar manufacturing units, gur and khandsari units were free from government controls like excise duty, levy and molasses allotment. While sugar manufacturing units paid government stipulated price of Rs. 58 per quintal for sugarcane but gur and khandsari manufacturers were freely paying higher price to grab adequate quantity for their requirement. As a consequence, farmers too were naturally not inclined to sell their produce to the sugar mills, thus the supply of sugarcane for the mills remained uncertain and tended to slump down the sugar output.

To overcome this problem, the management set about to develop cordial relationship with the cane growers. They approached the farmers with schemes to enable them to increase their production. The proposal was well-received and the area under cultivation witnessed a rise from 8% to 15%. Supply of sugarcane to Babhanan Sugar Mills too rose by 50%. This whole approach had also ensured ready availability of sugarcane at their disposal.

Production to Capacity

Management had also ensured working of the plant close to its 100% capacity by nearly eliminating idle times due to machine failure by resorting to high spareparts inventory.

Quality Control and Marketing Skill

Strict quality control and skilful marketing effort had placed Babhanan Sugar Mills in a position to command a premium even in a surplus market.

In 1992-93, within three years of takeover by the present management, the company registered a net profit of over Rs. 5 crores after wiping out a total loss of Rs. 4.5 crores. Flushed by success, the crushing capacity was raised from 25 lakh quintals to 33 lakh quintals, a record in its history, with its stock price crossing ten times its issue price.

Babhanan Sugar Mills' incredible voyage towards success owes much to the company's maxim "Classic management, pure and simple". But, the company was to pass through an acid test in 1994 with the country's output dropping by 8%. Notwithstanding this fact, BSML's march towards progress continued unabated with the crushing capacity rising by 27% as also the production.

Profit after tax also reached Rs. 14.04 crore surpassing the established majors in the business. The company's expansion plan for higher capacity of 42 lakh quintals had also been commissioned by the beginning of 1994-95.

The company's real strength lay in its people and in its management. While others insisted on 'control, regulate, manage' the new management deemed it essential to ensure flexibility through decentralization of operations. The managers were made to set their own targets. Consequently when the management was apprehensive about the production of 38 lakh tonnes, the actual production was 41 lakh tonnes. But one has to look beyond the four walls of BSML factory in order to recognize a major factor that had contributed to its growth—the relationship between the company and the farmers that has developed over the years. The farmers were willing to offer their produce to Babhanan rather than to any other producer, resulting in increased production for Babhanan even when production all over the country was showing a downward trend.

Babhanan Sugar Mills (asset base 50 crore) merged with Balrampur Chini Mills Ltd. (asset base 70 crore) in April 1, 1994 with the objective of emerging as the largest sugar company in the country by 1995-96. According to Mr. K.N. Saraogi, the merger has been effected in order to facilitate the use of the opportunities that has sprung up owing to the liberalization and to face international competition with combined strength. Further, the merger is likely to broadbase share holding, reduce overhead costs and help to save taxes. The management is envisaging further expansion of capacity at both the plants. The expansion plan is for about 5000-6000 tonnes extra capacity with an outlay of Rs. 110 crores. An industrial alcohol plant of Rs. 14 crores with a capacity of 60 kilo litres a day had been built, the full impact of which is to be felt in 1995-96.

With the entry of MNCs, dealing with food products, the company does not apprehend any difficulty in marketing its additional production.

It is evident from the above discussion that there is a transparency in the external and internal objectives of Babhanan Sugar Mills Limited. Furthermore, the position of the concern according to BCG model resembles the cashcow. Even when the country's sugar output dropped by 8%, Babhanan's production rose by 24%.

	1992-93	*1993-94*
Production of Sugar ('000 tonnes) All over India	10,609	9,389.70
Production of Sugar ('000 tonnes) At Babhanan	33	41

This situation indicates that the concern has a strong competitive position which has helped it to erase the past losses. But something that arouses our interest is whether the company has any weakness and if it has, whether it has any opportunity or threat from the environment. Having said all this, we now go for ETOP, SAP and SWOT analysis.

Some Financial Data is Represented here

	Financial Year		
Particulars	*1991-92 (Rs.)*	*1992-93 (Rs.)*	*1993-94 (Rs.)*
Share Capital	1,40,00,000	6,40,00,000	8,40,00,000
Reserve and Surplus	19,76,959	93,99,069	12,82,77,613
Loan funds	28,12,45,291	44,37,25,767	45,58,90,737
Profit after tax	4,37,51,504	97,73,315	14,67,19,844
Interest and other charges	59,49,734	2,53,39,636	5,52,04,779
Proposed Dividend	—	20,71,233	1,92,00,000

Current Assets	8,69,86,414	26,42,81,843	39,60,88,948
Inventory of fixed goods	5,12,01,806	22,19,74,725	35,18,55,596
Sundry Debtors	15,57,283	22,42,790	9,08,282
Current Liabilities	3,62,63,356	6,94,30,027	8,89,60,486
Sundry Creditors	3,45,40,476	5,57,56,441	4,87,91,369
Total Purchase	8,87,72,738	18,95,45,536	27,31,69,976
Turnover	13,84,69,528	17,22,15,936	45,62,83,314

Company	*Year*	*Sales*	*Int.*	*Dep.*	*Tax*	*NP*	*Equity*
Bannari	93-94	54.77	7.72	3.81	—	0.94	7.54
Amman	92-93	42.58	4.94	4.15	—	2.08	3.75
Dharampur	93-94	69.90	5.19	3.80	—	9.02	6.67
Sugars	92-93	146.52	10.23	4.64	—	15.78	4.44
Empee	93-94*	15.75	4.40	1.40	—	2.20	16.96
Sugars	92-93	11.22	6.86	2.68	—	12.65	14.93
Kothari	93-94*	70.38	8.51	3.73	—	7.14	14.6
Sugars	92-93	59.98	9.03	4.37	—	4.29	9.79
Rana Sugars	93-94	8.20	1.20	0.85	—	0.22	21.00
Sakthi	93-94	144.30	14.15	2.82	—	20.45	10.49
Sugars	92-93	107.20	10.61	4.11	0.01	6.15	10.50
Simbholi	93-94	96.69	4.16	2.03	3.75	5.01	5.57
Sugars	92-93	77.92	4.93	2.43	0.30	1.75	5.03
Ponni	93-94	37.30	2.29	1.48	—	3.07	9.99
Sugars	92-93	45.31	3.43	1.72	0.30	2.03	4.04
Balrampur	93-94	70.80	2.03	1.75	4.30	8.42	2.33
Chini	92-93	59.00	5.05	2.88	—	2.94	1.83
Babhanan	93-94	45.63	5.52	1.68	—	13.77	6.40
Sugar	92-93	17.22	2.53	1.16	—	5.34	6.40

*Figures of 6 months workings (September 1993-March 1994)

SAP Analysis

Factors	*Impact*	*Reasons*
Finance/ Accounting factors	+40	The organization was having both internal and external funds of Rs. 64.8 crores and registered a profit of Rs. 14.07 crores which was Rs (4.5) crores in 1989. Capital structure represented 2.3:1 debt-equity ratio and net profit ratio was 30.8%. This exhibited an efficient utilization of debt capital and an effective capital structure. Financial leverage represented 1.4:1 and this again depicted that the interest rate was not very high. The current ratio was 4.5:1 and the working capital was Rs. 30.7 crores. The high value of current ratio was due to the irregularities of cane production and led to maintain a high inventory for finished goods, i.e., sugar. With the debtor's turnover ratio at 0.72 days, and the creditor's turnover ratio at 65 days, the company enjoyed a high credit period without a risk of bad debt.
Marketing distribution factors	+30	Although the total market share of the organization was not very significant, the market share of this concern was increasing. Very high quality product was being produced here and the marketing skills were continuously developing. Four per cent of the product was purchased by the government directly and the rest by the confectionaries and soft-drink makers and sometimes sold in the open market, where always a very high demand was present. No customer loyalty was needed in this industry and only some packaging and advertisement might be introduced to attract the upper chunk of the society. But these things were not so important as producers would not directly sell it in the open market.
Production/ Operation Management factors	+25	(i) Lower total cost than competitors. (ii) Easy availability of raw materials. (iii) Loyalty of workers. (iv) Increasing production by utilising 100% capacity.

		(v) Efficient and effective quality control. (vi) Efficient vertical integration (vii) Alcohol plant under construction. (viii) Supply of raw material is very smooth and adequate. But the inventory control system was not very satisfactory as indicated by high sugar stock. But this was due to supply of sugar during peak demand period, such as pooja occasion, but in this regard profit is more than the cost to maintain this inventory.
Personnel/ Labour Relation	+40	A very good work-ethos was established over the years, managers were able to set their own targets. Skilled labourers were employed in order to make the cost of low labour. And there was a good inter-personal; relationship among the employees. Overall the employees were satisfied with the management.
Corporate resources	+25	So far the organization was able to reach its objectives. Furthermore, the management was very liberal and the staff-management relation was very good. Organization structure and climate helped to achieve the proposed objectives. And thus management enhanced the corporate image and prestige of the concern, by turning a sick unit into a profitable one.

So internal strength was more than enough and this helped to overcome the environmental hindrances and turned these hindrances as an advantage for the organization.

ETOP Analysis—helps to Determine Environmental Threat and Opportunity

Factors	*Impact*	*Reasons*
Economic factors	+20	The following are the inflation rates: Foodgrains—12% General Commodities—13% Sugar Cane (SAP)—18% Sugar—18% Interest rates are also at the higher side. So, overall it is absorbed. When there is increase in the business growth. It is

		known inflation occurs when aggregate demand is higher than that required to buy the full-employment output at the current level of prices. But in our economy though inflation exists, the problem of unemployment also prevails. As the per capita income increases, it undoubtedly increases sugar demand.
Governmental/ Legal factors	-25	Government had a great effect on the Sugar Industry. Producers were incurring a loss because of the levy-quota, which was 40% of output as per government notification. And owing to this levy-quota system, the selling price was below the cost of production. To meet the demand of the customer, the import of sugar was permitted by the government without any customs or excise duty. But it posed severe threat to the Indian sugar manufacturers whose output attracted excise duty. In addition to it, cane price was made higher by the government.
Market/ Competitive factors	+35	There was a change in population; Total population increased. This consumer good was not very much effected by the age and shift of population and therefore this view had negligible effect. But per-capita income had increased and there was a steady upward demand for sugar. And there was no remarkable entry of any strong competitors.
Supplier/ Techno-logical factors	+30	Here the price demanded by supplier was fixed up by the government. So the supplier would not be able to give pressure to the producers of sugar except in the supply of cane. Gur and khandsari manufacturers were able to give more price per quintal of cane as there was no government control. Furthermore, production of cane was very much fluctuating and depended on climate. But this organization had a very good relationship with the suppliers of cane. So in spite of the government policy on increasing demand of cane for gur, which was smuggled to the neighbouring country for producing illicit liquor, did not hamper the production

		schedule of the organization. From technological point of view, there was not much threat on the producers.
Geographic factor	+00	This was not essential in this consumer goods industry.
Social and other factors	-10	Nowadays upper-middle class people are conscious about their health and this might affect the sugar consumption and people would use the substitute of sugar i.e. saccarine for fear of diabetes.

This overall ETOP represent that in the environment opportunities were more than the threats.

Now we go for SWOT analysis to see the combined environmental threats and opportunities that the organization experienced and simultaneously to see the internal strengths and weaknesses to expolit the external/environmental factors. This is represented below.

SWOT Analysis

Environmental Factors	*Impact*	*Internal Factors*	*Impact*
1. Economic factor	+20	1. Finance/Accounting Factors	+40
2. Governmental/ Legal factor	-25	2. Marketing/ Distribution factors	+30
3. Market/Competitive factors	+30	3. Production/ Operation Management factors	+25
4. Geographic factors	+00	4. Personnel/ Labour relation	+40
5. Social and other factors	-10	5. Corporate resources	+25

The above analysis represents a more or less stable environment except in the area of government/legal factors. So, in this situation, it could be said that the organization should adopt a stable growth strategy. But, as is evident from the SWOT analysis, it is more desirable to follow a growth strategy as the organization has not acquired the status of a cashcow, as yet, and is just proving its position from dog. However, there is scope for improvement though business growth rate is low as there is demand for its product. In fact, the company too has, as expected, pursued a growth strategy. The company has been able to achieve a sustainable internal growth rate by increasing sales and profits and decreasing the cost of production. SWOT analysis also shows that it should have opted for a broader financial base with a merger which, however, was opted by the BSML management. Furthermore, it will save tax and at the same time reduce the cost of production.

The other area where it has diversified is alcohol. It is likely to be most profitable for the company as the raw materials for the project is to be supplied internally with an additional advantage that there is no government control in the alcohol sector as is the case with sugar.

Another area where it can make inroads is the confectionary business where the multinationals are coming in, as it has access to a primal ingredient, sugar, with an added advantage of cheap labour which is likely to give them a competitive edge.

20

Managing Strategic Alliances

Jyotirmay Mondal

TVS-SUZUKI, the first Indian 100cc motorcycle company can be regarded as a refulgent example of a successful management of strategic alliances lately. The company had to consider every aspect of its business to stage a comeback and this case is a remarkable story of corporate revival and a total turnaround from the brink of closure.

February 1990, for TVS-SUZUKI Ltd. part of the powerful 800 crores (Rs.) TVS group, being in financial doldrums was like cancer. It only happened to others and then everything went wrong.

A 100-day strike—a result of warring labour unions put the company back by six months in the fiercely competitive two-wheeler market. It resulted in revenue losses amounting to Rs. 80-90 crores, a profit loss of around Rs. 5-6 crores and above-all an opportunity loss. Current assets dropped from Rs. 32 crores to Rs. 21 crores in fifteen months. Of the Rs. 18 crores in sales, Rs. 12 crores were outstanding. Suddenly, TVS-SUZUKI was on the verge.

Labour disputes was not the only problem. TVS-SUZUKI, quite like the other engineering firms, viewed sales as a natural corollary to manufacturing operations. Consequently, it had grown inward looking and complacent. There was gross overstaffing; expenses were unbridled. The best employees were leaving, others were demoralized and demotivated. Products were weakly positioned and out of fashion.

Everything was not bleak, for, TVS had maintained its market share in Mopeds, its principal product, which was around 34%. Its TVS-XL, an improvement over the original TVS-50, targeted at the rural and semi-urban markets, was the country's largest selling moped at about 7000 units a month. TVS Champ, aimed at the urban market was selling at 4000 units a month. Apart from these, TVS had a reputation for engineering excellence and product quality. It was respected for its financial integrity. It had a fine plant facility and dedicated workforce. The way to success was carved out by pitting these against the negatives.

The potency of TVS in the moped market was demonstrated, when Bajaj Sunny could hardly make a dent in its sales. Sunny snapped up 15% of the moped market in 1992-93 at the cost of the Kinetic group. But this time TVS was not to be caught unawares by sliding back into complacency. It upgraded its product by introducing a new engine with 10% extra power.

But a completely distinct situation prevailed in the 100cc motorcycle market, the other two-wheeler market, where TVS had a presence. Though it was the first Indian company to introduce the 100cc bikes on the Indian roads with its launch of Ind-Suzuki in 1984, its share had dropped to a mere 12% by 1991-92. As it was first of its kind, the brand did not have much to say for itself aside the fact that it is distinct from 250 or 350cc bikes.

Then in 1985 came the "fill it, shut it, forget it" Hero Honda bike which snapped up about 50% of the 2.6 lakh units of 100cc motorcycle market, with its fuel efficiency positioning. Then came in the Yamaha RX 100 with a power positioning which by 1991-92 had acquired 24% of the market share. Kawasaki Bajaj RTZ launched in 1987 had 9% market share in 1991-92.

The Survival Phase

The main objective was to cut costs, and yet ensuring that the company re-entered the market with a bang. Consequently it reduced dealer's credit from 25 to 10 days. It borrowed Rs. 14 crores to invest in its R & D and human resources. The plant was integrated, cutting surplus manning, the assembly line made feasible enough to be able to shift from one product to the other. In the field of human resources, voluntary retirement scheme and Golden Handshake was introduced to reduce the employee strength from 1,915 to 1,195 by 1993.

In a period of 16 weeks, fixed costs were brought down from Rs. 78 lakhs to Rs. 64 lakhs a week. It became a much more flatter organization with constant interaction with the employees, suppliers and dealers.

In spite of the fact that every conceivable expense was cut, one area where it escalated was R & D, for, it was the product strategy of TVS to stage a comeback in such a way as to consolidate its position in the segments where it had secured a niche as well as to make its presence felt in other lucrative segments so as to emerge a complete two-wheeler company.

The Comeback

Ind-Suzuki, the original TVS 100cc bike was strong both on fuel efficiency and power, but was best in neither. Therefore, it required a dramatic repositioning.

First of all, it was fitted with a more powerful engine that gave 57 kmpl (more than before). After upgrading its original product, it set about to identify clear market segments and the bikes that could fulfil the need of each.

Through market research, the company could come across the need for chiefly 3 types of bikes.

First, the very low maintenance, reasonably fuel efficient, powerful, inexpensive, value for money, bike for the rural and small city dweller.

The second, low maintenance, fuel efficient bike for commuting in the cities. And last, but not the least, was the requirement for a powerful, stylish, performance-oriented bike for the rich college students in large towns and metros.

In eight months starting August 1992, TVS launched three bikes, each tailor-made, to meet the requirements of the customers and fitting into the identified slots. The first bike launched was Suzuki Max-100, with a Suzuki engine, flat seat, provisions for a carrier and all this for a mere Rs. 30,000 (the regular 100cc cost around Rs. 35,000) Max 100 with its evocative ad line *Aaj Ka Sikandar* (Today's Alexander the Great) was designed to hit Escorts' Rajdoot in the Hindi belt are. By 1993, Max 100 was selling at about 1000 units a month (average monthly 100cc motorcycle market, April-November 1993 : 22,000 units).

By September TVS introduced the 'no problem' Suzuki-Samurai, the urban community motorcycle, high on fuel efficiency and power, low on maintenance and with a strong emphasis on its Japanese lineage. Within a year Samurai had snapped up customers from its three main competitors; Hero Honda, Kawasaki Bajaj and Yamaha and was selling at about Rs. 35,625 (Bangalore price) with the company selling about 2200 units per month.

In March 1993, Suzuki-Shogun (Rs. 38,215 on road in Bangalore) was launched. Its positioning evident in "the most powerful bike of its kind" stood for power, style and uniqueness. The Shogun notched up a monthly average of 500 units.

In April 1993, TVS sold 2300 bikes, by November, it was selling 5000 a month.

Chart 1

Year	*Duration (month)*	*Turnover (Rs. crore)*	*Profit (Rs. crore)*
1987-89	13	177	2.8
1989-90	12	143	(5.2)
1990-91	12	141	(2.5)
1991-92	12	169	3.2
1992-93	12	189	3.8
1993 (Apr.-Aug.)	6	117	6.0

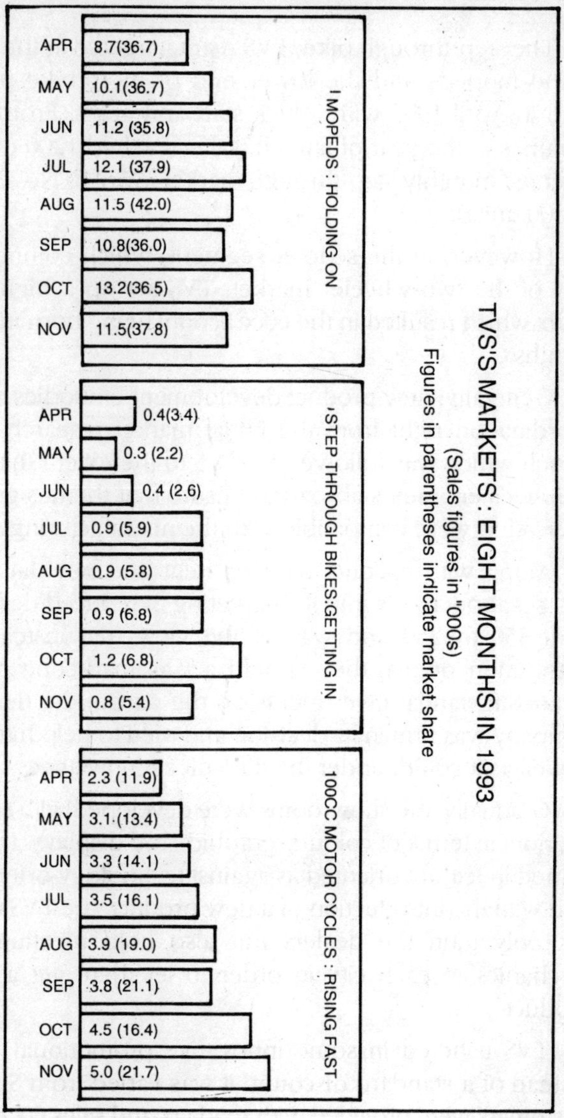
Chart – 2
TVS'S MARKETS : EIGHT MONTHS IN 1993
(Sales figures in "000s)
Figures in parentheses indicate market share
MOPEDS : HOLDING ON
APR 8.7(36.7)
MAY 10.1(36.7)
JUN 11.2 (35.8)
JUL 12.1 (37.9)
AUG 11.5 (42.0)
SEP 10.8(36.0)
OCT 13.2(36.5)
NOV 11.5(37.8)
STEP THROUGH BIKES:GETTING IN
APR 0.4(3.4)
MAY 0.3 (2.2)
JUN 0.4 (2.6)
JUL 0.9 (5.9)
AUG 0.9 (5.8)
SEP 0.9 (6.8)
OCT 1.2 (6.8)
NOV 0.8 (5.4)
100CC MOTOR CYCLES : RISING FAST
APR 2.3 (11.9)
MAY 3.1 (13.4)
JUN 3.3 (14.1)
JUL 3.5 (16.1)
AUG 3.9 (19.0)
SEP 3.8 (21.1)
OCT 4.5 (16.4)
NOV 5.0 (21.7)

The step-through bike, TVS Astra, targeted at the higher end of the mopeds and the lower end of motorbike market, was born in April 1992 with a kick start and gears. From a monthly 400 units in the year of launch, sales reached 1200 units in 1993 (average monthly step-through market, April to November 1993: 14,600 units).

However, in the scooter segment, which commands about 50% of the two-wheeler market, TVS set up a high level task-force, which resulted in the 60cc Scooty being born in just twenty months.

Generally, new product development embodies a systematic coordination right from the initial market research to product launch which was followed by TVS to the extent that it sent the supplier's engineers abroad to ensure that the designs they had to develop were compatible with the manufacturing systems.

Along with product development and new launches, TVS also set about to revamp its marketing. It reduced dealer strength from 350 to 250 and was of the view that instead of being distribution points, they should act as marketing points. This meant substantial investments on the part of the dealer but the company was firm in its decision and tried to help him financially as well as it could, under the difficult circumstances.

Gradually, the showrooms were developed with standardized interiors in terms of colours, graphics and displays. Dealers were trained in feature oriented as against technology-oriented selling. And with the introduction of a new product, the TVS team would not only train the dealers but also hold meetings with the mechanics in each city in order to let them get a feel of the product.

TVS ushered in some innovative promotional techniques. Instead of a standard discount, it was varied from State to State. Customers were provided with road tax and sales tax exemptions; the local press would announce, "No sales tax for TVS-Suzuki". It made the company seem caring and concerned. During product launches, free test rides; as in the case of Suzuki-Shogun, and give-away-posters were also offered. In addition television commercials were also on air quite regularly.

Above all the company refurnished its work culture based on the Japanese philosophy of 'Kaizen' or continuous improvement. And as part of total quality control (TQC), used as a measure to restore both the company's sagging fortunes and the employee's morale, problem areas were identified and given as projects to a group of five or six workers under a supervisor.

All the measures undertaken by the TVS-Suzuki management to stage a successful comeback started showing results for the turnover and profits were up. Sales per employee grew by 160% since 1990; with return on investment being more than doubled. As regarding the workforce, it is much more motivated with only by 6% absenteeism and the high entropy levels of yesteryears been convented into high energy levels.

21

SWOT Analysis for Hindustan Gas and Industries Ltd.

Tanmoy Roy
and
Anita Mukherjee

It is said that there are three types of companies, those which make things happen; those which watch things happen and those which wonder what happened. The industrial gas manufacturer, Hindustan Gas and Industries Limited, belonging to the Aditya Birla Group falls in the first category and is a success story among the Calcutta-based engineering companies.

The company was incorporated on the 14th day of June 1944 under the Indian Companies Act, 1913 under the name of 'Hind Gas Co. Ltd.', and this name was changed to 'Hindustan Gas Co. Ltd.', on 3rd January, 1945 and again to 'Hindustan Gas and Industries Ltd.', on the 15th of November, 1961 to commemorate its expanding-cum-diversifying activities.

It is known that successful companies know how to adapt and respond to a continually changing market place. Hindustan Gas and Industries Limited is one such successful company which practices the art of market-oriented strategic planning. In June 1944, the company thus purchased, as a growing concern, the business of 'Bengal Aerating Gas Factory Ltd.' which was then managed by Andrew Yule and Co. Ltd., with its factory at 42, Garden Reach, Calcutta, and manufacturing CO_2 gas and aerated water and repair of soda water machines. Subsequently, a new plant was installed at 22, New Tangra Road, Calcutta-46 and the site of the old factory was sold.

The company's success is due to three key ideas. The first is to see as to which business entities deserve to be built, maintained, phased down or terminated. In 1948, an ice plant was set up at 22, New Tangra Road, site to manufacture ice in block but this plant was closed down in 1978. In 1951, the company built cold storages to provide facilities for storage and preservation of goods under improved scientific methods. In 1956, a cold storage was established in Patna City.

The second idea was to assess the future profit potential of each business. The company commissioned its Oxygen plant at Tangra in 1962 and Acetylene plant in 1963 at Nangi, Budge Budge, to reduce the gap of demand and supply of industrial gases, particularly for Oxygen and Acetylene. In 1968, the company started manufacturing Argon and Nitrogen at Nangi as an expansion measure. A Hydrogen plant was set up in Calcutta to meet the growing demand of special gas segment. A CO_2 project was commissioned in 1991 at Murbad. The turnover of this division increased by 31% in 1991-92 over the previous year due to continuous marketing efforts and improved product mix. Thus from manufacturing CO_2 in its initial stage of development in 1944 the company started manufacturing Acetylene, Nitrogen and recently in 1990, in order to broaden its product range, the company started manufacturing Helium gas and speciality gases and its mixture at their existing Murbad premises.

The third idea was that of strategy. The company developed a game plan for achieving its long-run objectives. The game plan was that of diversification, and innovation. In response to the rapid industrialization and planned economic growth of the country the company installed a mechanised plant in 1954 to manufacture Engineer's Steel files. In 1982-83, the company successfully commissioned a major diversification project—a foundry unit at Holol at Baroda. It is one of the most modern plants in the country for manufacturing malleable and heavy duty iron castings. The foundry division's turnover registered an increase of 29% in 1991-92 and 17% in 1992-93 in comparison to their previous years inspite of the depressed market condition in the automobile and Insulator Industries. The company is still strengthening its position in existing products and is also expanding its activities. The company's industrial gases division in Calcutta had already introduced high purity CO_2 gas and ultra high purity Argon as part of this product range.

Corporate New Business Plan

It is generally seen that a company's plans for its existing businesses, will allow it to project its total sales and profits. However, the projected sales and profit will be less than what the management wants to achieve in the desired time period. This gap between the desired sales and projected sales have to be bridged by developing or acquiring new businesses.

Fig. 1. : The figure illustrates the planning gap for Hindustan Gas and Industries Ltd. The lowest curve projects the expected sales over the next ten years and the highest curve describes the company's desired sales over the next ten years.

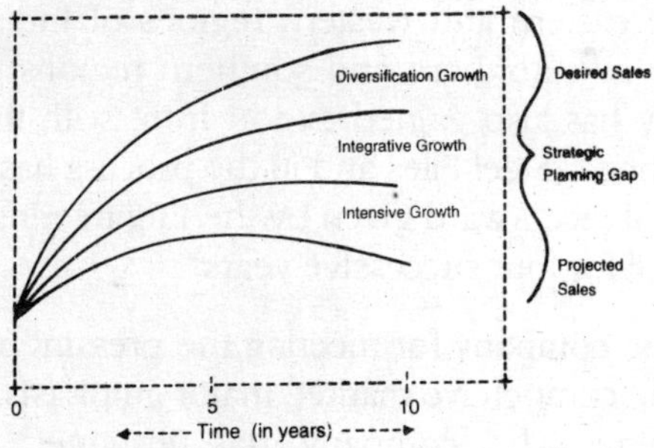

The Strategic Planning Gap

Reference : (Philip Kotler : 7th edition : P. 45)

The company has plans to fill in the gap in three ways. First, the company has identified growth opportunities within the company's current business, through gaining more market share with its current products in current markets and to develop new markets for its current products. The company is planning to set up centre for production of special gas and gas mixtures used in more specialised applications at Delhi and Bangalore for which foreign collaborator is sought. Apart from this the company has plans for Argon recovery from its sister concern Indo-Gulf Fertiliser whose planned capacity would be 3.5 million Cu. M.P.A. It also has plans for setting up a Nitrous Oxide plant at Budge Budge. The company has just entered into an agreement to export Argon and other special gas to SAARC countries. The company has identified newer areas in the overseas market and this had resulted in the growth of exports from 2.88 crores in 1991-92 to Rs. 4.68 crores in 1992-93, a substantial increase of 62%.

Second, it is to acquire businesses that are related to the company's current businesses and the third way is to identify opportunities to add businesses that are not related to the Company's current businesses, i.e., diversification strategy. The company is considering entry into non-ferrous castings at Baroda. It is also planning to set up a tonnage plant at Jamshedpur.

Today, the company is one of the main supplier of industrial gases both in the eastern and western regions of India and is considering entry into northern and southern regions. Besides this, the company has also gained export front with the rising export of its Engineers' Steel Files and in the process has bagged the Regional Excellence Award given by the Engineering Export Promotion Council for four successive years.

To gear up the company for meeting the pressing needs of expansion and the competitive market, major emphasis is being placed on training. The company has instituted suitable programmes aimed at developing specific skills as well as supervisory skills. The company has at present 45 persons in managerial category, 117 persons in technical, 73 in non-technical, 60 in junior level technical and 1, 912 persons in workmen and clerical level.

Table 1

The Financial Aspects of the Company

(Rs. in Lakhs)

	1992-93	*1991-92*	*1990-91*	*1989-90*	*1988-89*
1. Turnover	4388.32	3936.08	3217.12	2557.12	2182.17
2. Gross Profit	413.00	509.82	461.43	218.10	186.93
3. Profit after Depreciation & Tax	154.80	192.74	256.88	49.89	43.81
4. Total Capital Employed					
Gross Block	3794.02	3459.15	3201.62	2768.07	2512.20
Net Block	1718.06	1546.49	1417.60	1164.62	1060.39
Investments	4.91	4.91	4.91	4.91	4.91
Net Current Assets	1672.85	1354.87	1032.81	802.51	750.68
5. Financed by					
Share Capital	169.43	169.43	122.18	122.18	122.18
Reserves	777.65	660.08	532.82	438.06	413.59
Borrowings	2448.73	2076.76	1800.32	1411.80	1280.21
6. Per Equity Share					
Net Worth	59.37	51.91	40.83	34.81	33.26
Earning	9.72	13.33	16.20	3.05	2.67
Dividend	2.25	2.25	2.00	1.50	1.50

The Company's present manufacturing activities are:

Oxygen
Medical Oxygen
Nitrogen
Argon Gas
Dissolved Acetylene Gas
Hydrogen Gas
Helium Gas
Speciality Gas Mixture

Carbon Dioxide Gas
Dry Ice
Engineers' Steel files
Malleable and S.G. Iron Castings
In addition, they are the owners of cold storage.

Major Gas Manufacturers

In the eastern region the major gas manufacturers are BOC Ltd., Asiatic Oxygen and Acetylene Co. Ltd., Allenburry's Industrial Gases Ltd., Bihar Air Products Ltd., apart from Hindustan Gas and Industries Ltd. and in the western region the major industrial gas manufacturers are Bombay Oxygen Ltd., Gujarat Flurochem Ltd., Ramkrishna Oxygen Ltd., Superior Air Ltd. Among these, BOC Ltd., a member of the British Oxygen Co. group is the India's largest industrial gas manufacturer and it is nearly five times the size of HGI Ltd., its nearest competitor in the business.

Table 2

Market share of HGI Ltd., alongwith major competitors in West Bengal for Liquid Oxygen, Liquid Nitrogen and Argon :

Liquid Oxygen			
	IOL	-	73.73 %
	HGI	-	10.82 %
	Asiatic Oxygen & Acetylene Co. Ltd.	-	4.73 %
	Allenburry's	-	4.39 %
	Others	-	6.33%
Liquid Nitrogen			
	IOL	-	0.45 %
	HGI	-	99.53 %
	Others	-	0.02 %
Argon			
	IOL	-	58.66 %
	HGI	-	34.57 %
	Others	-	6.77 %

Please see figure 2-4

MKT. SHARE OF SUPPLIERS (%) FOR LOX IN CALCUTTA REGION

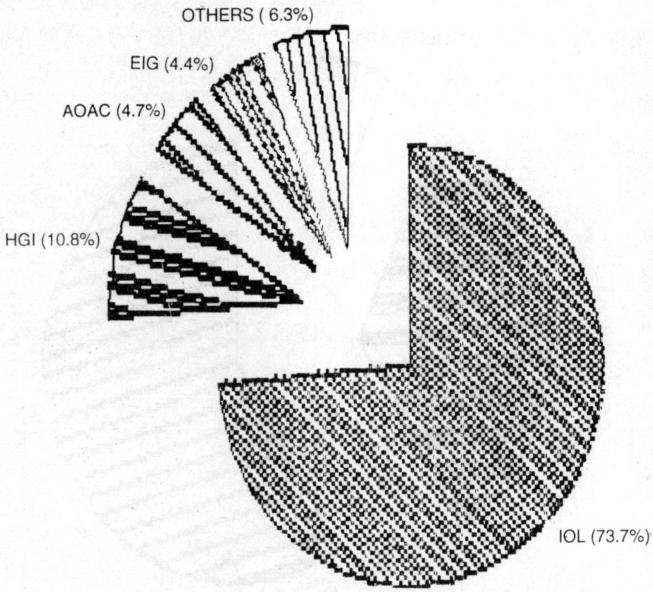

MARKET SHARE OF SUPPLIERS (%) FOR LIN IN CALCUTTA REGION

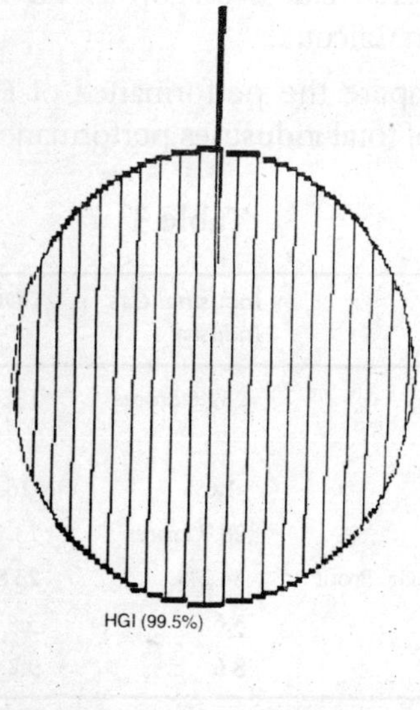

MKT. SHARE OF SUPPLIERS (%) FOR AR IN CALCUTTA REGION

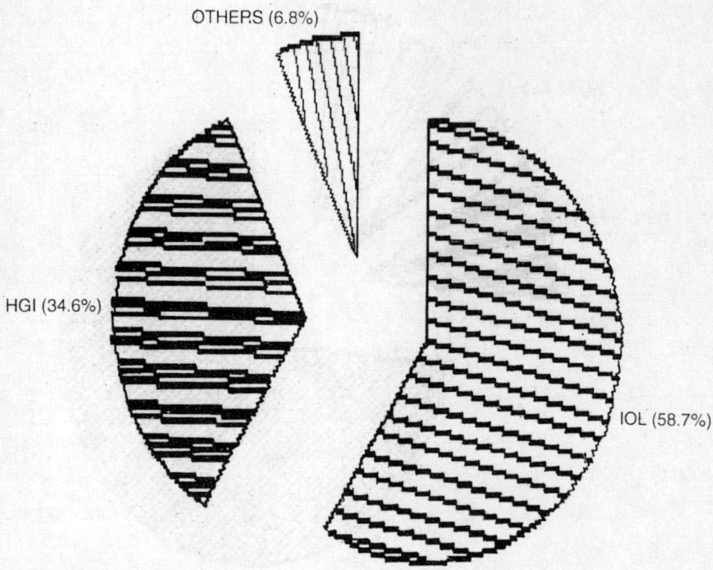

Thus, it is evident that in the case of liquid Oxygen and Argon, BOC Ltd. is clearly the leader whereas in the case of liquid Nitrogen, HGI Ltd. is on top as BOC does not produce liquid Nitrogen in Calcutta.

We will compare the performance of HGI Ltd. with BOC Ltd. in the light of total industries performance as in March 1992.

Table 3

	Industrial Gas Industry	*BOC Ltd.*	*HGI Ltd.*
Sales:	259.6 crores	152.7 crores	39.4 crores
Percentage change in Sales:	-1.6%	-16.8%	22.4%
Gross Profit	28.7 crores	13.5 crores	5.4 crores
Percentage change in Gr. Profit	34.2%	23.8%	16.1%
Net EPS (Rs.)	3.6	3.5	17.5
EPS (Rs.)	8.6	9.2	39.5

The diagnosis of HGI's strength and weaknesses can be fruitfully utilized only if the environmental opportunities and threats are considered alongwith its internal strengths and weaknesses. This will result in strengths and weaknesses, opportunities and threats (SWOT) analysis. In a way SWOT analysis may be said to consist of interlinking of Environmental Threat and Opportunity Profile (ETOP) and Strategic Advantage Profile (SAP).

The ETOP is a convenient means by which attention of top management may be drawn to the most critical factors and their potential impact on the strategy of firm as a whole and key aspects of its operations.

The profile consisting of environmental factors and their impacts are shown here.

Table 4
ETOP

	Environmental Factors	*Impact*
1.	Economic Factors	+ 30
2.	Government/Legal Factors	+ 35
3.	Market/Competitive Factors	+ 10
4.	Supplier/Technological Factors	+20
5.	Geographical Factors	+ 25
6.	Social Factors	0

+ 50 indicates very strong opportunity.
0 indicates no impact.
-50 indicates very strong threat.

The economic factor offers opportunities because of 3-4% growth in industrial output in 1992-93 was mainly from production of steel, aluminium, textiles and few other items. This is significant because steel manufacturers are the largest purchaser of industrial gases. This opportunity was somewhat reduced by the recession in industrial offtake which resulted in accumulation of inventory. Due to the liberalization of technology-import policy and partial decontrol of the steel sectors, the scope and opportunities of HGI increased. Even though the demand for industrial gases is high in the market, there are many small industrial gas manufacturers after delicencing and organizations intentions to keep minimum inventory reduces the promise for HGI. Due to the easy availability of raw materials, opportunity for technological upgradation is high. These in turn provide, major opportunities to set up plants in Jamshedpur and in Calcutta region.

SAP is a tool for making systematic evaluation of the strategic factors like the company's Finance/Accounting, Marketing/ Distribution, Production/Operation, Personnel/ Labour relation and Corporate resource to determine where the firm has significant strengths (and weaknesses) so it can most effectively exploit the opportunities and meet the environmental threats pressing the company.

Such a profile of HGI is given here :

Table 5
SAP

SAP Factors	*Impact*
Finance/Accounting Factors	+ 5
Marketing/Distribution Factors	+ 10
Production/Operation Management Factors	+25
Personnel/Labour Relations Factors	0
Corporate Resources	+ 10

Although the turnover increased over the years the profit after tax depreciation decreased in 1992-93. In the case of raising funds the company has placed less reliance on raising funds from public and its need for fund is largely compensated by the Aditya Birla Group of Industries whose total turnover amount to about 1700 crores. Even though the company has adequate sales force in Calcutta region, the awareness among the customers about HGI is low in regions other than Calcutta. The delivery schedule of the company is not at all satisfactory. Young, knowledgeable, ambitious executives of the company adds to its strategic advantage, in the face of the company steadily increasing the existing production capacity and going in for expansion programme.

SWOT Analysis

It is one thing to find out opportunities in the environment and it is another thing to have the competency to succeed in the opportunities. The company has to evaluate its strength and weakness periodically. SWOT analysis is a process of matching internal capabilities and environmental conditions which is reflected in the following ETOP-SAP interlinking. In examining the strengths and weaknesses, the company neither have to correct all its weaknesses nor gloat about its strengths. The question is as to whether the company should limit itself to those opportunities where it possesses the strengths or should consider the opportunities where it might develop strengths.

ETOP Factors	*Impact*	*SAP Factors*	*Impact*
1. Economic Factors	+ 30	Finance/Accounting Factors	+5
2. Government/Legal Factors	+35	Marketing/Distribution Factors	+ 10
3. Market/Competitive Factors	+ 10	Production/Operation Management Factors	+ 25
4. Supplier/Technological Factors	+ 20	Personnel/Labour Relation Factors	0
5. Geographical Factors	+ 25	Corporate Resource	+ 10
6. Social Factors	0		

The above analysis represent an extreme case where all the factors of ETOP and SAP are positive but few matches across. Since government or legal factors pave way for increased production, the company should follow growth strategy as the grand strategy and more precisely internal growth strategy through increase in production capacity and setting up of new plants as the sub-strategy.

The implementation of the aforesaid strategy and sub-strategy would call for leadership, functional policy and organizational implementation. In order to implement the strategy effectively one should ensure that right strategies are in the right position. As far as Resource Deployment is concerned, due emphasis should be given to production units in terms of allocating funds and technology oriented personnel. In this regard HGI should seek to implement the strategy of growth (internal growth) by transforming its present divisional type of organization structure to simple type of organization structure (innovative organizational structure).

22

Synergy from Merger : A Study of Lipton and Brooke Bond India Limited

Arup Mukherjee

Lipton and Brooke Bond International, both beverage giants, were adversaries, in spite of the fact that both belonged to the Unilever group, giving rise to a bewildering situation. This situation was, however, reconciled with the merger of these two beverage giants which resulted in the emergence of Brooke Bond Lipton India Ltd. (BBLIL) to work towards the company's establishment of a strong presence in the beverages market. As a consequence, of the estimated two lakh tonnes per annum packaged tea market, BBLIL had a share of 53.9% in 1993-94 followed by TATA Tea with 20% (ORG figures).

The necessity of a coalescence was an outcome of the 1993-94 depression in the tea-market. Additionally, the management rightly perceived that a large number of plantation companies in India have started their own brands of tea, and these new 'plantation packers', with regional presence, (ORG research too shows), are the ones that are growing rather than the large established brands.

BBLIL : Popular among Consumers

The plateauing of growth has seen BBLIL to launch itself

into frantic activity, in an attempt to consolidate its position. Though the merger brought together in its fold a portfolio of 31 tea brands like the company has concentrated on eight to nine major brands like; Taj Mahal, Lipton Yellow Label, Lipton Taaza, Super Dust, Three Roses and Lipton's Ruby Dust. This policy, according to the management, aims at achieving growth through a concerted effort towards concentrating focus on only a few sharply defined brands.

As far as coffee is concerned, BBLIL's Bru Instant is the market leader commanding a sizeable portion of the market share. Apart from Bru Instant, the other roasted brand, Green Label Coffee, more popular in the south, a mix of coffee and chicory, is likely to give them an edge over 100% coffee brands, for a sharp increase in the price of coffee beans is less likely to hit their pricing. The company intends to push both the brands to remain the brand leader.

Along with tea and coffee, BBLIL has also diversified into areas such as frozen desserts (Walls) and other food items like Bird's Eye Green Valley Frozen Vegetables and Kissan Food Products. The argument behind this expansion of activities, according to the management lies in the fact that internationally the Uniliver strength is in foods which account for 53% of its global annual turnover of Rs. 123000 crores. Food business of the Unilever group is composed of five key areas: tea, frozen desserts, oil and dye products, meal related products and professional market products such as specialized bakery fats.

The logic behind this diversification is made more transparent by an executive who says that the tea market is currently growing at around 3% annually, therefore, it needs over areas where it can step in confidently, with access to Unilever's expertise and experience.

On the beverages front, the company is creating a higher interface with the consumer, through research. Consumers' preferences are likely to decide the subsequent relaunch of the core brands with the requisite alterations. The company is also gearing up to face the possibility of tea drinkers shifting to other beverages, including soft drinks, as affluence spreads.

Recent activities of the company's beverage division have included the launch of Lipton Yellow Label, an internationally successful brand, and the relaunch of Red Label, Taj Mahal, Super Dust and Three Roses.

Yellow Label, a premium tea, positioned as an international brand "Now also in India" through advertisement was launched in 1993 in Bombay and Delhi and then extended across the country. In view of the fact that it could make the positioning of BBLIL's prevailing premium tea, Taj Mahal, indistinct, a need was felt for sharper positioning of Taj Mahal.

Zakir Hussain: From Classical Music to Modelling

The positioning of Taj Mahal was mainly made operative through television advertising, which took on a sharply contrasting ethnic tough while continuing with *tabla* master Zakir Hussain as its endorser. The sign-off takes the message *Wah Taj* to *Wah Naya Taj.* (Taj is an excellent beverage to New Taj is wonderful). The latest in this series zooms in on the new vacuum packaging that preserves freshness for a longer time.

The consumer preferences are highly regionalised, as such, the Taj Mahal blend has been changed for northern India in accordance with the consumer demand for a clearer leaf structure and milder strength. For Bombay, however, the blend remains strong in flavour.

Considering the fact that, the brand image of Red Label (the largest selling brand in the packaged tea market with a market share of 13.1% in 1993-94 : ORG figures) had eroded but it was relaunched in October 1993. It was repositioned as a 100% strong energy reviver.

Without digressing from its original design and colour combination the packaging has been upgraded so that it can be associated with value by the consumers. The tea blend has also been upgraded and the company claims has been received well. ORG figures, according to the company, reveal an increase of 12.3% in September-end quarter of 1994, in the market share of post relaunch of Red Label.

Super Dust, the other brand to be repositioned, popular in

Maharashtra and South India, was faced with the same problem of deteriorating image and quality. For this purpose, the company had two alternatives; either to project Super Dust as a tea that gives hightened strength that remains for a longer duration or to project it as a tea that enables a person to do super human feats. The second option was chosen which has resulted in the brand's new ad campaign which features film actress Raveena Tandon as a damsel in distress rescued by the Super Dust hero against all odds.

The use of Raveena Tandon is strategic as Maharashtra is still fascinated with the fantasy elements of films and super heroes.

In order to take advantage of the growth of the rural market and keeping in mind the lower per capita income of the rural masses, BBLIL is promoting Super Dust in smaller 50 gms packs. Printing on the foil too is done to prevent piracy. Given the fact that Super Dust is already a much admired brand in the rural markets, the rural commercial is a sixty second one, with the television version reduced to thirty seconds.

The ad repositioning of Three Roses, a premium tea brand popular in the south, uses three attributes—*Rang, Swad, Dum* (Colour taste, stamina) personified by three ladies who represent the three expectations of consumers from the tea.

After the merger, apart from relaunches, the distribution channels have also been reinforced. This calls to attention the fact that before the merger the two companies had been using two distinctly non-identical methods of distribution. While Lipton used stockists, Brooke Bond had its depots. However, the merged BBLIL uses common stockists/distributors. According to the management of BBLIL, they have more bazaar power, and can approach distributors with a much larger price list of more successful brands. As a consequence, the transportation too has become more cost effective.

The management also draws a distinction between the BBLIL consumer and the customer. For the customer, being the distributor, it is important to keep him happy. This is ensured through timely delivery, training of the distributors' sales people and taking responsibility for the problems when they arise. Besides this, attractive incentives and promotional schemes are also being implemented.

Food is an another area where BBLIL has been causing a lot of excitement, chiefly through the launch of Walls frozen deserts in Bombay. Though not an ice-cream, for it contains less than the required milk fat, it is giving a stiff challenge to the established ice-cream brands.

Walls has been a runaway success in Bombay. But accompanied with this success came a problem; arising out of the gap between demand and supply, as demand was underestimated by the company, its retailers and distributors. The major drawback in this case, as described by the management, was not production but the unavailability of special trucks to carry the product from the company's Nasik factory to the points of sale.

Dollops, its other brand in this range of products, acquired from Cadbury in July 1993, adds to its ice-cream portfolio. The management is of the opinion that it has its strength in the scoops and parlour business and thus they have no reason not to sustain Dollops, which is an established brand and has a distinct image.

Frozen Vegetables: A New Trend

Frozen vegetables are a comparatively new concept in India, although smaller players such as MAFCO in Maharashtra have sold frozen peas successfully. The launch of Green Valley Peas, Carrots and Spinach in Delhi in April 1994 and soon after in Lucknow and Kanpur, marked the beginning of BBLIL's endeavour to popularize this concept in India. The vegetables, specially peas, have been well-received in Delhi. Apart from this, market survey indicated a demand for mixed vegetable packs (cauliflower, peas, carrots and beans) which led to subsequent launch of Green Valley mixed vegetable packs.

The management, however, was confident, for they believed that Green Valley's off-season availability, consistent quality and an escape from price fluctuations of the market makes it a prized commodity. The fact that the vegetables are cleaned and frozen within twelve hours of packing, also provided an extra edge. The company also has adopted backward integration, helping farmers sow the right variety and quality of seeds.

The takeover of Kissan, by BBLIL in April 1993, has seen Kissan to spring into renascent activity for it has been provided a complete overhaul by the BBLIL management since July 1993. The products : Jams, Squashes and Tomato Sauce have been upgraded in quality and repositioned through strong advertising. Pre-relaunch, the Kissan brand lacked clear positioning. There was virtually no advertising as consumers viewed Kissan as an old and trusted brand.

BBLIL through its new advertising campaigns, has aimed at developing a competitive positioning for the brand. The tomato sauce, therefore, has been positioned as a 'deliciously thick' ketchup; the squash as 'real refreshment for real fruit'; and the jam as the 'fruitiest jam' with the message 'fruits by nature, jams from Kissan'.

Since the relaunch the growth rate of the brand has been 30% in 1994 as compared to the same period in 1993. And this too, at a time when the food products market is showing a growth rate of 10%.

It is evident from the above discussion that BBLIL's involvement with the food processing business is here to stay, for in the changing environment in India, processed foods are likely to be the in-thing. This, however, does not mean that they are moving away from beverages, as it is the backbone of their business.

With large sums of money being invested in launches and relaunches of various brands, the company expects handsome return in volume and profit to manifest themselves after some time.

The structural changes affected by the company led to a healthy increase in sales and profits. Sales increased from Rs. 639 crores in 1992 to Rs. 1264 crores in 1993 for twelve months ended December. It increased even better during the six months ended June 1994 to reach Rs. 858 crores from

Rs. 380 crores for the same period in 1993. Net profit too rose to Rs. 104 crores (Rs. 43 crores) while equity stood at Rs. 120 crores.

Share Price Movement of BBLIL :

The price pattern of BBLIL suggested a technical price target of Rs. 650, and shortly since November 1993, it moved up from Rs. 350 to Rs. 570. Thereafter it fell to a level of Rs. 470 and then moved within a narrow range, consolidating between Rs. 470, a support area (where investors buy) and Rs. 515, a resistance area (where investors sell and take profits). But the consolidation phase is over and it is all set to move forward.

SWOT

Strength :	Market leader with established brand names, and after the merger, commands a sizable chunk of the tea market.
Weakness :	Being an agro-based company its fortunes are dependent on the monsoons.
Opportunity :	Its foray into the food processing business has been at the right moment as this sector is considered to be a Sun-rise industry. Packaged tea sector where the company has established itself is likely to witness a 6% annual growth in future.
Threat :	Though competition from established companies like Nestle, Tata Tea and ITC.

Conclusion

We have seen that the "Structural Changes" at BBLIL has lead to the consolidation of the company's overall position in the market and the company is all set for a "move ahead".

A brief analysis of the Strengths, Weaknesses, Opportunities and Threats does put up the advantageous position of the company in the present market scenario. But since a company has to look forward, think and plan for the future—it is suggested that BBLIL should move strategically and plan for future "Growth Strategy after a pause". A more integrated approach in the functioning of BBLIL and other subsidiaries of the worldwide Unilever Group is suggested, so as to avert the threats from other leading and established companies.

Addenduk

BBLIL seems to have proceeded in lines with the SWOT analysis given in the conclusion of the case. During the later half of 1996 the company has merged with Hindustan Levers Limited, another Unilever Inc subsidiary and both have jointly taken up a more integrated approach in exploring and leading the market.

■■

List of Contributors

P.C. Sen	Former Chairman and Managing Director of the Peerless Group
Shyamal Sen	Company Secretary of Brooke Bond Lipton India Limited, Calcutta
Rakhal Datta	Professor of Economics, Calcutta University and Director (SEBI Nominated) of Calcutta Stock Exchange Association
Sarmila Banerjee	Reader, Department of Economics, Calcutta University
T. Mallikarjunappa	Chairman, Department of Business Administration, Mangalore University, Karnataka
Dilip Roy	Fellow of IIM Calcutta, Professor and Head of the Department of Business Administration, Burdwan University, West Bengal
Mrinmoy K. Sarma	Attached with Department of Business Administration, School of Management Sciences, Tezpur University, Assam
Anjan Raichadhuri	Managing Director of Business Horizons (P) Ltd., Calcutta
Sanjib Raj	Engineer, Incharge-Amtron Service Centre (AEDC Ltd.), Tezpur, Assam
Gautam Chakroborty	Senior Sales Officer, HPCL, Calcutta
Rituparna Chowdhary Raj	Lecturer, Department of Business Administration, School of Management Sciences, Tezpur University, Assam

Sajal Kumar Das	Calcutta-based free-lance journalist and Full-time Faculty of Newport University's Calcutta Centre
S. Mallick	Dy. Director (Statistics), Directorate General of Mines Safety, Dhanbad
K. Mukherjee	Professor and Head, Department of Industrial Engineering and Management, Indian School of Mines, Dhanbad
A.M. Shah	Reader, Department of Management Studies, University of Kashmir, Srinagar
G.S. Shergill	Reader, Department of Commerce and Business Management, Guru Nanak Dev University, Amritsar
Maninder S. Sarkaria	Teacher, Government Senior Secondary School, Ajnala, Amritsar
G.S. Batra	Reader, Department of Business Administration, Punjabi University, Patiala, Punjab
Sukti Ghosh	Member, Research Team, MBA Department, University of Burdwan
Harendra Dey	Supervisor, IA & Sales, K S & Distributors, Ground floor, Hotel Center Point Building, Police bazaar, Shillong-1
Saikat Banerjee	Executive, International Trade, Polar Industries Limited, Calcutta-16
Samata Bhattacharya	Calcutta based free-lance journalist
Jyotirmay Mondal	Executive, Wembly Interiors Pvt. Ltd., 6/1B, British Indian Street, Calcutta-69
Tanmay Roy	Sky Industries Ltd., BE-348, Salt Lake City, Sector-1, Calcutta-64
Anita Mukherjee	Sky Industries Ltd., BE-348, Salt Lake City, Sector-1, Calcutta-64
Arup Mukherjee	Creative Manager, IDEAS, Gopalpur, G T Road, Muchipara, Durgapur-713212

Index